The Poet and the Dream Girl

The Poet and the Dream Girl

THE LOVE LETTERS OF

Lilian Steichen
&
Carl Sandburg

Edited by Margaret Sandburg

University of Illinois Press
Urbana and Chicago

Manufactured in the United States of America
C 5 4 3 2 1

This book is printed on acid-free paper.

Library of Congress Cataloging-in-Publication Data

Steichen, Lilian, 1883–1977.
The poet and the dream girl.

Includes index.
1. Sandburg, Carl, 1878–1967—Correspondence.
2. Steichen, Lilian, 1883–1977—Correspondence.
3. Authors, American—20th century—Correspondence.
I. Sandburg, Carl, 1878–1967. II. Sandburg, Margaret.
III. Title.
PS3537.A618Z496 1987 811'.52 [B] 86-25001
ISBN 0-252-01386-7 (alk. paper)

Contents

Acknowledgments

For all the encouragement and assistance given while working with these letters in the Carl Sandburg Collection, I wish to express my deep gratitude to Dr. John Hoffmann and all those in the Rare Book Room of the University of Illinois Library.

I owe special thanks to Dr. George Hendrick, professor of English at the University of Illinois, for assistance in certain editorial problems, and for invaluable advice as well as important information. He and Willene Hendrick encouraged me at a time when this was much needed, and proofread the manuscript in the early stage as well as in the final one.

For her unfailing assistance in research on some of the notes and many time-saving suggestions, I would like to thank Penelope Niven McJunkin of the Carl Sandburg Oral History Project at the University of Illinois.

I am deeply indebted to the Wisconsin State Historical Society in Madison, and wish to thank the staff there for courteous assistance in researching newspapers of the period, especially the Milwaukee *Social-Democractic Herald* for my father's column, "The Lake Shore and Fox River Valley Department," and Carl D. Thompson's column, in which there are references to my father. I also thank the Milwaukee County Historical Society for the photographs of some of the socialists my father and mother knew in Milwaukee, Carl D. Thompson, the minister who married them, Charles D. Whitnall, Emil Seidel, Frederick Heath, and Winfield Gaylord.

Also, I would like to acknowledge the kindness of Mrs. Elmer Gant, Ms. Mary Williams, and the Bureau County Historical Society for the reproduction of the Princeton High School faculty from the 1907 yearbook, which included my mother, her friend Elsie Stern, and the principal, Hugh Macgill.

I deeply appreciate permission from Joanna Steichen to reprint the early Steichen photographs of my father, mother, and grandmother.

Introduction

These letters reveal the thoughts of two fine, strong minds drawn to each other at first by their interest in socialism, then by their love of poetry and a similarity of ethics and ideals. My mother recognized this in his early prose and poetry. They learned so much about each other from these letters, yet it seems extraordinary that there was so little personal contact. My father's visit to the Steichen farm in late March, at the time of my mother's spring vacation, which coincided with her brother's birthday visit, lasted a week. But after that they were able to see each other only once before their June wedding, and this was in May at the National Socialist Convention in Chicago.

Their dream of socialism was then shared by notable American writers of the day, including William Dean Howells, Edwin Markham, Jack London, Edward Bellamy, and Upton Sinclair. Because of the scandals that were exposed by the muckrakers, thinking people felt a need for reform, and there was hope for this in the air. My mother longed to do something, "tho ever so little," to help bring this about. Her impatience with life at Princeton shows throughout the letters. She had attended socialist meetings in Milwaukee, Chicago, and Valley City, North Dakota, and had led discussions of socialist literature. She also knew something of the way the party worked. But until he came to Wisconsin, my father had never belonged to a socialist organization nor made a socialist speech. He had, however, attended lectures by Charles Zueblin, Arthur M. Lewis, and others and had written a short essay on the various kinds of socialism for the *Lombard Review* and an article for *To-morrow Magazine,* "The Onset of Socialism." They had read many books by well-known socialists of the time, some of whom are mentioned in the letters.

The first letters are not really love letters. They are just getting acquainted, and we see them becoming more and more interested in each other. While at first she meant only to encourage him in his work as a socialist organizer, the poems he sent surprised and delighted her. "You discover to me the only poetry that has ever satisfied me since I learned to think twentieth century thoughts," she wrote. Then she encouraged him to keep on with his poetry, "such beautiful, vital poems." He had not often met with this kind of enthusiasm, even from friends, and certainly not from any of the editors to whom he sent his poems.

The actual love letters do not appear until after his visit to the Steichen farm in Menomonee Falls, on March 27, my uncle's birthday. They were caught in a thunderstorm on the way to the farm and always referred to it afterward as "the Baptismal Rain," because they considered it the beginning of the realization of their love. Years later, in Michigan, when my sister Janet mentioned that it was "Uncle Ed's birthday," he looked at my mother and asked, with a smile, "Paula, do you remember the Baptismal Rain?" She broke into a little laugh, her blue eyes twinkling, as she replied, "Oh, yes, Carl, that was the beginning of *everything* for us."

We know so little of what happened during that visit, which meant so much to them. Of course there must have been a big birthday celebration with a big birthday cake made by my grandmother. She would have asked about the family in the Villa L'Oiseau Bleu at Voulangis in France and his exhibit then on at the Photo-Secession Little Galleries in New York City, and my uncle would have talked about Alfred Stieglitz and had some good stories on hand about some of the foreign artists and writers whom he had met in the course of his work. At some time he took several photographs of my father, probably guessing that there was nothing my mother would rather have than some Steichen prints of him. But according to my mother, they were wholly absorbed in each other, taking long rambling walks so that they could be alone, exchanging confidences, and learning about the plans, experiences, friends, and families of the other. It must have interested my father to learn that when she was at the University of Chicago, my mother had had English classes under Oscar Lovell Triggs, whom he had known later at *To-morrow Magazine,* and also a year of philosophy under Thorstein Veblen, whose book, *The Theory of the Leisure Class,* he had read and admired. He wrote to her later, "The coincidences of our ideas and plans and whims is something I would not have believed till—the Wonder Woman came." At some time he gave "from the rostrum," as he called it, some of his poems, including "Among The Hills" and "You." My mother told me that he also gave Langdon Smith's "Evolution," which was a favorite of his at the time; he knew all fourteen verses and enjoyed springing it on friends, usually exclaiming after he finished, "But why did he take the girl to ritzy Delmonico's?" He could, in giving it, compliment her on her dark hair and blue eyes with the lines, "Your eyes are deep as the Devon springs,/ Your hair as black as jet." She seems to remember the poem in some of her letters and on May 3 wrote that she would like to hear him give it again if he came to Princeton. By the time his visit was over, he was fully rested.

Since her letters were all written from Princeton, they were always referred to as "the Princeton letters." Her first long letter after his visit (fifty handwritten pages) gives a fine picture of a socialist meeting of the time, through the enthusiastic eyes of this young socialist. Throughout these letters, in her many moods, whether enthusiastic, serious, loving, or mischievous and playful, the high spirits of youth can be seen. Her modesty was surprising in a person of her brilliance, and my father found that he could not pay her a compliment without arousing a fear that she might not live up to his expectations. When he put her ahead of May Wood Simons, who had written articles on socialism for several magazines, she wrote a thirty-page letter giving her views on equality of the sexes, which she regarded as something usually discussed without clear thinking, and saying that she was not a "woman-genius." At another time she wrote a fifteen-page letter to make it clear to him that she could not write! Yet she was not afraid to criticize his work if he asked for it, as in Letter 46. More than once he shows his appreciation of this and at one time calls her "a Teacher."

His letters were hardly the kind that might have been expected to impress a young lady, written as they were on hotel stationery, postals, or the poorest of note-tablet paper, with a few on the stationery of the Wisconsin Social-Democratic party. But my mother was an unusual young woman, and though she preferred plain, simple stationery for her own use, she once wrote him that she liked "the free democratic way you have of using anything that comes to hand for writing—what you write transforms the poster into a beautiful wax tablet." Sometimes he used no form of salutation; in fact, this became a habit with him after the farm visit, and she picked it up from him after a while.

During the 1960s, when preparation was being made for the publication of a collection of my father's letters, and copies of those to her had been made, I realized that some could not be fully understood or correctly dated without careful reading of her letters to him, so I asked my mother if I could read and make copies of them. When she assented, we went to her room, where from the back of the top bureau drawer she drew an old stationery box, holding all her old letters, neatly folded, with most of them still in the envelopes.

The earliest letters are missing. When I asked my mother about this, she explained, "Neither of us could have known then what we would come to mean to each other. And correspondence isn't usually kept, unless for a good reason." But unfortunately some of his subsequent letters are missing also, how many cannot be determined, and what happened to them can only be speculation, for it is a long time since 1908. My father did not write as many or as long letters as my mother, owing partly to his work, but also to the fact that she was a prolific letter writer. In this collection of their love letters, written in the winter and spring of 1908, there are ninety-five of her letters and thirty-nine of his (the original letters are now in the Rare Book Room of the University of Illinois at Urbana-Champaign). Twelve of these appear in *The Letters of Carl Sandburg* (1968), edited by Herbert Mitgang.

These letters have been difficult to edit, because few of my father's letters are dated, and some are without any reference that could help in placing them. It is fortunate that my mother dated almost all of her letters, and her habit of referring to something that he had said in his last letter has proven very helpful. Certainly without her letter informing him that she had just received "the Cherry Blossom letter," it could not have been placed. Sometimes she makes us very aware of the missing letters, as when she mentions "the Commune Manifesto letter," quoting, "L.S. and C.S., Unite! You have nothing to lose but your chains—You have a World to gain!" If it were not for her letter, we would not know that he had written this. When answering his letter about her mother, she wrote that she has "the big-hearted letter about mother from Carl who *understands*." This helped to place his undated letter. In a case like this, I have put the date in brackets. There were times when she seemed to be picking up his habit of not dating the letters, and then I had to look for some clue in the contents. Some principal points of reference were the sophomore boys' play and the girls' elocution contest on April 24 at Princeton High School, the "menseversary" of the farm visit on May 12–16, and the Wisconsin Social-Democratic state convention in Milwaukee, beginning on June 13.

Although I worked on these letters for so long that I knew the dates of various events very well, relying on my memory seemed to me insufficient for a real study of the letters. After I made a 1908 calendar, marking each week during April and May with the Roman numerals they used for counting the weeks until the day of the wedding in June, putting down quotes from the letters on the days they were written, and on the day of a lecture, the towns, cities, or organizations where they were given, this helped immeasureably, and I could refer to it at any time of uncertainty.

The Poems

At first my father sent *Incidentals* and some of his poetry that had been published in *To-morrow Magazine* and *The Lyceumite* to my mother, then some of his unpublished poems. These not only aroused admiration and delight, but also a wonder that he considered poetry as a part of his past, and this encouragement was all he needed to continue. He began writing poems especially for her. These poems were never published, nor did he mention them to others, because he considered them as personal as the love letters. In later years when he was asked if he had ever written any love poems, he would hedge, evade, and if driven to the wall would say that he might have done some, but he never mentioned these, or the love letters. To him they were too private to be discussed, even with his daughters many years later. "These are something personal between your mother and me." As a result, some biographers concluded that he had never written any love letters or love poems. The poems belong with the letters, but there is no way of knowing which poems were sent with what letters, except in a few instances, for at some time they were separated from the letters, and kept in an envelope and folder marked in his large script "Paula."

When one of these poems is mentioned, or has been quoted by my mother or father in a letter, that poem has been placed after it, so that the reader may understand the reference. There are some exceptions. "On a Wagon" has been placed after the first letter he wrote to her after his visit to the Steichen farm, because in it he had mentioned a poem, and this one about the drive "from Menomonee to Home" seems fitting. Since "Back to the Beach" was in the mood of Letter 53, and moreover my father had written below the poem, "Two Rivers in 1908," it seemed logical to put it after this letter. Those love poems that I have been unable to place have been put in Appendix C. The early poems mentioned in the first letters, which he termed "juvenilia," are in Appendix A. Some related letters and writings of the time are in Appendix B.

Prologue

These were the peaceful days of 1908, when there was little concern about war, since it was before World War I and the Russian Revolution, and socialists and communists were regarded merely as impractical agitators. My father and mother were socialists—being idealists who wished to help to bring about better conditions for the working people. In their world the words "comrade" and "commune" had not yet been taken over by communists. Workingmen were fighting to better conditions in factories and elsewhere; often workingwomen were not able to earn a living wage. There was no workingmen's compensation in case of accident, serious illness, or unemployment. That would have been considered revolutionary. Children from eight to twelve years labored in factories for nine or ten hours, when they should have been in the fresh air or in school. It has taken a long time, but this country now has many of the things my father and others were fighting for back then.

Sometimes my father was irritated with anyone who called him a socialist, for some socialist movements he had never liked. "What *kind* of a socialist?" he would ask. "Why doesn't he say that?" I think myself that he could have been called a Fabian, since these socialists believed in bringing about the desired result by gradual reform.

In *Ever the Winds of Chance,* he tells of going to the Masonic Temple in Chicago to listen to a lecture at the Chicago Anthropological Society meeting. "After the one-hour lecture came a two-hour free-for-all of speeches from the floor—anarchists, single taxers, radical socialists, Christian socialists, criers for cooperative stores, for birth control, for the rights of labor to organize, to strike, to picket, for the rights of women to vote, for church property to be taxed, for priests and ministers to be refused 10 per cent discount on railway fares, for the death penalty to be abolished, for heavy income and inheritance taxes on the rich, for war to be outlawed by international agreement." This may give some idea of the times.

My father came in April 1906 to the old brownstone house at 2238 Calumet Avenue in Chicago, known as the Spencer-Whitman Center, which was the home of *To-morrow,* a small magazine owned and published by Parker Sercombe and edited by Oscar Lovell Triggs. Some of his poems and essays had been published by *To-morrow* during the past year, and Triggs had written an introductory note to the first three poems. His first book, *In Reckless Ecstasy,* had been published in 1904 by the Asgard Press, but *To-morrow* was the first Chicago magazine to publish any of his poems, so it seemed a large step forward, even though it was a very small magazine. It hardly matters that in later years he called these poems "juvenilia." Any comparison with *Chicago Poems* can only serve to remind us of his fast growing skill with words.

Sercombe now offered him free bed and board in return for editing, proofreading, and handling manuscripts. He decided to stay, for some interesting people were there, and he thought the experience would be worthwhile. Here he wrote other poems, literary portraits, and a column, "Views and Reviews," which came out in every issue. This was the time of the muckrakers, and the scandals exposed by such writers as Lincoln Steffens, Ida Tarbell, David Graham Phillips, and others could not help but influence his writing at this time. One of his portraits was of David Graham Phillips; he reviewed Upton Sinclair's *The Jungle* and about this time wrote a poem called "The Muckrake Man." When the University of Chicago accepted a large gift from John D. Rockefeller, it was dubbed "Kerosene Kollege" by one of *To-morrow*'s writers, Frank Stuhlman, who headed his article, "Gifts of the Greeks," with the old quote from Virgil, "Beware of the Greeks when they come bearing gifts."

Before fall came on, my father left, to continue selling stereoscopic photographs, or stereographs, for Underwood, and by October he had given his first lecture. Those early lectures were an odd assortment. "Black Marks" was about the development of the small black marks, which make up the various forms of writing, and their effect on mankind. "An American Vagabond" was about Walt Whitman, and a third was "The Three Blunders of Civilization: War, Child Labor, and the Death Penalty." He worked hard at them, trying to develop his own style of oratory, and listened to other orators with an ear tuned to learning from them. Years later, when complimented on his voice, he replied, "I worked *hard* to make it like that—no one knows how hard."

In December he was offered the job of advertising manager at *The Lyceumite* by Edwin Barker, who in the next issue introduced the new manager as a poet and published "A Dream Girl." Here my father met various platform personalities: Elias Day, an impersonator; Harry Holbrook, Billy Sunday's manager; two artists, Ross Crane and Alton Packard, who did some sketches of him for *The Lyceumite* and later designed the cover for *Incidentals;* Joseffy, a magician; and two socialists, the journalist and writer Charles Edward Russell and a Wisconsin Social-Democrat, Winfield Gaylord. He did a monthly series of portrait sketches on Lyceum performers titled "Unimportant Portraits of Important People" as well as some short sketches. The magician Joseffy interested him, and they became good friends. My father did a portrait sketch of him that he hoped would be published in *The Lyceumite,* but it was not accepted. Barker told him that an article about another magician had been published not long ago, and it would not do to favor one profession above the others, but this my father took with a grain of salt. Later *Joseffy* was published by the Asgard Press (1910). In April Barker was forced to sell *The Lyceumite,* and in the upheaval of transition my father was again without a job.

Philosophically, he took up where he had left off in the winter with Underwood and continued giving lectures. That summer he was asked to give two of his lectures at the Roycroft Chapel in East Aurora, before Elbert Hubbard and the Roycrofters. On July 6 he gave the Whitman lecture and was roundly applauded by these followers of the William Morris tradition in America. At the Socialist Symposium given there on July 13, he gave his lecture on Civilization.

By August he was back in Chicago, having joined Edwin Barker, who was now on *The Billboard,* and he was corresponding with Philip Green Wright about *Incidentals,* which was to be published by the Asgard Press early in November. His mind was also on the 1907 chautauqua, as he was on the publicity committee. The chautauqua opened in Joliet, at Delwood Park, August 30, with Billy Sunday's sermon, "Flies and Grinders, Hot from the Bat." There were many "stunt-fests" by platform personalities, and on September 6 my father gave "An American Vagabond." Many years after, when Billy Sunday was mentioned, he would sometimes say, laughing, "I once spoke from the same platform as Billy Sunday," and then tantalize by not going into particulars.

In the early fall of 1907 Winfield Gaylord came to see him at *The Billboard*. Since he appears in the letters many times, perhaps it would be best to give my father's description of him. "He was a deep-voiced, upstanding man, breezy and easy with a shining face, a former Congregationalist minister living in Milwaukee where he had been elected a senator of the Wisconsin legislature on the Social-Democratic ticket. He gave me the first personal information I had about a socialist movement that was practical and constructive. The Wisconsin Social-Democrats were members of the national Socialist party at the extreme right; they were 'Opportunists' opposed to the members of the extreme left whom they called 'Impossibilists.'"

My father liked what he heard about the Social-Democratic movement, which had been fighting corrupt Democrats led by Dave Rose, and Republicans not much better led by Sherburn M. Becker. Gaylord told him that organizers were needed in three districts in the state and that he would like to see him try organizing in the Fox River Valley district. My father asked, "Organize? How do you organize?" Gaylord explained in some detail about meetings in halls or homes of comrades, soapboxing on street corners, visiting local branches, trying to get new members, getting members to organize a local if there was none. "So that's how you organize," said my father, and Gaylord replied, "Yes, if you're good at it, all you do is work morning, afternoon and night."

He decided to take his time and think this over. He was now working on a new lecture, on Bernard Shaw. In October he had a lecture in Manitowoc, Wisconsin, and while there he met the editor of the Manitowoc *Daily Tribune,* Chester Wright, and had a long talk with him, which probably gave him another push in the direction of the Social-Democrats. Wright was an intellectual, witty, well up on affairs in Wisconsin, and he was also a Social-

Democrat. It was the beginning of a lifetime friendship. My father wrote to the Social-Democratic party in Milwaukee. Around the end of November, Miss Elizabeth Thomas, the party secretary, got in touch with him, and soon after he also heard from Carl D. Thompson, the state organizer. By December he was in Wisconsin.

A note among my father's papers gives his thoughts about this transition.

> So there I was, riding the North Shore Line to Milwaukee, where I was to join the Social-Democratic Party not merely as a member but as an organizer, one who 'stirreth up the people.' What would it be like, to carry a soap box to a street corner, stand on the box and call to people to come and hear a gospel of freedom to come? I had never made a socialist speech. In the Brooks Street fire department I had for six months read The Worker, the leading journal of the socialist party of New York city and state, the Social-Democratic Herald, weekly organ of the Wisconsin socialists—and I had read classics of socialism by Marx, Engels, Liebknecht.

Arriving in Milwaukee, he went to Brisbane Hall, the socialist headquarters, where he met Miss Thomas and other Social-Democrats, among them Carl D. Thompson and Victor Berger. Not long after, he became officially the organizer for the party in the Lake Shore and Fox River Valley district, with Oshkosh as his headquarters. Aside from organizing, he wrote a weekly report about what went on in his district, which was printed in the *Social-Democratic Herald* under the heading "Lake Shore and Fox River Valley Department."

Near the end of December my father came again to Brisbane Hall to talk something over with Victor Berger. Miss Thomas told him that he was in his office with a friend and that she would let them know that he had arrived. They did not keep him waiting long. Soon Miss Thomas returned with Berger and an attractive young woman whom she introduced as Miss Lilian Steichen. At that time my mother wore her long black hair in a simple Gretchen braid around her head, and when she spoke of the work he would be doing, her blue eyes were alight with enthusiasm. I once asked my mother what her first impression of my father had been, and she said, "Well, of course I was interested in him as the new organizer, and more organizers were needed in Wisconsin, so I wanted to encourage him in his work—but I felt sorry for him—he looked tired and worn, as if he worked too hard, and didn't take care of himself. I wasn't really attracted to him then, it was a casual, brief meeting."

My father, however, was very attracted by this enthusiastic young woman with the sparkling blue eyes that were so much a part of her charm and wanted to know more of her. She told him that she taught at a high school in Princeton, Illinois, and was home for the Christmas holidays. Later he saw her to the door and asked her if she would have dinner with him. She refused, saying that she had a previous engagement for dinner and a concert afterward with some old friends of the family. She said to me later, "That was true. Oma and I had been invited to dinner at the Delères, and Mr. Delère had also invited us to a concert that evening. But if I had been free, I would not have accepted. In those days no really nice girl would have had dinner with someone she had just met. Your father didn't think of that at the time." When he asked if he might write to her, she gave him her address.

Victor Berger, Miss Thomas, Carl D. Thompson, and others with whom he was becoming acquainted were her old friends, for Milwaukee, where many Germans and Luxembourgers had settled, was her hometown. My mother's firm resolve to acquire an education brought her first to an academy in Chatham, Ontario, and later to the University of Illinois for a year. She transferred to the University of Chicago in September 1901, where she had a class in philosophy under Thorstein Veblen, and an English class under Oscar Lovell Triggs. In December 1903 she graduated, receiving a bachelor of philosophy (Phi Beta Kappa) and with honors in Latin and English. During the first part of the next year she had various jobs of translating from Latin and German, and then she went home and began looking for a position as a teacher. In September she went to Normal, in Valley City, North Dakota, where she taught for two years before going to Princeton in 1906 to teach literature and expression.

Her Christmas vacation ended, she went back to Princeton, and he continued as organizer of the Lake Shore and Fox River Valley district. However, he did not allow this work to absorb him entirely, for he still wrote poetry and various forms of prose, sometimes essays, sometimes portraits. He was corresponding with Philip Green Wright about *Incidentals,* and *The Plaint of a Rose,* which was to come out in January, and sent him a copy of his “A Little Sermon,” which had been published at Christmas in the Manitowoc *Daily Tribune*. In addition to his regular organization work, he wrote “Labor and Politics,” an article that was published by the Social-Democratic Press as a leaflet and distributed at meetings.

But he often thought of Miss Steichen and her enthusiasm and charm and wrote her as soon as possible. When she replied, it was at first with the purpose of encouraging a comrade in the movement, though this changed as her interest and admiration were aroused. And so these letters began. They tell their own story.

I.

Princeton, Ill.
January 7, 1908

Dear Mr. Sandburg,

I have your leaflets "Labor and Politics"[1] and "A Little Sermon."[2] Do tell me how you contrive to be a moral philosopher and a political agitator at one and the same time—and especially how you contrive to write such Poets' English one minute and the plain vernacular the next. The combination is baffling! Artist, poet-prophet, on the one hand; man of action on the other. You must explain yourself else I shall "have such misery" trying to crack the hard nut myself.

Thank you for the leaflets. And Good-luck to you in all your work.

Yours cordially,
Lilian Steichen

1. *Labor and Politics* was a socialist leaflet written by my father and printed by the Milwaukee *Social-Democratic Herald* press for party organization purposes; it was distributed by the comrades at meetings.

2. "A Little Sermon" was first published in the Manitowoc *Daily Tribune* on Dec. 24, 1907, as "A Little Christmas Sermon." My father wrote to Philip Green Wright, "I have had some extras run off on laundry paper here." Later it was published under the original title in Elbert Hubbard's *The Fra:*

> Remember who you are. Remember you are one of the latest products of millions of years of toil and play and regurgitations of universal forces. The rain and stars and dust of a thousand worlds that have perished have contributed to the making of you.
>
> Be true to yourself and then it will follow as the trailing star-pageants of night follow the sundown shadows on the western sky that the stuff of your life will be the stuff of great, real dreams to be revealed in great, real actions.
>
> Deep-stained in changing days of triumph and disaster, the high, rare moments of life encrimsoned on the dark fabric of remembrance are the times you were strong enough to give yourself to others and know the result as growth and gain.
>
> This is the pathway of companionship, love, and attainment. Even so.

2.

Princeton, Ill.
Feb. 15, 1908

My dear Mr. Sandburg,

I have your letter and the "opuscula" in prose and verse. Also *Labor and Politics,* which I acknowledge separately because it cannot be classed with the rest having been done with that same utilitarian *broom* you spoke of, not with the artist's brush!

You need not apologize to me for cynical utterances regarding art. I understand! I agree with you that ours is not an epoch adapted to art. This is an *age of action*—not of dreaming or contemplation or gratulation. I too have written my apostrophizings (however crude) to the Stars etc. I have even labored lovingly setting together little word-melodies with nothing to them but the sensuous music of the words. (I can't send you samples from here for I left them all at home. Next time I am home I can send you some if you are interested.) But now—let alone *writing* verses—it's only once or twice a year that I *read* pure poetry like Shelley, Lanier, Keats. Not that I no longer appreciate the lyric loveliness of Shelley's *"Life of life thy lips enkindle"*[1] or of Lanier's *Marshes of Glynn*—but that I am called away from such aesthetic enjoyment by a Voice from the World of Action—a Voice unmusical, strident even, but *Compelling* for it is the *Cry of Life*. There you have it. Art now-a-days (indeed ever since the decadence of communal folk-poetry) is by and for the privileged minority—it is a thing of Snobbery—a diversion of the leisure class. Give me something more inclusive, more universal! Something that is for the Masses! And so Shelley lies neglected, dusty, on the shelf, and Enrico Ferri[2] or W. J. Ghent,[3] or Robert Hunter[4] is read.

You may laugh then at your youthful aesthetic productions without apologies to me, Please! It's good to have loved the poets' Poets and to have soared a little on the wings of poesy oneself! But it's good too, and better, to grow toward maturity (I ought to know being on the eve of maturity! i.e. nearly 25), and move on to greater things—the every-day life of Action—the politics of constructive socialism! If I had the choice between, on the one hand accelerating (tho by ever so little) the progress of the socialist movement, and on the other writing another "Prometheus

Unbound"—I should choose the former. The time for writing lyric dramas is past.

Still, believe me, I was interested in reading the *Dream Girl* for the proof it gives of the powers of expression which you are using *now* in the propaganda of socialism. The *Arrangements in Words*[5] will be interesting for the same reason.

Your *Dream-Girl*[6]—since you laugh, I may smile at her, may I not?—is indeed a dream girl—not of our world to-day but of the Millennial Epoch of Rest. In our Epoch of Struggle girls must be made of sterner stuff. Too bad, but it's so. My hope is that socialism will gradually create an environment favorable to the development of such a Millennial *Dream-Girl*. But meanwhile under capitalism your Dream-Girl must be a leisure class product. "The hill-flower grace," "the murmuring speech," "nuances spoken with shoulder and neck"[7]—all bespeak a delicate loveliness so frail that it could not grow unsheltered. And the "universal" girl—I mean the girl of the People—*is* unsheltered to-day.

So while I have no praise for the *Dream-Girl* itself (from the standpoint of democratic art)—yet I have plenty of appreciation for the intelligence that created it—for the powers for good in that intelligence when employed in socialist propaganda!

As for *Incidentals*[8]—it is all right. I believe in its optimist philosophy. (You see the point, don't you? "*I* believe in it. *Ergo* it's all right.")

But—of course you've guessed it—I like *Labor and Politics* best. It belongs to the sphere of Politics, of Action.

Pardon these comments. My excuse is, you asked for them when we met in Milwaukee. I took you at your word.

You ask when I shall be in Milwaukee again. Our spring vacation lasts from March 27 to April 6. I shall spend it partly in Milwaukee and partly at home. I told you—didn't I?—that my home is in the country—a little farm—four acres—3 miles from Menomonee Falls—about 15 miles from Milwaukee. If you should be in Mil. at any time during my vacation I should be so glad to see you there or to have you come to see us at the farm.

I am sending you the February Century[9] containing an article about my brother—this in lieu of samples of my own writing—for I have nothing of my own here. I haven't written anything for about four years (I've done some translation from the German—

purely scientific—so I don't count that). I quit writing because I became convinced that I lacked talent for it. I believe I was meant by Nature for other work.

When you read the article about my brother you'll come across a reference to myself. I must tell you that the credit I am given is not deserved. Everything else in the article is true—but this is pure fiction. I was at school while my brother was studying in Europe—both of us supported by our mother. All the credit belongs to her and brother himself. The article does not tell the half of our mother's wonderful goodness.

One thing I have done for my brother. I've helped make a socialist of him—just as I helped make one of mother. And I hope some day brother will help the movement with his art. He photographed the leading socialists at the Stuttgart Convention last August—something may come of that.[10] Robert Hunter expects to use these portraits in a book of biographies of the great socialists.[11] And they can be used in socialist magazines—and so help our party press.

Forgive this long letter. When residing among "retired farmers" one must live in books and letters.

Sincerely yours,
Lilian Steichen

1. *Prometheus Unbound* by Percy Bysshe Shelley.

2. Enrico Ferri (1856–1929), Italian socialist and criminologist, editor of *Avanti,* the party paper in Rome, and author of *Socialism and Modern Science.* My mother had a copy of this, which she had read carefully and with thought.

3. W. J. Ghent, an American socialist, the author of *Our Benevolent Feudalism* (1902) and *Mass and Class* (1904).

4. Robert Hunter (1874–1943), American sociologist, writer, and well-known socialist lecturer on poor living conditions and socialism. His books came out in the *Social-Democratic Herald* before publication. He was the author of *Tenement Conditions in Chicago* (1901) and *Poverty* (1904), on which my father wrote an article for the *Lombard Review* in 1905.

5. "Arrangements in Words" is an early work with which I am not familiar, as it is not among my father's early papers. It is mentioned in a letter to Philip Green Wright, Feb. 9, 1908, as one that he expected to be published by Elbert Hubbard in *The Fra.*

6. "A Dream Girl" was first published in *The Lyceumite* (Jan. 1907) and later in *Chicago Poems* (1916).

7. From "A Dream Girl."

8. *Incidentals,* a "little book" of essays by my father, was published by the

Asgard Press in November 1907. It was small enough to put in an ordinary letter envelope and had a brown paper cover; it was designed by Alton Packard, whom he had known at *The Lyceumite*.

9. The February *Century* article was "Progress In Photography with Special Reference to the Work of Eduard Steichen."

10. In 1907 nearly a thousand delegates representing thirty nations attended the Socialist Convention in Stuttgart, and over fifty thousand people came to hear them. It was known that they represented many others; one delegate there represented a million votes.

11. This was *Socialists at Work,* which would be published later in 1908.

3.

Hotel Ahearn
Oshkosh, Wisconsin
2—21—1908

Dear Miss Steichen:—

It is a very good letter you send me—softens the intensity of this guerilla warfare I am carrying on up here. Never until in this work of S-D organization have I realized and felt the attitude & experience of a *Teacher.* With those outside the party, I am an Advocate. But those within "the organization" have so much to learn, and to show those who have intelligence what to do, and to get the hypercritical into constructive work, and to give cheer to the desperate and rousal to the stolid sometimes I know just what it is to be a Teacher.

I see you employ the exclamation point as freely as I do!—You chip away at an idea in sculptor-fashion. You leave the thing unfinished and half-put, neither neat, correct, discriminative, nor scholastic! I indict you as fellow-felon!

The Dream Girl is Millennial—formed in the mist of an impressionist's reverie. Millennial, and at this time, impossible. But, my good girl, she is not of the leisure-class, as we know the l-c. She is a disreputable gipsy, and can walk, shoot, ride, row, hoe in the garden, wash dishes, grimace, haggle, live on half-rations, and laugh at Luck.

You remind me of two types of women—seem to sort o' blend the two in your cosmos. Actresses of the modern school of repression, Fiske,[1] Kalich,[2] and Ashwell.[3] And the Russian revolutionist!

Am going to send you The Plaint of a Rose.[4] It was written as and marks the half-way point on the journey "from Poetry to Economics." A protest and justification of the universe!

I shall plan to be in Milwaukee the last days in March and one or two in April, and will hope to see you then. Will tell you then about some of the curious and interesting phases of the work up this way. Will also make some inquiries of you, pertinent and quasi-impertinent with reference to democratic art. One can't lecture on Whitman or Shaw without attaining facts and convictions.

I will forgive you (out of inborn generosity and largeness of nature) for writing such a long letter, provided, as hereinafter stated, that you repeat the offense! And don't forget your exclamation points!

Charles Sandburg

P.S. Am going to have the district headquarters here from now on. My permanent address will be

248 Wisconsin Ave.
Oshkosh.

P.S.: P.S.:—Once in my callow days and for many years I thot *Oshkosh* was like Heaven, Nirvana, Sheol,[5] the North Pole; mythical, imaginary, fictive, and hopeless of attainment.—But here it is! bustling & populated, stern and real, a factual entity stretching away from my window with lands, bldgs, laws, and noises!

1. Minnie Maddern Fiske, an American actress of the time who did much to make Henrik Ibsen popular. My father had seen her as Mrs. Karslake in *The New York Idea*.

2. Bertha Kalich, an American actress whom my father saw in *The Kreutzer Sonata* in 1907 in Chicago.

3. Lena Ashewell, a British actress my father admired. He was so stirred by her performance with Guy Standing in *The Shulamite* that he wrote a commentary on it.

4. *The Plaint of a Rose,* his third published work, had been published in the first week of January 1908 by the Asgard Press. It had a cover design by Elizabeth Wright (Mrs. Philip Green Wright).

5. Sheol, in Hebrew theology the abode of departed spirits of the dead.

4.

Princeton, Ill.
Feb. 24, 1908

Dear Mr. Sandburg,

The poems—the poems are wonderful! They are different from the poems in the books that stand dusty on my bookshelf—how different! Yes, from the best of them too—from Shelley, from Whitman, from Carpenter![1] Oh, if I had a volume of your poems, dear Poet-of-Our-World-Today, it would not stand on the shelf dusty but would be read and wrestled with for the life-strength it could give!

(Lucky I have free and unlimited license to use exclamation points. There is such need of them! Without them how could I hope to convey to you any idea of how your poems have affected me. As it is you'll doubtless find all this inarticulate enough.)

"Enclosed is some stuff"—and you discover to me the only poetry that has ever satisfied me since I learned to think twentieth century thoughts. Truly an unceremonious introduction! But of course I couldn't expect you to grow ecstatic over your own work!

But however bluntly presented, the Poems are here. Great thanks to you!—

And to think that I wrote so despairingly of poetry to you. Now, tho, you've "shown me." Yet you anticipated me in despairing of poetry—did you not? or didn't I understand rightly? I *am* bewildered. Do explain yourself. You refer to your poetic period as a "past" period. Will you tell me why you've turned from poetry—you who knew all the while these poems that I read today for the first time. I can understand *my* despairing of poetry—But You!

I suppose you have reasons to give—undreamed of by me—quite as wonderful as the poems. And when you've explained yourself I'll say again "Now you've shown me."—

My own case was simple enough. The poets I knew bored me. They gave me pictures of life which were less wonderful, less poignant than the picture I made for myself out of the stuff of experience and study—study of twentieth century social science for instance! In their day these poets' pictures were more wonderful than the ones that people could make for themselves—for these poets saw all that the contemporary scientists saw, and saw it transmuted, emotionalized, humanized moreover. But the world moves on. It has moved very rapidly in the last fifty years—most rapidly in the last ten years. The old science—the old Weltanschauung[2] is outdated: so too the old poetry.

And the new poetry? Edward Carpenter was the only poet I knew who was abreast [?] of advanced thought. And he is romantic—sentimental—lachrymose! I knew no realistic poetry till I saw yours and I concluded (not very logically) that all modern poetry was romantic rot!

Another indictment I had against poetry—especially modern rhymeless poetry—was its verbosity—its diffuseness. Now modernism stands for succinctness—Ibsen, Shaw in drama—Jack London in fiction. I knew some mystic romantic modern poetry—and mysticism and diffuseness (words, words, words!) go together! Just as realism pairs with directness, simplicity. Your poems have that elemental quality of being direct and simple.

I may keep them a little while—may I not? Could I keep them one week? I shall want to read them often. The *Cry of Life* will not call me from your poems—it is *in* your poems—poignant, intense!

Have you really turned from poetry for good? Shaw is our dramatist—why shouldn't you be our Poet? The American movement doesn't seem to be in pressing need of a poet, at the present moment—*perhaps. Perhaps!* But surely the time isn't far off when it will need its Poet. Germany could use a socialist poet today. (I really know very little about the German movement. I make this assertion with nothing to back it up except the fact the (fortnightly) magazine as well as the pamphlets and books published by the *Verlag der Sozialistischen Monatshefte*[3] are all gotten up very artistically. There is one other scrap of evidence which I had nearly forgotten: the articles on democratic art that come out from time to time in the *Monatshefte*.—Now you know the evidence so take my assertion for what it's worth).

And yet—it's *great* work what you are doing now—as S.D.P. organizer! You seem to have a genius for that work too (I received the Manitowoc newspaper[4] with your article—an article that ought to take hold sure). Would it be possible to be both organizer and poet? Or is it a case of having to forego one service in order to do the other? And if you have decided to forego being a poet, why? Why?

More anon—
And great thanks for the wonderful wonderful poems.

Sincerely
Lilian Steichen

1. Edward Carpenter (1844–1929), an English poet and writer, was interested in socialist movements, especially those of William Morris and Henry M. Hyndman. He lectured on socialism and was the author of various books of poetry and literary essays, *Chants of Labor; Angels' Wings; Love's Coming of Age; Iolaus; The Art of Creation,* a socialist work; *Civilization, Its Cause and Cure;* and *Towards Democracy*. My mother and father were well acquainted with his work, in particular *Towards Democracy*.

2. World philosophy.

3. A German Social-Democrat monthly publication.

4. Probably the article she refers to is the one Carl D. Thompson mentioned in his *Social-Democratic Herald* column: "Comrade Sandburg and the local organization are certainly doing great work for the cause here (Manitowoc). . . . A splendid article on 'What Is Social Democracy?' appears on the front page of the Daily Tribune." Before my father became a socialist organizer, he had met Chester Wright, the editor of the Manitowoc *Daily Tribune,* in November 1907, when he gave his Whitman lecture in Manitowoc. Wright was a socialist also, and the two became close friends; my father occasionally wrote for the Manitowoc paper and even had his *Herald* mail sent to the Manitowoc *Daily Tribune*.

5.

Princeton, Ill.
Feb. 25, 1908

Dear Mr. Sandburg,

I had to quit writing yesterday evening before I could say half of what I wanted to say. It was bed-time and past bed-time—so I stopped, threatening "More anon." The threat was not an empty one (unlike most of my threats at school which I seldom have the heart to carry out. You see the whole existing educational system is based on discipline which involves threats. But I don't believe in *discipline*. Would substitute *interest*. Hence the dualism—the antagonism—the inconsistency. The system makes me threaten. My convictions rebel. The pupils are at a loss to understand me—

I seem to be of the system and yet not of it. Result—discipline breaks down. The pupils don't stand in awe of me. Rather they speak to me "as man to man"—not without misgivings, however, because according to all precedent I should be classified as an Olympian[1] by virtue of my office. So it's only a wavering faith that my boys and girls can give me after all!).

I hope you don't mind long parentheses like the above. For I'm apt to go off on a tangent thus every now and then.

I had to read your poems over before school this morning, at noon and again this evening—each time to reassure myself that it was really so—that it wasn't some passing glamor that made the poems seem so wonderful—that they really were the wonderful poems I thought them. And every time the reassurance was complete. The hour had come to say: "Hail, Poet!" The three poems in "An Autumn Handful," the poems "The Pagan and Sunrise," "The Rebel's Funeral," "A Fling at the Riddle," "The Road and the End"[2]—all great, great, great! "Hail, Poet!"

Of course I must retract what I said about your Dream Girl. I didn't interpret rightly—your explanation in your letter was a revelation, a surprise. I got a wholly different conception from the poem—the conception of a girl fragile, ethereal, not having in her the stuff of womanhood, lacking the elemental vitality for developing into a woman who would be Mate and Mother.

This view may not seem to harmonize with what I said about the Dream Girl's being Millennial. But I can't stop to explain—and you don't seem to object to my "half-putting" things—suggesting and leaving you to fill in the picture. And mind! don't you go and fill in the picture wrong as I stupidly did in the case of your Dream Girl. How stupid it was of me! (And I'm not usually stupid. Dull I am often—stupid rarely).

I'm glad you are interested in photography as an art—a distinctively modern art. And that you appreciate my brother's work. The few remarks you made were enough to show that you understand!—

I have some faint hope that my brother will come over to America this spring. He was planning for an exhibition in New York but the Panic unsettled his plans. In a letter about two weeks ago he wrote that he was undecided whether to come or not. So we don't know. If he does come he will plan to be home at the farm during my vacation. I should so much like to have him meet you—he would appreciate your poems and love you as an S.D.P. organizer! Too bad it's so uncertain whether he'll come.

Anyway you must see the really good reproductions of my brother's photographic work in "Camera Work." The reproductions in The Century are mere shadows compared with those in C.-W. And the real prints are immeasureably beyond these! You must see what prints we have. I would like to send "Camera Work" to you to look over—but it is too big and heavy to send thru the mail. Anyway the treat will keep till my vacation.

You say you will want to hear some of my word-melodies in vacation. I'm beginning to feel uncomfortable over the prospect. But no! Why should I be ashamed of those early efforts—(why should one be ashamed of anything in one's past?) If you wish to hear them, you shall. *Only remember* that I mentioned my poetic efforts simply to prove that I was once a devoted *reader* of poetry—so sincerely devoted that I tried my own hand at it. All my poems fall within the years 15–20. You remember I wrote you that I haven't written anything the last four or five years—because I've known for so long that I have no ability in expression. In my teens I used to dream of being a poet—I suppose because I loved poetry. And dear-Brother-Mine shared these dreams. He was sure I was a genius. It has been the hardest job disillusioning him. As a matter of fact he isn't wholly disillusioned yet. You see brother and I are very sympathetic—we've watched storms come up together—we've made pilgrimages together on moonlit nights to birch woods listening in the Silence for the heavy fall of a dewdrop—we've looked at his pictures together. So he knows that our tastes are akin—that I too have some poetic insight, appreciation. And brother jumps at the conclusion that I'm an artist! But there are thousands who have insight to one who can express himself thru some medium of art—thousands who love poems or pictures to one who can paint or write. Simple enough and natural enough! I wish brother could see it. For my part I'm content to be, instead of a genius, an average human being. There's wonder and joy enough in being a mere human being—a Woman! Anyway there is something tragic to me in the combination Woman-Genius. The constant struggle between two kinds of work she has to do: as mother of children, as master-workman.

Of course the true Woman-Genius takes up her double life-work—accepts it—rejoices in it—just as the true Mere-Woman her one work! The double task carries with it strengths for both and for the conflict between both. And it must be glorious to be such a woman-genius these days—doing her woman's work of bearing strong children to carry forward the Movement in the next generation; and doing besides the man's work of carrying on the Movement now. Tanner and Ann[3] united in one Human Being! Something that a mere Super-Man could never attain!

I see I'm rambling on and on and on. And it's past bed-time again! Good-bye.

Sincerely,
Lilian Steichen

1. Olympian, a term for an adult invented by Kenneth Grahame in *The Golden Age* (1895). Her use of the word would seem to show that she had read the book.

2. The three poems in "An Autumn Handful" were "Perspectives," "Backyard Vagaries," and "In Illinois." "The Pagan and the Sunrise," "The Rebel's Funeral," and "A Fling at the Riddle" were published by *To-morrow,* a small Chicago magazine, in March and April 1905. "The Road and the End" is in *Chicago Poems* (1916).

3. Tanner and Ann, in George Bernard Shaw's play *Man and Superman.*

6.

Princeton, Ill.
Feb. 29, 1908

Dear Comrade:—

I am happy to hear you say that my letters have given you something. You have given me so much—I like to feel that there has been something given, tho ever so little, on my side.

The poems came this morning, and I've read and reread them over and over again. It's Saturday—so I have time. What joy for me to read and know by reading that there are more and still more such wonderful poems as those in the first bunch that so completely upset my notions about modern poetry! And I see beyond this last bunch even, more and more such beautiful vital poems "coming, coming, coming"[1] out of the great source within you—*if* your strenuous life as agitator leaves you energy for it. And a formidable IF I know this is!

As if it were not enough to be possessed with one sort of divine madness! You must needs add to the divine madness of poesy the diviner madness of revolutionary agitation—Bless you!

I like to let my eyes rest on the bunch of poems I have here and think over the ones that appeal most to me (*The Road and the End, The Pagan and the Sunrise, Fragments* "In a far time I was a cave-man," *Departures, All Day Long* etc. etc.).[2] I like to get the thought of all this great great poetry in my mind—and then think of you knocking about in the "Lake Country"[3] (I have your postal) not as a wandering minstrel, but as a plain practical S.D.P. organizer giving talks to hard-headed workingmen and organizing them for political action. Wonderful! How Shelley would have envied you! He tried so hard, poor boy, to do what you are doing now—to be a man of action helping to carry forward the political movement of his day. But it wasn't given him to do such work—he wasn't hardheaded himself—lacked genius for practical action.—You see the gods have been very good to you!

I like the plan you suggest about the poems first-rate. Thank you so much for letting me keep them these weeks till we meet in Milwaukee. And I hope we'll find Comrade Thompson[4] appreciative too. Have you any idea whether he has sense for art? Of course my range of experience is small but so far the socialists having a sense for art, that I have met, have been half-baked in their science; and the scientific constructive sane socialists have been not even so much as half-baked in their ideas on art. Oh there *have* been a few exceptions: yourself, my brother and—? I fear I've come to the end of the list. For goodness' sake, don't show this to any of our mutual friends in Milwaukee!!

It occurs to me just now that it's possible that my experience in this matter may have been partially responsible for my past cynical attitude toward literary art—and toward art in general (The summer my brother was at home I jeered at him so much that he lost faith—or nearly lost faith in art too. He was asked to give a talk on Art before the Milwaukee Camera Club. And what do you suppose he did? Scored art and artists both mercilessly, indiscriminately! I wish I had preserved the newspaper report of it—It was so funny—The reporter tried so hard to make something creditable, academic, out of it.) [P.S. Fortunately brother recovered his poise abroad.] I can understand how finding practically all good socialists lacking in artistic feeling might influence a person like myself to take a cynical attitude toward art.

By the way I must not forget to define "opuscula" for you. It's a term applied to literary pieces of no great length by a person who takes a cynical attitude toward literary art in general and who has not yet come to recognize the genius of the author of the pieces aforesaid.

Now you know what "opuscula" means, or more accurately, what I meant by the word when I used it. Needless to say I shall never use the term with reference to any work of yours in future. For I confess your genius. Moreover you've converted me from a cynic, as regards art, to a true believer. For this too great thanks! Cynicism is naturally distasteful to me—I feel better rid of it—more free more human. Cynicism is of a piece with snobbery. Yes, yes—great thanks to you again!

And for Weltanschauung. Must I really dispense with good homely German words in writing to you? I like Weltanschauung so much better than the scholastic "Philosophy" or the clumsy "conception of the world." And of course to one from Milwaukee—a plain, homely German word sounds less foreign than a Greek or Latin word that has been naturalized in English. However I'll forbear hereafter. Was glad to note that you are of Swedish stock—A Teuton therefore anyway! More about the Teutons some other time.

Regards to your friend the General[5] wot was in the army with you and thank him for the trouble delivering to you this letter.

L.S.

1. Lines from "A Fling at the Riddle," an early poem that he later classed as "juvenilia"; it does not appear among his published works.

> Some stray blithe romance, coming, coming, coming—
> Some shining gleam of a woman's hair.

2. Of these, only "Fragments" is unpublished. "All Day Long" and "Departures" (with the title changed to "Docks") were published in the "Other Days" section of *Chicago Poems* (1916).

3. The "Lake Country" was the Lake Shore and Fox River Valley District, which he was trying to organize.

4. Carl D. Thompson, a Congregationalist minister in Milwaukee, was the state organizer of the Social-Democratic party of Wisconsin. Local organizers kept him informed as to what had happened at successful meetings and when and where future meetings would be held, and this information would appear in his column, "The State Organizer's Department" of the *Social-Democratic Herald*. So my mother knew from the *Herald* not only something of where my father had been working, but also that he was to go north to Oconto County to lecture as a visiting organizer in Suring, Mountain, Green Bay, and Marinette.

5. One of his letters is obviously missing, and since it is the only one that refers to "the General," he must remain a mystery.

7.

Princeton, Ill.
March 3, 1908

My dear Comrade,

Just a word of cheer to you in the midst of your arduous labors in the faraway North! I can imagine what difficulties you have to battle against—so that a word of glad thanks to you for the good work you are doing, will not be unwelcome.

Glad thanks to you for every thought-awakening word you spoke and will speak on this northern trip, at Green Bay, at Marinette and wherever else your work takes you! Glad thanks for the thought you give to the improvement of our propaganda (I note what you say about the lack of what you call "style" in our propaganda—and I appreciate the force of your criticism).

"A something of compressed and striking presentation, with as much daring and force as we now have, with hope and good-sense and gayety added"—Yes that's just it—exactly what we want!

And you are working toward the realization of this! You *say* it and you *do* it. You have the discernment to see what is needed—and the heart and the will to supply the need. Bravo! The world could not move on without You! Without Your help!

It's *your* Religion—or call it Joy-in-Life[1]—that makes you do it, I suppose. For the socialist propaganda and pilgrimages to birch-woods have the same well-spring. Am I religious?—Yes, I believe I have always been religious—more or less—more, I think as I grew older—tho already at twelve I was pretty seriously religious. Of course the forms have changed considerably since. [All the theology is gone—not a shred remains—not so much as the word "God." But theology seems to me to be more a question of science than of religion. Hence a relatively insignificant question. I am not worried about theology—believe me. Religion is the important thing.]

A long digression again! But I thought an explanation necessary. I have a horror of being misunderstood on this point—of being mistaken for a militant atheist or some such monstrosity! Which I am not! I am not hostile to theology. I simply have no theology. I recognize a universal religion of humanism and joy-in-life—a religion common to all—to those who accept theologies and to those who have no theology.

I set out just to send the word of cheer—not to write an exposition of my views on theology. But this last got itself done somehow—so let it stand. I wish though you'd try to imagine that this latter part of my letter is in fine print—a modest footnote. And let the word of cheer stand out in large capitals—as the real message to you pioneering on the frontier—to you in Marinette! Glad thanks!

Lilian Steichen

P.S. And Marinette isn't a mere dot on the map to me. I see it (as I see all the towns you work in)—"a factual entity with lands, buildings, laws and noises."[2] Your graphic description of Oshkosh serves to make Marinette and the rest live communities for me instead of names or places on the map.

1. Her combination of the words "Joy-in-Life" seems reminiscent of Edward Carpenter's phrase, "joy of the liberated soul" in *Towards Democracy*.

2. The quote in the P.S. is from Letter 3.

8.

Princeton, Ill.
March 4, 1908

My dear Comrade—

This mail brought your first letter from the North (you see I count on more,* so I specify "*first*")—also the Social Democratic Herald. I always read your notes in the Herald and from them conclude that you are, what Thompson calls you in this issue, a Hustler![1] I was glad to read that Thompson appreciates what an energetic worker you are—Thompson's enthusiasm over your work means a lot—he is such a splendid worker himself. Doesn't it please you to have a man like him recognize your work? He's in the field himself and knows what it all means.

When I read the Herald I said—"Now I've got to write to Green Bay again—and say again *Bravo!*" I had written yesterday evening and mailed the letter this morning—(By the way I addressed that letter to Marinette not to Green Bay. I hope it will reach you all right.)

And your letter tells me that I'm helping you. I like to hear that. So I shall be able to help the world on a little, through you. Directly I don't touch the world these days. Princeton is outside the bounds of the world. Oh, there is one other hope of course—that some of my boys and girls will leave Princeton when they grow up and become a part of the World. And so my work at school may count a little.

Thanks for the "Sunshine-Slanting-Across-Shadows" and "The Crimson Turban in a Corot Landscape"[2]—I accept both! With a glad heart! My Religion is *Joy-in-Life* you know.

I have had the best news from my brother—he is on his way to America! Now I am waiting to hear definitely whether business in New York will not interfere with his being home during my vacation. It is just barely possible—or my fears make it seem so—

* But don't write when it's a burden to write—I mean when you are busy (or too busy) anyway. I shall understand. What with correspondence and platform talks etc. an organizer's life must be ever so busy. Write only when it's a real pleasure!

that he may have to hold his exhibition that week. So I'm waiting anxiously.

The short spring vacation promises so much this year!

You *MUST manage* to spend a day at the farm. It's not very accessible—no trolley line and a poor schedule on the railroad. (I inclose schedule so you can see for yourself). There are two good morning trains from Milwaukee. The 7:40 train arrives at Granville 8:15 and is met there by a mail coach from Menomonee Falls which takes passengers and mail both arriving Menomonee Falls about 9 o'clock. The train that leaves Milwaukee at 9:05 arrives Granville about 9:30. You have to wait there till train leaves Granville about 10:35 for Menomonee Falls. This train is scheduled to arrive at Men. Falls about 10:35 but it is usually late, from a quarter to a half hour. I think the 7:40 train is the better. It is the mail train—therefore sure and quick.

The farm is three miles from Menomonee Falls—a fine walk in good weather (for folks who like to walk—do you?). I think it would be a fine way to begin "the day at the farm" with this walk together. But if you're not a pedestrian, or if the weather is unfavorable or the road in bad condition, I'll call for you with horse and buggy.

If you are equal to these difficulties, all right! We are ready for "the day on the farm."

There are no hills, alas. Just farm-land for miles around—cultivated fields and pastures—and a few small remnants of woods. But there's the sky and the wide horizon and the Open Road! And the small remnants of woods aforesaid! Abundantly enough for glad hearts!

I suppose you'll look at the schedule for trains back to Milwaukee. If so, don't imagine that we'll let you leave on the *afternoon* train from Menomonee Falls. It's so early that it's out of the question. You'll either have to stay overnight with us or leave from another station, Granville (6 miles from the farm—a comfortable drive) on an *evening* train. The better plan would be to stay overnight—*if we can lodge you comfortably enough*. The farmhouse is small—it's a dear little, old little, white farm house. Kitchen, big living-room and one bed-room down-stairs. Upstairs attic and two small bed-rooms. Papa sleeps in one of the upstairs bedrooms and you could have the other. But papa doesn't mind the cold—and maybe you do. (The up-stairs isn't heated). So whether we can lodge you comfortably enough will depend on how cold the weather is—and on how much cold you can stand. There are plenty blankets and quilts by the way—if you can get any comfort out of that thought!

Perhaps you can put up with such "simple life"—can you? If you will come to the farm in summer again, we'll be able to do better. We have a tent up in the orchard then for sleeping out-of-doors. And Papa is the only member of the family who prefers sleeping in-doors. The house "is good enough" for him—he does not take up with new-fangled notions as mother does. So in summer we can say very grandly to our friends who come to the farm: "Where would you sleep, in-doors or out-of-doors; if in-doors—up-stairs or down-stairs? Choose!"

I must see that story MSS—with the portrait "approximating" me! . . . Yes, you must see brother's portraits of me. I wonder what you'll see in them and what things you'll expect to find in them and be disappointed? Strange things have been said about those portraits! and by those who are wont to understand too!

How long do you expect to remain in Milwaukee? Do you know?

Chop Sooey and Thomas Orchestra![3] I learned what the latter meant in the years I lived in Chicago—and I know from present experience what it means to be *without* Thomas Concerts. But the companion-extravagance of Chop Sooey, I have never indulged in. So it will be a Voyage of Discovery for me—how alluring the prospect you can imagine!

Spring is here too—and Gladness! From glad heart to glad heart—Greetings!

L.S.

1. Carl D. Thompson's column in the *Social-Democractic Herald*, Feb. 29, 1908, reads as follows: "Comrade Sandburg is certainly a hustler. You hear of him one day at Manitowoc, the next at Fond du Lac. He says 'will be here Monday and Tuesday of next week; in Appleton the 27th and 28th.' On the 27th he is to give a lecture on Bernard Shaw for a literary society of which some of our comrades are members. On the 28th at the Trades Union Hall, 'I shall do some building,' he says. At Appleton a prohibition trade unionist, who seemed to be quite impossible a while ago, joined the branch and is making a worthy addition. . . . The comrades are distributing the leaflet by Comrade Sandburg, on 'Labor and Politics.'"

2. I am not familiar with "Sunshine-Slanting-Across-Shadows" and "Crimson Turban in a Corot Landscape." They are not with my father's early poems and essays among his papers, and I do not know whether they were some of his early work. But from what my mother says here, I would think so.

3. The Chicago Public Concerts were free and available to poor working people and students; they were begun by Christian Frederic Theodore Thomas (1835–1905) and continued in his name after his death.

9.

Princeton, Ill.
March 7, 1908

Dear Comrade—

I have it—your "latest" and best! "*Let It Be Said*"[1] has caught, enmeshed in its words and rhythms, the spirit of joy in living. Oh, it makes me more than ever in love with Life—"the difficult splendid thing!" And *you,* happiest Poet, do not only live this brave proud free life—you also find the words and the rhythms to infect one with the elation! One is swept along as by the wind!—a freshening wind from the sea!

I see the well-spring of poetry is not dry in you! You have surpassed yourself!—

And the word from Swing anent the "lumberyacks" gave me a vivid realization of how keenly alive you were to the Challenge of the work you were going to do that evening—the talk to those lumberyacks![2] I can imagine how you met that Challenge! They "sat up"—now didn't they?

I am glad for a glimpse like this into your life on the field of action—and shall be glad for more such glimpses—of the disappointments and of the successes. (The gray days mean as intensely—as the bright ones.)

Yes indeed I liked the sketch "Fashion"—every word of it. And I'm glad to hear you say that I am a far cry from that *Figures without Eyes.*[3] My own consciousness tells me so too. I think for myself. I dare to have natural feelings. And I'm not afraid to speak my thoughts and feelings. I give Nature a fair chance to work in me. No artificialities for me! No corsets, no French heels, no patent medicines! No formal receptions! No mad chase after the very latest styles in dress! In short I appeal from Fashion to my own Reason and my own Instincts.

The other evening I came in to supper after a splendid walk—in an exuberance of joy! It had been raining hard all day till late in the afternoon. The streets were muddy and pools of water were everywhere. The air was sweet and fresh after the rain. At sunset the sky had cleared in the west along the horizon—The rest of the sky was still overcast with great heavy clouds—slate blue. I was walking toward the sun-set. The street was bordered with elm trees. Thru this vista of arching elms, I saw the sky aglow! And the ruts in the road caught the glow—two ribbons of burning gold. And my heart caught the glow—burning intense—So there I stood and looked and looked. "Let it be said I have lived"![4]

I walked on again—and on till I came to the end of the avenue of elms. No more Gothic arches overhead. The open country! Wind-swept! The darkening slate-blue sky heavy with clouds overhead—great fields of yellow corn-stubble stretching afar on both sides of the road—and the West a great lake of burning gold! And always the wind blowing wildly! Such a wind, fresh after the rain, and impetuous, is irresistible. I am blown along—The wind challenges—I run hard returning the challenge. . . . Then slow down—vanquished—beaten—laughing at myself—at the Wind too!

I turn homeward—gay at heart. A friendly dog has joined me—a sympathetic fellow—ready to run when I run or to walk. But readier to run! We are gay, we two! My coat flaps against the dog—and I laugh aloud in merriment! After which I laugh again—this time *inwardly*—pleased that so simple a thing should have moved me to loud laughter—pleased that for one gay moment I have been a *simple child* responding exuberantly to the play of the Wind!

I feel glad for the life that is given me to live. I think of how I shall soon see my brother. I think of the splendid letter—the last one—from you, my good comrade. And I think of how I shall see you soon. I feel exuberantly glad for it all.

So I came into supper after this splendid walk—my hair windblown covered with fine sleet (for a sleet has begun to fall soft and fresh—caressing one's cheeks). I'm late of course. The table talk at the boarding house is about an evening wedding reception—very swell—hats must be worn (in-doors at night!) swell evening hats—the women are worried—they are sure their hats won't do—some are going to send to Chicago for new hats—some can't afford that and don't know what to do. God help them! Then there's talk about the afternoon receptions—there have been four or five of these each week for the last month. The women are *tired* of them—tired to death—but they wouldn't miss one! The high school teachers are all invited to these afternoon receptions—so as a matter of course I got invitations to the first two or three. I declined—"too busy." The other teachers go—some to all—the rest to most of these receptions. But I stay at home—walk—read—work—do as I please. And Princeton doesn't mind—they accept me as I am. Put me down as "peculiar" of course but don't molest me. I walk the streets hatless most of the time—a thing I couldn't do in Milwaukee without attracting attention. Here it's hardly noticed. I don't go to church Sundays—that isn't noticed either. I talk socialism, and radicalism generally, whenever I get a chance—that doesn't disturb Princeton either.—Of course there's a reason why Princeton is imperturbable respecting my "eccentricities." Princeton is sure that it is in the right. I am regarded as harmless—they do not see that my non-conformity is part and parcel of a large, really formidable movement—a movement that threatens to overturn their institutions. If they scented the danger, they would cease to be tolerant.—Meantime I enjoy toleration here as I would not in a place where there is a labor movement that has made itself felt. (Of course this is a vegetating existence! I'd rather meet intolerance and wrestle with it and try to down it. The toleration of ignorance can only be temporary anyway).

To return from this digression anent Princetonian tolerance. You see the point—the contrast between me and the women whom I meet at table after my walk! They are more or less "Figures without Eyes."

This morning I saw my first robin for this spring! And it's warm and sunny, with south winds, to-day. If the weather is anything like this when you come out to the farm we won't have any difficulty making you comfortable for the night. By leaving the door from the living-room to the stairs open, we can arrange to have the up-stairs bedrooms reasonably warm and fairly well ventilated too. With a hot fire in the living room and windows open—you'll get fresh and warmed air up-stairs all right.—

And I wish you would plan to stay several days instead of one! Provided you would enjoy it, of course!

L.S.

1. "Let It Be Said," an early poem, was never published.

2. He had spoken at Suring on March 5 and then at Mountain in Oconto County on "The Social Democrats—Who They Are And What They Want."

3. "Fashion" and "Figures without Eyes" are early works, never published and now lost.

4. From "Let It Be Said."

10.

Princeton
March 12, 1908

Dear Poet and Comrade,

I have your good letter from the land of "lumber, tanbark and cranberries"—I catch from it something of the spirit of the hardy north—the scent of pine forests and all![1] Clean and strong and sweet, your North!—I love it.

And I love no less these earliest soft spring days here. Tender pussy-willows! And meadow-larks! And warm velvety south-winds! And little green things pushing up thru the moist rich humus of dead decayed leaves! Over all a glamor of something—I know not what—call it Spring!—of stir or light or life?

This is the time when the country road calls irresistibly. "Then longen folk to go on pilgrimages"![2] Straight from school I take the Open Road these days. The hedges are full of joyous little gray and brown birds (I don't know their names—do you know the names of all the pretty little gray and brown birds? I don't expect ever to know one little feathered gray brother from another by name—I have no turn for remembering names—and it doesn't bother me much. I love the birds. It is enough for me!)

The "lines on a Paradox"[3] are well worth while! You are a

Joyous Heart—a Sweet Boy—to have thought the thoughts in them! And a rare Poet to have found the sweet simple words that tell the thoughts! Again Glad thanks!

P.S. There are a few lines just before the three last lines that puzzle me. I shall ask you for light on them at the convention.

And the prose inclosure is splendid. Strong, simple, direct, and full of joy and wisdom—it shows the noble strength and stature of your soul.

I had not seen the essay by Sinclair you sent me from Oconto. It helped so much to clear up my confused ideas on the subject of democratic art etc. Am so glad I didn't miss this splendid work, thanks to you! By his historical method, Sinclair makes everything so plain—I see it now solved! The problem of modern literature!

Yes, it's a go. I'll try always to say "hard work" instead of "arduous labors" hereafter. "I'll try," I say. But doubtless I'll blunder into scholasticisms now and then. That's what schooling did for me. This was the way of it. My mother tongue is Luxembourger—a German dialect. English is an acquired tongue—and as I was a book-worm from about twelve years old till I got thru college, I got my English from books, largely academic books at that. I've tried to get free from Latinisms—and talk idiomatic English. It's been up-hill work. But I'm at it still—will try harder than ever, I promise you. And you trip me up, please—when you see me going in the wrong direction. And don't give up hope for me if I sin often—backslide often—you know *Why* I'm liable to now—No more to-day. Good-night.

L.S.

1. My father had written his sister Esther on March 11 that he was writing "on a sleigh stage crossing Green Bay from Marinette to Sturgeon Bay."

2. From Chaucer's Prologue to *The Canterbury Tales*.

3. "Lines on a Paradox" was an early poem, never published, but obviously written on inspiration after reading over some of her letters.

Lines on a Paradox

All the beautiful thoughts you send,
In a sheaf I gather and give back to you.
Yet I keep them, too,
For that is the way with beautiful thoughts;

Into and out of their trackless routes
They pass and repass and no man loses.
        Whatever they touch
Will lighten and gleam and reply somewhere
On the tide of the years, today or tomorrow.

Even the shadows would not be shadows
Were it not for the magic of shimmering moons
And the face of a stagnant, wayside pool
Will catch and reflect an evening star.

Splendor and terror and gold and folly,
Poise that is ready and love that is sure—
They are answers from out of a final voice
That utters the world's great will.

All of the beautiful thoughts you send,
In a sheaf I gather and give back to you.
        Yet I keep them, too.

II.

Princeton, Ill.
March 15, 1908

Dear Comrade—

I have your note saying "we will *walk* from Menomonee Falls." Good! And the date—March 28—isn't so far off any more. Then you'll have to tell me about your work as organizer—in Manitowoc—in Oshkosh and among the lumberjacks. I'm looking forward to it eagerly. I hope we'll have favorable weather so you'll be able to *enjoy the country* to the fullest extent while you're resting from your hard hustling life as agitator.

Resting? I fear if you do all the talking I want you to do—telling me about yourself generally and about democratic art and about S.D.P. organization work—you won't get much rest! But there will be the pictures to look at—that will be rest for you!

Today I got a short note from my brother saying that his photographic exhibition[1] opened last week (I inclose announcement) and that it will continue till April 2. I hope the exhibition won't prevent his coming home March 27 as he first planned. His note didn't mention this possibility. It was very typical of Edward's notes—short—brisk—full of the rush of work—"hastily but lovingly, Gaesjack."[2] When you've read the note you've gotten a vivid impression of the rush, rush, rush—of getting up an exhibition in very short time. But you haven't any facts—practical points like dates. He's a wild boy—*Gaesjack!* (That's his "pet" name—Luxembourger). I wish he were a little less wild—a little more practical—and would write definitely whether he'll have to stay in New York till the exhibition closes. An artistic temperament has its drawbacks!

By the way, do 20th century artists have "temperaments" too? Necessarily? I don't see why a modern realist artist need have any such romantic nonsense about him!

On second thought I believe I did my brother an injustice in referring his shortcomings to his supposed artist's temperament. I'll take that back—say his shortcomings are due to plain "*cussedness*." That sounds lots better—Edward would like it better too. And it's much nearer the truth. For Edward hasn't any nonsense about him.—

Now *you* haven't *Edward's* sort of "cussedness." Your letters are always satisfying—they come to the point. However I take for granted that you have a peculiar brand of "cussedness" all your own. It's only a question of finding out wherein lies your "cussedness." It's not human nor comradely to be angelic—and until the contrary is proved beyond a possibility of doubt I'll consider you innocent of any such uncomradely deficiency in plain human "cussedness."

That's all for to-day.

Here's Good Luck to you and your work!

L.S.

1. This was a one-man exhibition of photographs in monochrome and color at the Photo-Secession Little Galleries, New York City, from March 12 to April 2, 1908.

2. "Gaesjack" (pronounced Gay-shawk), meaning "little Jack," was a common nickname for John in Europe, when a son had been given this name after his father. My uncle's baptismal name was Eduard Jean Steichen, after a Steichen cousin who was his godfather, and my grandfather, Jean Pierre Steichen. The names were Anglicized in this country.

12.

Princeton, Ill.
March 16, 1908.

Dear Charles Sandburg,

Your two beautiful letters which came together today have left me full of Wonder and Hope! To think that one day can hold so much happiness!—and it's You, my Poet, so free with the warm human gifts of your dear words and rhythms, that have filled the day brimful with Joy for me!

"So glad am I that on the great wide way we have met, touched hands and spoken."[1] This thought "I give back to you—yet I keep it too"—[2]

And I have really some part in the making of your warm human poems! Really? This thought is what fills me with such sweet wonder and hope—

I have been conscious in rare poignant moments in my life of something very beautiful deep deep within me—but the Voice from those depths has always been so small, so still—more a *hush* than a *voice*—that I never dreamed that anyone but myself would *hear* it. But so finely attuned was that heart of yours, you caught the fine vibrant note from the depths—and—gave it strength and quality. In your poems somehow (I dare *hope—believe* it!) the sweet still hush of my heart has become blended with the clear strong proud Music of yours and so is heard! It is heard—and the farthest star and the last son of man will vibrate to it. But for you, the sweet small hush yearning upward toward light and utterance would have subsided back to the dark depths—subsided and subsided—till it lost what small strength for upward yearning it had—and so died forever! So glad thanks to you—for Voice! for Life! This is the Wonder and the Hope!

No more to-night. It is late and I have a hard day of work before me—

Good-night! Blessings on you, dear boy.

L.S.

1. There are obviously two letters missing here, one from which she is quoting.

2. From "Lines on a Paradox."

13.

Princeton
March 17, 1908

Wunderkind!

I've got to call you that even if you don't know what it means. The name has been on my lips before when I read some account of what you were doing—or when I read some splendid poem of yours. But I kept from calling you the name aloud—because of the Weltanschauung episode. Besides I found substitute names in English that seem fairly adequate to the occasion. Now that I've read "In Reckless Ecstasy"[1] and the rest you sent to-day—why nothing short of *Wunderkind* will do! If there's an English equivalent I don't know it—my English vocabulary is small.

Yes, of course, *Wunderkind* can be explained in English—the which I shall try to do presently. But an *explanation* isn't a *name*. When I'm thru with my explanation, you'll tell me if you know a name in English that means all that. I'll be so glad to learn—because I don't like to throw German names at you—names that you liken to Coal-Wagons! Unhandy missiles!!

You call a *Wunderkind*, a boy that makes you lift up your heart to him and sing: "Hail, Thou Young God!" Such worship and rapture and wonderment are embodied in *Wunder-kind*. "Wonder-child" would be the literal translation—but English has not crystallized a thought, a name in any such word combination. The German soul had greater need for the word—so it made for itself the word! The German soul—you get it in a Wagner opera—knows how to feel the passion, the tumult, the rapture of Worship. And there is nothing under the sun that has so good a right to inspire such Worship as a proud, free, tender, strong, brave Boy! This Boy the Germans call *Wunderkind!* The Germans who know how to worship, the Germans who have given us the Wagner opera *too!*

(And you are Norse! Splendid! That is the superlative of German!—It was not enough—it seems for you to be a young god—you add to this that your race is the young God among the nations! You glorious young Norse God!)

I want to say so *much* more—but I must stop. I've read and read "In Reckless Ecstasy" (O, you Wunderkind!) and read the

Circulars—and have thought and thought looking at you in your different aspects together—Lyceum speaker, Poet, S.D.P. organizer, Boy—and it's to You—this complete many-sided *You*—that I say in glad worship recognizing in you a glorious achievement and a still more glorious *Hope:*—"Wunderkind! Wunderkind!"

What with reading and thinking, it's late. More anon. Goodnight!

L.S.

P.S. I shall take very good care of all the Mss you send me—be sure! It will not be my fault if they are missing at the Great Assizes.—*Send more!* P.S.P.S. But don't send "*You.*"[2] I'd rather hear you read that yourself as you suggest "from the rostrum"!

1. *In Reckless Ecstasy* (1904), his first published book.
2. "You," an early poem written for her.

You

You are slanting sun across the dark,
You are dew and calm and fragrance,
You are fire and gold and sunset peace,
    You lure and you lead
And the look of your eye is light
On the path of the dream we dream.

The touch of your hand is hope
And the sheen of your hair is glory
You are the sea with its mystic song,
You are the stars and dawn and morning.
You are a woman, you are a comrade,
We will do, we will hope, we will live,
We will rest in the hearts of remembering men
Who saw us as we passed.

14.

Princeton
March 18, 1908

Dear Comrade—

I've been reading *In Reckless Ecstasy* again to-day. How this Voice of your past self helps me to understand you as You are to-day. I feel surer of you. You aristocrat, you! This monument out of the past shows that your blue blood is not of yesterday—Wright[1] testifies that your blue blood showed itself to him when he first met you in '98—ten years ago! So I'm sure that your present self is built on sure solid foundations. You, Charles Sandburg, as I have known you these few weeks, are a real individual—not a phantasm, or a passing mood—You have a past self—that contained the embryo of your present self. It was a natural growth and gives sure promise of further beautiful growth—

Not that your manhood needs any such literary certification from the past—your manhood can stand of itself! alone, approve itself! The certification is so much extra—that's all.

In but a little more than a week we shall see each other face to face! This time I shall really see You. The first glimpse I had of you was not *seeing*. That we will be good comrades I know. For the rest, we know not. Perhaps we shall shortly know—perhaps—I like your Shavian "Nothing matters much." It's honest. It means that you know you'll get what's coming to you—and more than that, you don't want. The man who wants more than is coming to him is a fool—if he gets his wish, there'll be the devil to pay afterward! But you, my dear Shavian comrade, are honest! are wise!—We aren't worried or hurried. We are ready any minute for all things—the great and the small—and glad for all things! We have faith in the gods—that they will serve up to each man the dishes suited to his digestion, "all the elephants of Hindustan"[2] or—a peck of turnips! As the case may be!—Also the gods know best when each of us is ready for his heavy meal—whether it shall be breakfast or dinner or supper!—Woe to the dishonest mortal who tries to cheat the gods and devours an elephant not meant for his turnip-stomach! or breaks fast with a course dinner before his digestive apparatus is ready for hard work! "There'll be the devil to pay!"—The wise wait till the gods serve up the dishes—to each his proper dish at the proper time.—Everything comes to those who wait—that is to those who wait *actively* (the Shavian-honest); of course those who wait only *passively* (the Philistine-honest) miss the chances being asleep when the gods make them offers!

Once more—*so* glad you're a Shavian! So glad you have a proud, free, careless, joyous heart! alert and ready too! but above all free, proud, honest! and Careless!

It will be great to see you! I shall probably arrive in Milwaukee at 4:45 P.M. Friday, the 27th. I *may* have to go straight thru to Brookfield (a station on the main line C.M. & St. P.—6 miles from the farm) where father could call for me with horse and buggy. It will depend on whether brother will be at home then (the 27th is his Birthday—a great event in the family! so if he were home I'd have to hurry home as fast as possible to celebrate with Mother and him). If brother isn't home—as seems likely now—I'd like to wait over in Milwaukee till a later train to Brookfield, either the 6 or 7 o'clock train. That would give us time to see each other—maybe time for Leif Ericson—possibly for Chop Suey?—I'll have to think it over and see what mother says. Mother gets very lonesome on the farm—and very hungry for me! Mother *is such a mother!* She wants me the first minute she can have me.—But I would like to be with you in Milwaukee till seven o'clock anyway. Perhaps we could walk down to the Lake.—I must write mother and see what she says.

I hope you'll like it at the farm well enough to stay there most of the time till you return to Oshkosh. You will want to stay probably—if you find me as good a comrade when you see me face to face, as you think I am now that the miles separate us! We shall see!

You will like my mother I believe. She has such a Heart! And such strength and dauntlessness! And such Hope! Mother comes from plain unlettered peasant stock in medieval priest-ridden Catholic Luxembourg, with its religious processions and pilgrimages and the rest! Yet mother understands me an "infidel"—and is half an infidel herself, tho she won't quite admit it! And she's a party member and a private Agitator!—And such a Heart! In her best years, starved for love! Lived only to work for her children—and joyous always, glad for the work, and for what it brought us! It was long before I came to understand mother—and before I came to love her with an understanding love—I was too much of a child before.

I notice you dedicated *In Reckless Ecstasy* to your mother. What a mother she must be—to have such a Wunderkind as You! What a Mother! "One who has kept a serene soul in a life of stress—wrested beauty from the common-place—scattered her gladness without stint or measure"[3]—How proud she must be of having born You!

I suppose you'll be in Manitowoc, when this reaches you, hard at work again!—To think of your making a speech—2 hours & 10 min. long—as you did at Green Bay—and then a shorter speech the very next day at noon! and keeping this sort of thing a-going!—It's glorious—but I'm glad you are to take a rest soon.—Meanwhile Good-luck!

L.S.

1. Philip Green Wright, a professor of mathematics at Lombard College, had influenced my father in his formative years and was a very dear friend. He ran the Asgard Press in his basement and published my father's first three books, *In Reckless Ecstasy* (1904), *Incidentals* (1907), and *The Plaint of a Rose* (1908). The quote is from Wright's foreword to *In Reckless Ecstasy.* On receiving this letter my father wrote to Wright to send her *The Dreamer,* a book of poems by Wright for which my father had written the foreword.

2. This line is from the third page of *Incidentals:* "Failure and success wear the same face to one thoroughly alive, and I may say with Heinrich Heine, 'Red life flows in my veins. I could eat all the elephants in Hindustan and pick my teeth with the spires of Strassburg cathedral.'"

3. From the dedication to his mother of *In Reckless Ecstasy.*

15.

Princeton
March 20 [1908]
5:30 P.M.

Just a word—will try to get it off by the 6 o'clock mail—so it will surely reach you at Manitowoc.—Have just gotten home from a hard day's work at school.

First a *DON'T. Don't* work so hard. *Don't* rob yourself of sleep & rest. Of course all this activity (this ferment of the Yeast as the old Sea-Wolf would say)[1] is Life. And its Glorious! But there's a Nemesis—the Greek un-moral Nemesis—for Too-Much-Life.

I have the best right to give this piece of advice, having kept too-late hours myself last week and cheated my body of exercise! This has been grade-week with us—which means tests—exams—averaging grades etc.! Besides I've just launched the Sophomore dramatic work (Scenes from *She Stoops to Conquer.* I've tried Ibsen's *An Enemy of the People* in my day. I know better now! It's not worth while). Had to adapt and re-arrange and fix up an end for the scenes—also assign parts! You won't appreciate what all this means, as *you've* never been a pedagog! *Pedagog—Me* a *Pedagog!* If you'd see how my classes act sometimes you wouldn't think I came under that classification either! Such lawlessness! and such fun! When I'm just one of *them*—one of "the youngsters"! But assigning parts in a play—that's different!

But what I started out to write you—You ask about my train. I arrive Mil. 4:45 P.M.—C. Mil. & St. Paul station—(a week from to-day!)

How do you like this plan? We visit in Milwaukee together till 6 o'clock—or *possibly* 7 o'clock—train to Brookfield (Better 6 o'clock!). Then take train *together* and reach the farm that evening *together* (*not* walking!—that would be fun for us, tho our luggage might be a hindrance—but mother WOULD NOT HEAR TO IT, I KNOW. Still it would be a lark!) Father or someone would call for us at Brookfield—and we'd have the ride home together. Wouldn't that be better than the old plan of having you come out to the farm the next morning? Write me what you say to this.

I inclose a letter home from my brother. So you can see what his plans are. He writes that his nose is "to the grindstone"—the letter shows it. It's surely work—work—work—with him these days. As you probably *don't know*—I'll tell you what "Paus'l" stands for. It's *me.*

Edward writes we are to keep what he says about McClure's to *ourselves* for the present. Not having heard of you at the time he wrote the letter, he probably didn't mean to include *you.* But I know it's all right—you'll not let it get any farther.

Must stop now—or I won't make the mail—More later.

L.S.

1. In Jack London's *The Sea-Wolf* (1904), Wolf Larson says, "I believe that life is a mess. It is like yeast, a ferment that moves and may move for a minute, an hour, a year, or a hundred years but in the end will cease to move."

16.

Manitowoc, March 21. 1908

Dear girl:—I will look for you on the 4:45 at the C.M. & St. Paul station on Friday the 27th. I expect to have everything cleared up and be ready for anything that can happen, gallows or throne, sky or sea-bottom! Yours Thoughtfully alias Paus'l will be dictator and mistress of ceremonies. You will announce the events and the gladiators will gladiate like blazes! The joy-bells on high will clang like joy. Motley will have vent and psalms will be sung and three or four peans [*sic*] will go up to the stars out of pure gladiosity.—I believe you asked about my cussedness. This is some of it. I am cussedest when I am glad, and so are those around me. Admonish me gently to behave and I may or I may not. For whatever is in must come out. That is the snub and sumstance of expression and great is expression.—I promise tho, that while we are on the cars and respectable people who pride themselves on demeanor are about, I will not "Rah! rah rah!" nor sing "The mother was chasing her boy round the room" with all forty-four verses. Thus much is certain. The honorific norm of dignity shall have recognizance, all it wants.—As we pass triumphantly, we shall leave the leavings.—Haven't had anything, never touch anything, just glad, L.S., just glad, that's all! that's all!

Well, what do you think of a paper on Love—from me—me going in on this age-old subject and grappling, juggling and tossing the theme like the strong man at the circus with the iron balls. You started it! You started it! That will be one answer to any reproach you may utter that I pontificate unduly.—Honest tho, I rather like it. A few months of rest and then some retouching and it may compete with Virginibus Puerisque,[1] etc.

So interesting a brother you have! The letter gives me a glimpse of him. "My tricks and carelessness" how naturally that drops from him—with those he loves confessing a little waywardness, knowing they love him for it.

Will you bring along and wear once that Graeco-Gothic white thing you have on in that picture?[2] Just frinstance!

When you rebuke me on the gibbosity of this letter—for these are awful babblings—and chide me for gayety that spills and splashes—I shall take refuge in the authority of your Richard Wagner, the man who wrote operas occ. Rebuke not too rebukingly for Wagner is explicit on the point. I will quote it on the way out of Brookfield.—

To Her Thoughtfulness alias Pausl—
from
C.S.*

* Such as he is.

1. *Virginibus Puerisque* (first published in 1881) was a collection of essays by Robert Louis Stevenson. The third of these was "On Falling in Love." This is the reason that my father wrote with some humor that after a few changes his "paper on Love" might "compete with *Virginibus Puerisque*."

2. This refers to a Steichen print of my mother taken at the farm in 1907, when she was wearing a long, full, light print dress, being blown by the wind, with barefoot sandals on her feet. She must have sent him a reproduction of the print, probably as an example of her brother's photographic art.

17.

Princeton
March 22, 1908

Did you get my letter at Manitowoc, asking whether you will second my plan to go thru to the farm with me Friday evening instead of waiting over in Milwaukee and coming to the farm Saturday morning. If you like the plan we'll take the 6 P.M. train together to Brookfield.—

So if you haven't already done so, write me whether the farm is to expect you Friday or Saturday. Mother will want to know.

What you say about your father and mother brings you so much nearer to me—you—Charles August Sandburg! Our past, our forbears, so much the same and now "sitting together on the same rock high on the mountain roadway"[1]—we ought to understand each other! I have had comrades who thought they understood me, and yet failed to understand and love my past. "The wooden shoe ascending"[2]—that is one of the things I worship! I am proud of my peasant grandfather[3]—My *mother* I *worship* for the way she has unfolded from a peasant girl! and for the way she has helped her children get on—toward the Mountain Roadway!

And you understand—feel—all this—the glory of it perhaps more wonderful in your home than in ours—And you, dear warm-human Poet, you give the Past—a Poet's worship! God bless you!

No more to-day—I must get out into the streets—under the budding trees—in the warm living sun-shine and fresh wind! I must not let myself be tired by Friday from lack of outdoor life—the last week I was indoors altogether too much working on grades, tests etc. And we're not thru yet. This week we enter the grades—we keep three distinct and separate records of grades in this school!

Maybe I'll write another little note tomorrow. There's so much to answer in your last letters, I feel I can't hope to get caught up with it by letter. And all this will keep till we can talk face to face—You'll have to tell me about all the Great Companions then—and more about your Mother too!

TAKE GOOD CARE OF YOURSELF—and be at hand for roll-call when the Convention opens Friday 4:45 P.M.! The Convention-Salutatory is *Great!*

L.S.

I am inclosing a note from Elizabeth H. Thomas.[4]—Parts about the Campaign will interest you.

1. These words are apparently a quote from a letter of his, now missing. The "mountain roadway" allegory, like "mountain-top," was much used at the time.

2. These quoted words are probably from the same letter. An article by Jack London in *Cosmopolitan Magazine* (Mar. 1906), "What Life Means To Me," quotes an unidentified Frenchman as saying, "The stairway of Time is ever echoing with the wooden shoe going up and the polished boot going down."

Years later, in response to an inquiry by Upton Sinclair about the source, my father replied, "The quote you refer to about the wooden shoe going up and the polished boot coming down the stairway of time first came to my attention in some essay or story of Jack London's. Since then, which was quite likely thirty years ago, I have met several variants of it. Where Jack London got it he did not indicate though I recall distinctly he used it as a quotation without giving his source" (Dec. 2, 1940).

3. Peter Kemp of Monerich, Luxembourg, her mother's father.

4. Elizabeth Thomas, secretary of the Wisconsin Social-Democratic party in Milwaukee. She had corresponded with my father about organization work, but my mother had known her much longer, and the summer before had her at the farm for a week's visit.

18.

Princeton
Monday March 23, 1908

Dear Charles August Sandburg!

What a glorious name it is!—Strong and proud and free—just the right name for you whom I call in loving worship, "Wunderkind"!

I have your poster letter (I like the free democratic way you have of using anything that comes to hand for writing paper—what you write transforms the poster into a beautiful wax tablet!)

I know why I'm glad that you are of the race of the Far-North Teutons. It's because Scandinavia has given us Ibsen, Björnson in drama—and in music so many names of the newest Pioneers—I don't remember the names of these 20th century Scandinavian composers—I do remember getting the general impression from Thomas Concerts that the most daring moderns, who *carry forward* the Wagnerian idea, are Scandinavians. What you remarked about individuals is true of nations too—"the polished boot descending, the wooden shoe ascending." Germany is in its *prime now*—Scandinavia fresh and vigorous in its magnificent *youth*. Hence the *daring*, the pioneer-spirit of Scandinavian art! And you are an incarnation of that spirit—you Wunderkind!

As for an "obsession of nationality"—of *course not!* You know how every true-patriot among the Germans hates Heine for the way he has satirized German nationality—more particularly the *phlegmatic middle class* of Germany. And I—I love Heine![1] But mention Heine to a typical German and he will cry "Renegade!—traitor!" Yet Heine and I both *so* love Germany! *So* love the passion and ardor of the German soul! The very reason why we would mercilessly lash her phlegmatic flesh!

And wasn't Ibsen just such a patriot? Living in voluntary exile from his country—and trying to prod her to action! Yet *so* loving her!

But Americanism! What does American nationality stand for? Anyway!—Is it "our *Puritan* fore-fathers"? I prefer Ibsen—Hauptmann—Sudermann[2]—That is—I prefer "Joy-in-Life." I prefer Life to Death; service to self-sacrifice—etc—So for me German-Scandinavian! instead of Anglo-Saxon. Yes, I'm glad I am German and you Swede!

Of course there is something to be said for our Puritan brothers! As a human being, I take pride in their achievement too—I'm broad enough for that, thank God. It is possible—to love one's own people and take pride in other peoples too—Fourth-of-July patriots to-the-contrary, notwithstanding!

And I do feel an enthusiasm for the American nationality that *is to be*—a grand conglomerate of Puritan-Swede-Italian-German-Russian etc etc etc—But that is yet to be!

Must change the subject abruptly—

I have your glad glad glad letter—all alive with *a very cussedness of gladness!* and the "Paper on Love" inclosed!

I like your kind of cussedness! It's fine—dear-boy—*magnificent!* You *are* a Gay-Heart!

And for the "Paper on Love"[3]—Such Wisdom! You've shot way ahead of Stevenson!—

I feel like writing a whole lot in comment—in praise—in glowing tribute. But—all I'll say is that—

You're a Wunderkind!

Good-night!
L.S.

And Good-bye till Friday—I do believe—God keep you well, meantime!

1. "I love Heine!" My mother had a thick copy of Heinrich Heine in the Old Germanic script, which she could read, having had several years of German in

the Milwaukee school. She knew quite a few of Heine's poems from memory, but the only ones that come to mind now are "Du Bist Wie Eine Blume," "Die Schöne Fischermädchen," and "The Loreley," and I have heard her singing the opening words of "The Loreley," "Ich weiss nicht was soll es bedeuten" and others. Since my father had become very interested in Heine a few years before, her admission delighted him.

2. Hermann Sudermann and Gerhardt Hauptmann were considered the leaders of a new movement in German literature that voiced the democratic revolt and socialist idealism of the 1880s and 1890s. Henrik Ibsen, of course, was battling against hypocrisy, sophistry, and mistaken ideals.

3. The "Paper on Love" is among the missing papers.

19.

Princeton, Ill.
March 24, 1908
Tuesday—Evening

My mistake!—The train I am coming on *arrives at 5* instead of 4:45.

I hope this will reach you in time to save you the extra trip to the station at 4.

I dash this off in a great hurry! to make the early evening mail—

Yours,
L.S.

P.S. I can hardly wait till the 5 P.M. Friday!!!!

20.

Sheboygan Falls—3—25 [1908]

Three (3) beautiful letters passed out to me here. Been battering from town to town since Sunday, making two towns a day. Hadn't heard from you in three days! Slept last night looking out on a sky of stars and a winding river—saw the sun come up the other side of a ridge of hills. So I knew whatever was mine would come to me, "reply somewhere on the tide of the years, to-day or to-morrow." And it turned out to be to-day!—Anybody that can put it down in black and white "I—I love Heine!" has mounted far toward the summits of freedom.—Dear, beautiful girl-heart—proud, mystery-woven girl-heart—Lilian Steichen—we see great days of big things—so shall we be like what we see.

The Five (5) O'Clock, C.M. & St. Paul, Friday.

Cully.*

[Written on back of page:] *You don't know what Cully[1] stands for, so I'll explain. It's me!—Thus do I square myself on your darting pertinacious Paus'l explanation.—Paus'l![2] What in Gehenna is its source & derivation?

1. Cully was an old nickname that went back as far as his boyhood days with the "Dirty Dozen," and old friends in Galesburg called him this, though the family usually called him Charlie.

2. The Steichen family's "pet name" for my mother was Paus'l, an old-fashioned Luxembourg endearing name used somewhat like "Honey" or "Pussy," though the meaning is not the same. When they were at the farm together, she gave him as good an explanation of the name as she could and then told him about her little niece Mary, on her first visit. She was just learning to talk and managed "Oma" and "Opa" for the grandparents, but when they tried to teach her to say "Aunt Paus'l," it came out "Paula" instead. My father, always interested in stories about children, liked that very much, and said to her, "That's what *I'm* going to call you."

The visit to the Steichen farm in Menomonee Falls meant much to my mother and father. On the way to the farm they were caught in a thunderstorm, which they afterward referred to as "the Baptismal Rain," because something happened then that was the beginning of the realization of their love. When they came to the little old white farmhouse, my father met her mother and father, and later Edward, of whom he had heard so much. There was a birthday celebration. At some time during this visit, my uncle took three photographs of him. In the meantime they were absorbed in each other, taking long, rambling walks together, alone, exchanging confidences, each learning about the plans, experiences, and family stories of the other. At her request, my father would at times give some of his poetry "from the rostrum." From here on, the letters have an entirely different tone, because they are in love, and there are many references in them to what happened during this visit, which in one letter my father designated "the Great Week."

21.

[April 5, 1908]
Sunday Night

So here, Kid, is a poem. Such a day as today during the past week would have been too much and killed us dead, for sure. Not "Hasn't it been glorious?" but "*Isn't* it glorious?"—Well-apparelled April follows on the heels of limping Winter.—The lake was so blue, such balms floated on the breezes, the sunset fell in such ruddy beauty, to-day.—And over all of it, as a capsheaf of glory, is The Great Fact—we have met—YOU ARE!!!

Cully.

To Lilian A.M.E.* Steichen[1]

*American Methodist Episcopal

1. The postscript is a gentle joke on her long baptismal name, Anna Maria Elizabeth, which she disliked and the length of which she found amusing. I have heard her say, "I should have turned out better, having been put in the charge of the Virgin and her mother and grandmother." Her mother liked the name Lily and used it as often as Paus'l; when she went to school this was lengthened to Lilian. At the University of Chicago she thought that she would not have to use the baptismal name, but since they asked for her full name she gave it, and her Phi Beta Kappa is under the name of Lilian Anna Maria Elizabeth Steichen. She must have told him some of this during that week at the farm.

On a Wagon

In a wagon, on a roadway
  From Menomonee to Home,
With the mist upon your hair
And the wind upon your brow
And the wonder and the welcome
  Of the calling wanderlust,
You keep a-looking forward

On the winding wayworn road,
By house and hill and random boy
  That drives the cattle home.

O tousled girl! dishevelled head!
What musses your hair and makes you look
  A thing for picture, poem, story?
For your face is set with glory
And your eyes are dusky mirrors,
Sky and wild and birds awing are there,

In a wagon, on a roadway
  From Menomonee to Home.

22.

[April 5, 1908]
10:30 P.M.—Sunday—Princeton, Ill.

Here I am back in Princeton—back in the old room—getting ready to take up the old routine life again! Good-bye to "the farm"! For sure!

And you, Carl, in your district again—how goes it? How did you get thru with your speech Saturday night?[1] Oh, *for sure,* it's "Goodbye" to "the farm"—to churning butter—to washing dishes—it's "good-bye" to the parcel's post and all! Good-bye—good-bye!

Only not to each other—It's not Good-bye to each other! Somehow the miles and the day more or less can't separate us. Last night I dreamed and dreamed of you—and it was so real! I awoke happy and refreshed—The waking hours are sweet with the same Presence. Always you are with me, Carl—and Cully too, Cully too!!

You—you Wonder! You Glory! I read and read the poem to me. Never was such a poem written to a woman before—Never! Do you know this? That it is the Best absolutely! *The best poem in the world!* Do you realize this—you Wunderkind you?—And I—I must make good—and shall!

I'm going to go to bed right now—and rest! I'm going to take good care of myself and will begin the health regime *right now.* I'm off to bed!

To-morrow I'll write again. I have much to tell you but I'm too tired to-night—and it's time to go to roost for the night any-way—Good-night and Love—Love—Love—to Cully from Liz

1. This was a speech given at Manitowoc before a large mass meeting.

23.

[April 5, 1908]
Sunday night

A day of sunshine—moist—lingering air—the grass getting greener as you look—all the girlish laughter of Spring in the air—And now it rains.

I'm stupid tonight—haven't kept fair with You-and-Me on the sleep proposition!—I moved from one room to another here—classified & eliminated stuff—things accumulate so—I told you, Pal, I'm stupid—informing you that things accumulate!

Stupid, foolish Cully; tired, tired boy—YOU are the *undersong* giving a lift to the weariness—*You,* sweet Paula,[1] who kissed me in the breaking storm of black clouds and lightning last Thursday night!!

You are the undersong toning your chord thru all the noise & clangor—

I love You. Alive & roused I love you—and tired & played out & done for, You are the Pal, the Love, the Comrade, the Presence, telling me this is only for now—Saying, "It comes like rain & grey sky & it will go like passing weather."

Sweet, sweet girl—dear hands—good arms—soft, warm lips, you are with me—Good-night, Paula—good-night, Paula—My Love—

Your Cully

So funny—so funny—I laugh at Paula, "I'll have to run to catch the mail!"—I hear her feet go patter-patter—I see her scamper—scamper—little wisps of hair flutter around her little ears—and the light in her eyes is the miracle-light, the light of a golden hope that glimmers and glimmers always in the heart of a Poet far off—You're a Wonder!—You're a Wonder!!

I mutter it. And I want to shout it sometimes: You're a Wonder!! You're a Wonder!!

1. This is the first time he has referred to her as Paula in the letters.

24.

April 6, 1908

Since March 27 when I left Princeton, ten days! Hem!—I wonder what mathematics are good for anyway!—Ten days according to arithmetic. Indeed!—But according to the Soul, how many days? or shall I say—how many years?—how many centuries?—How we lived! What eternities we lived! Eons and eons and eons!—Arithmetic with its days and years and centuries cannot measure it—You—Carl August[1]—*You are*—that's the fact that gives the lie to all mathematical calculations—and packs eons into—a week!

You Are! Or is it *Me?*—Is "*You*" me? Answer, Cully! I'm sure I'm not a "single separate person" any longer! How the world has changed! The atom commingling with another atom, become a Molecule! Oh the Wonder! Cully! Heart! *Me-in-Thee, Thee-in-Me[.]*

When I came upon you Saturday at 1:30 in the depot—so suddenly—face to face—how I yearned to you—Cully—that was a moment of eons and eons and eons—Love!—Heart!—

What a Glory that the Soul should be so transfused into the body! The Body no more a Hulk—no more a thing of Wood—but etherialized—a Speaking Flame! What a Consecration! A realist Pentecost!

Pentecost! Pentecost! The Convent lives and speaks to You. Carl August, Poet! The Convent with its calm and Spirit-Peace—

You Carl August—so good—so good—"I love you—I kiss your hair"—You—so clean—so pure—I am yours!

But that sudden Joy of coming upon you—1:30—Saturday—at the depot—My heart so yearning to you! Sweet!

And I had just seen W——[2] Mother & I had stepped in to explain that we would not stay overnight at his house—that we had not time to visit him this time. And I could see in his eyes the affection—and the *mother-in-me pitied* him *so*. I was moved. Edward used always to compare him with Christ. When Edward was about twenty W used to wear a beard so that he really resembled the old-master pictures of Christ—and Edward's greatest aspiration was to paint a Christ with W as model. It was one of those youthful Dreams that don't materialize—at least not in the particular shape & form. Edward has never painted a Christ.—But I mention it—it was a big deep artist-intuition. W is just *that: The Man of Sorrows*. We will give him sweet pity always—will we not, Heart?

Yes, I was moved—

And then this sudden coming upon you! Ah—Life—Life! What eternities I lived thru from 1 P.M. to 1:45 P.M. Saturday! I measured Death & Life against each other! Pity and Love! Sacrifice of self for another and Consecration of self *and* of another! Annihilation and Life!

And this is not Nietcheism [*sic*] either—We-two can do better than Nietche [*sic*]—We accept Pity too—do we not?

But ——— but ———

"The kelson of the Creation
is Love"![3]

We know that—You-Heart—"the kelson of the Creation is love"—

Isn't it?

1. This is the first time she has referred to him as Carl in the letters. When they were together at the farm, she learned that his baptismal name was Carl August, but that he had always Anglicized the name from early days, thinking that "Charles" seemed more American. My mother thought Carl a strong name that fitted his strong personality. She could not understand at first why he had changed it, and it must have been difficult to explain something that went back as far as childhood days.

2. Charles B. Whitnall, a good friend of the Steichens and very well-to-do, was a socialist who later became Milwaukee's city treasurer under Emil Seidel.

On his death he left the city of Milwaukee some beautiful grounds for city parks.

3. From Walt Whitman's *Song of Myself* (1855).

The first and second pages of this fifty-page letter are missing because my mother tore up the first sheet and meant to destroy the entire letter, afraid that something in it would be misinterpreted. I remember a feeling of panic as I tried to persuade her not to destroy it, urging that nothing showed her feelings about a socialist meeting or about how she felt about my father just after the farm visit as well as this letter. I said that I thought it a great letter and that she must be remembering something that was not in it. I do not know whether it was something I said that saved the rest or my alarm and real distress at the thought of the letter's destruction that moved her.

25.

[April 6, 1908]
[Monday night]

I'm glad—glad—glad—to do it! What an escape for him! As well as for others!

We went to Mayer's[1] house after we saw you off Saturday. And in the evening Mr. & Mrs. M., mother and I went to hear Seidel[2] in a small hall. There were no big meetings Saturday. When we got to the hall a Polish speaker was giving a speech—Anielewski[3] who has been brought to Mil. from Chic. for the campaign. I don't understand a word of Polish but I followed his speech fairly well—the general drift of it—from his gestures—his voice—and the proper names used. His manner was very simple—he just *talked*—but he had his audience listening hard—it seems to me that the point of his method was *clearness, directness, simplicity*—what he said seemed easy for the audience to follow—and it was solid constructive stuff. The audience was thinking—it was still in the hall—no hurrah speechifying.

When Anielewski finished, he went on to his next meeting—they were making each some four small meetings that evening.

Then Seidel began. In English. The splendid earnestness of the man—his sincerity—his zeal—all told on the audience. A really constructive speech it was. Principles—not personalities. No wonder the Milwaukee movement is so solid—this was straight socialist education work—not academic tho—no "holy words," no explanations of "the materialist conception of history" nor of surplus value—but solid education work not vote-catching. He didn't talk about class-consciousness, but his speech was interfused with the spirit of it—and it was a genuine class-consciousness (not a musty, bookist N.Y. Worker class-consciousness) that gave *fire—real fire*—to his speech. He was honestly in earnest—completely forgot himself—such earnestness takes hold. I was moved—so were we all—each in his own way. There were some 120 men in the hall (Mrs. M., mother & I were the only women) before Seidel got thru—at least 40 of these had come in since we came in. So the audience was a little more restive than at first—there were young boys—fourteen years old—mere kids—in the audience—so they'd talk and make a little noise at times. Seidel didn't seem to notice it—none seemed to. And there were great hushes whenever he was especially impressive—showing that they were listening. And a few times men in the audience put in a few words—backing Seidel up. Some earnest soul that exploded—couldn't hold in! Oh it was great! And this was in the Polish quarter—the priest-ridden Polish Catholic quarter! After the meeting—a young fellow begrimed of face—stunted of growth—but with fiery Isaiah-eyes—distributed literature. One of the silent heroes. He was a worker. Showed us his button—said he had been a worker in the party for eight years—and his eyes gleamed! Isaiah, without the prophet's tongue! Distributing literature! He was quiet— repressed—but the eyes! the eyes! Another incarnation of the old man in my Chicago local—A worker losing himself in the Cause! God bless him!

How a meeting like this stirs me! Such exaltation! Such hope—Such faith in man!—I *see* the dynamics of the movement! I *see* the yeast that will leaven the bread! And there is plenty of yeast! Plenty!

It was great—great—great—to see those Poles—some stolid, just a gleam of thought, a momentary rapt attention now and then—some passionately alive to every word—the majority somewhere between these extremes—but all at least *there*—listening or trying to listen—thinking—thinking—thinking—

Oh it's a great great time that we are living in—when workingmen sit in little halls on benches and stand stand[4] around the walls thinking—thinking—the thoughts of social-democracy!

When I left the hall, Charles, my head was striking the stars! Such exaltation—

The thought of you, Love—was with me thru it all (the thought of You is with me always—more or less consciously I feel the clasp of your hand always)[.] I thought of what Service we two together would do for the Cause, somehow, somewhere, sometime. We will do it! We may have to change our plans as to the *how* and the *time* and the *where*. But the Service we will render! We will!

So we may walk the earth, we two, our "sublime heads striking the stars"—

With your life-experiences, Cully, and your brain—your reason and tact and powers of expression—and your person and your voice and your heart—and with me to help with brain and heart and all—we two together will surely *do something* worth while. We will discharge the great debt we owe the World for having given us the best happiness—for having brought us two together.

I have the "Royal Bengals"—"A Royal Snake" here at hand to prove that it is really so. That *you are*. Cully—your laugh and heart and voice and brain and all. *You are*. It is true!—No dream those lips, those strong arms, those good eyes! Cully! Heart! Oh—*You to Love! You to Love!* Sunday morning we left the Mayers in time to see Mr. Delere (family friend—Luxembourger—nonsocialist) for an hour before we called for Miss T.[5] to take her to dinner as we had arranged. When we reached the office Miss T. and a number of the men were still hard at work. B[6] cornered mother in his office (as I afterwards learned) and asked a few questions about you—how long you were at "the farm" etc.—it seems the few words at the depot that other time (Monday noon) made him suspicious. When he heard how long you had been with us—he guessed the rest and practically got mother's confirmation of his guess—mother can't keep anything in—and besides B is past master in getting information of any and all sorts he wants. So afterward when he and mother came into the front office where Miss T and I were, he asked "Is it so?" And I said "Yes"—hoping to be understood at last—And so I was of course. I really felt grateful to mother for having talked too much. You—you understand—don't you?—I am a simple soul and like order and clearness in all affairs, Cully!

B. thereupon announced that he would go out to dinner with us. (Also by the way mother accepted an invitation to take supper Monday evening at his home and go with them to a meeting that evening). So out to dinner we went.

And what a dinner it was! Really *great* talk. The subject was: The Sex-question in general—our "possible" marriage in particular! What do you say to that, Cully? It was like a Shaw or a Sudermann play! Such talk! Such talk! And you were really there, Cully—for I was always saying "We," as if the "molecules" had been in existence indeed for ages and ages and ages—It came so naturally—I talked as if inspired—so I was—by *You*. I quoted liberally from *our* talks and *our* letters and the Paper on Love (of course never giving credit—why should I have?—I spoke the sentences as if they were original with me then—) I think we held our own well!

It was interesting when you think of it! Very dramatic! Each man of us represented a separate theory. Miss T stood for race suicide! a pessimist on the sex-question. But confessed to a lack of faith in her own theory in the end. Saw her own life a failure—(a sample of race suicide—) herself unhappy—lonely—starved for love! She spoke with terrible sincerity. That's what made the talk great. Each of us was terribly in earnest and sincere—talking on a vital question! And how rare a thing it is for people to talk on a vital question!—and doubly rare to talk on it with perfect sincerity!

Mother represented a modified form of the accepted conventional Church-view of marriage—modified, I said, somewhat.

B. stood for varietism—(I don't know whether I've got the right name, but you understand—the idea that a frequent change of mates is natural and desirable).

You get the alignment dear, don't you? Miss T: Race-suicide—No mating. Mother: Life-long mating by *contract, promise* before state or Church authorities. B: Change of mates as the mates change in character—and his idea was that the change of one mate would be in one direction, of the other in another direction—a haphazard change in no particular direction. The S-S idea that I voiced: Life-long mating the ideal—two people matching each other in mind & heart & body, the mates believing that they will continue till death perfect mates—not on the basis of contract—not because they promise each other anything—in fact they *promise* nothing—each is proud and free and wants the other to be proud and free—but they share the belief that the present identity of mind & heart will continue always. Why not? The two individuals have come along separate roads from separate sources—the two have been subject to somewhat different forces, *yet they they are so like each other.* They have grown steadily and rapidly—changing all the time—(but not haphazard)—in the direction of progress—the direction in which the whole world is moving—not this way and that—but always the same way! Very naturally! After all the forces to which the two individuals have been subject are not so very different. The big forces are universal—at work in Milwaukee the same as in Galesburg! But if the two individuals have become as one while living apart—will they not become more and more one living together? subject to the same forces etc. Life-long mating is normal, natural—if the two are really mated to begin with (nothing external taken into consideration)—and if after entering on the life together they share their brain-life & heart-life. The great reasons why there are so few life-long matings in reality, are two: people commonly marry for other considerations than love alone; and afterward they live wholly separate lives, touching only physically and to some extent socially—but the woman narrows down to the house, babies, sewing, fancy needle-work, pink teas—the man broadens out to business, politics, science, etc. No wonder they grow more & more apart.

You see the real fray was between B & myself. Miss T confessed her theory a failure. Besides *Life is* and the *Will to Live!* But her theory meant Death. *To be is better than not to be!* That is enough said to answer Miss T. As for mother's theory—no use wasting words on it—on the promise-vow-contract theory. For *love is* free always—spontaneous always—cannot be bought or bargained or contracted for!

The real fray was between B & myself.—I understand why he

and I could not agree. It is natural for him to be a varietist—because he cannot understand a modern woman—cannot really love as you & I love. A perfect satisfying mating of one man & one woman he cannot understand. He does not know what real love is! He hasn't that poise of mind & heart and body—It's too much a matter of body with him.

Of course each of the other three in his own way suggested that I *must be wrong*—at least I *couldn't talk with authority*—because *I am young*. We two, Cully, represented Youth and Hope—we spoke as Infants of what we *had not tried!* But they?—They had tried—and—*failed!* They all admitted as much! Which is better qualified to speak with authority: Age coupled with failure, or Youth coupled with inexperience?

Youth coupled with inexperience, of course! So say Emerson & Stevenson & Maeterlinck and the S-S molecule (or the Wunderkind-Thaumaturgist Combination!)[7]

And I said the conversation turned also on the application of these general principles to our possible marriage! Miss T's last word was—she was glad we two (You & I) would not heed the croakings of the old! (You see she *knew* her theory was wrong—all cynics do). B's advice was "to wait *at least six weeks before marrying*"! What he really meant was "Several years"—since varietism is impracticable, he argued, wait till you are thru with growing—till you won't change any more—then marry and you "stand a chance" of continuing happy in the prescribed monogamous marriage! Wait "till thirty-two" to marry, said B! "Nit" said I; "we'll wait only as long as we *have* to wait on account of financial considerations—but we'll not wait till we stop growing, for that won't be till we're dead!"—And what do you think of C.S. anyway, I asked B. He spoke the truth: said he really didn't know you, that he'd tell me his opinion next summer! So you may expect to be looked over by him next time he sees you! And I'm glad of that! Let him look you over! If he's fair he'll have to like you. *You Are*. There's no escaping that fact. The sooner he looks you over, the sooner he'll have to give you recognition! If he's fair! And if he's not fair? What then?—But he has judgment: there would be no use being unfair—he knows that—besides I don't think he would be unfair. But we shall see. As for Miss T. she praised you nobly! Also she seems to have changed her mind about your "talking over the heads of the workingmen"—She showed no signs of such a misconception—but praised you all around—really nobly, for her powers!

How I came to ask B's opinion? He said you weren't good enough for me! But when I put it up to him straight—he had to say "Honest—I don't know him." Oh, he did say he thought you "had religion" a little. I suppose he got that impression from you being such a good friend of Gaylord's.[8] I reassured him on that point—said you had about as much religion as he and I—that you were not aggressively anti-church because there was no use—the economic question was the one to settle now—better not antagonize the people with attacks on the churches—to which he agreed. And repeated—that he really didn't know you—no use venturing any opinion—as it would be a preconception. And I—of course I expressed complete faith in you. Told B that in ten years you would be another B—and of course we needed a race of B's! To which latter proposition he assented!—Now in reality—I believe that you have in you the making of more than a B—You are many men—B and Shaw and Whitman and Bebel and Jaures and Blatchford and Gaylord and Thompson and Anseele and Vanderveld and Bernstein and Keir Hardie[9] and Ibsen—You are all these! You, Cully! Love!—And then there's Me too! Part of You! Surely We-Two ought to achieve in the years to come something greater than a single separate B.!

But I said you would be a B in ten years—because B would *understand that*—if I had said *more* than that he would not have understood—and what is speech for, if not to convey meaning? I spoke the lingo he could understand.

I write all this, dear—because I believe you need to know it—You'll be prepared for B—and understand—if he carries out his purpose of "looking you over"! And he need not know that you know all this—eh?

My hope is that B will like you—that you'll work together well. B likes me—so if he's just he must like you. And if he's sensible he'll endorse the S.-S. molecule. In that case the S-S molecule will be a good comrade to him—which will mean the best Good of the Cause, and fun for us all besides! But if he doesn't accept the S-S molecule—if he doesn't honestly like you—then—you know, Cully—"Thy people shall be my people and thy god my god"—these are old words but they will convey to you what I mean. If B—can't appreciate you—then he doesn't understand the first thing about Me—and he is no longer a camerado of mine! Impersonally, as a genius, I shall always admire him. But as for personal comradeship—that depends on what he thinks of you.—In short when he judges you—he will in reality be delivering sentence upon himself!

For *You Are!* In comparison all other comrades are phantasms! You are the most Real Thing in the World to me!

It's a shame that I've stayed up so late writing—It isn't right I know. I'll not do it again—But I can't explain such complicated things briefly—and I thought you ought to know all this—I'm very very tired—and I daresay this letter is terribly dull especially the last pages! Page 50—isn't it awful!!

I'll never do it again!

I want to write more now about the poem I got from you today—and the sweet letter to your "delectable Liz"—but I'll leave that for another time. I *do* need sleep!

Cully, I kiss your lips—Good-night!

1. Louis Mayer, a Milwaukee artist and friend of the Steichen family.

2. Emil Seidel, then a Milwaukee alderman and later the city's first socialist mayor.

3. Henry Anielewski, a Polish socialist speaker, was very popular with Polish socialist locals or organizations. When he spoke before an audience in Racine, in February, there was standing room only, and the speech brought twenty-two more members to the party.

4. When enthusiastic, my mother repeated words for emphasis, as here.

5. Elizabeth Thomas.

6. Victor Berger, a Milwaukee alderman and a leading Social Democrat, was also a friend of the Steichen family.

7. My father wanted a word that would mean Wonder Girl, and since thaumaturgy meant the working of wonders or miracles, he decided on thaumaturgist.

8. Winfield Gaylord, a Congregationalist minister, was also a Social democrat. He first met my father at *The Lyceumite* and later at *The Billboard,* told him that more organizers were needed in Wisconsin for the Social-Democratic party, and suggested that he become one.

9. August Bebel, leader of the German Social-Democratic party at this time; Jean Jaures, leader of the French socialists and editor of *L'Humanite;* Robert Blatchford, a British socialist who started the *Clarion,* an effective organ for the socialists, who for a time wrote under the pen name of "Nunquam," and who was the author of *Merrie England;* Edouard Anseele, a Belgian socialist from Ghent; Emile Vandervelde, a Belgian socialist and the author of *Socialism Versus*

the State; Eduard Bernstein, a German socialist, known as the "Revisionist" from a confrontation with Karl Kautsky, a Marxist; James Keir Hardie, a British socialist who organized labor unions among the miners, who then became secretary of the Scottish Miners' Federation, and who also founded and edited *Labour Leader,* a party paper.

26.

[April 8, 1908]
Wednesday

No letter from you to-day, Cully, but it's all right! *You are* anyway. I don't need the daily letter to prove it—And while we're on the subject—*don't ever* write except when you *want to!* I'll write a lot—probably—long letters sometimes—wickedly long long ones sometimes—and then again the letters will be short—a few little lines—just as I feel. But however frequently I may write—don't you feel that you ought to keep up with my pace! There's a reason, you know. I am thinking of you all the time—can't help it—there's nothing here to take my mind off of Love! No work—no play—Nothing!—So I'll have to write very very often—on the safety valve principle—I'd explode if I didn't write lots of letters to you—Cully—But you—you have lots of work to do—you haven't time to brood about Me. See?—And doing work is really better for yourself and for the World than writing—writing—writing—letters!—(What *did* you think of that awful *long* letter I wrote you Monday night?!)—I can guess what's before me! What writing of letters! I wish there were something worth while to do here in Princeton—I'd throw myself into that!

I might try writing on "Art & Life"!—We shall see—we shall see—

Meantime understand that even if there's a constant flow of letters from me—I don't expect a return-flow from you for that reason—In fact I don't *expect* anything from you—You must do what you like—in your way—considering your work and manner of living. The one important fact remains: *YOU ARE. You are,* whether you write long letters or short letters—frequently or not frequently! *You are*—Heart—Love—And you love me—

as you alone can love me—But the day has but twenty-four hours—I would not have you take time that you need for rest and exercise and recreation or for work in the movement, and give it to writing me.

You know the circumstances of your life each day—whether at any moment it is best for you to study or to rest or to work or to write to your delectable Liz![1] You know. I don't know the circumstances—but I know you!—Which is enough!—Knowing You—I know it's all right whatever you do! You—impeccable One—You! (that's more than the Catholic Church says to its Pope—*He* is only *infallible* in matters of doctrine "ex cathedra"; but *You*—Carl August—you are *impeccable!!*)

I'm glad to have that photo of you—the one alone in the armchair, with hat & coat. It looks a little like the outer husk of You—more like than any other picture of you I've seen—Your eyes—Cully—looking right at me—eyes, so good—so good!—I ought to have a color photograph of You! to see your eyes as they really are! You!

A photograph is a queer business anyway! I look at you (in the foto) and say "Cully" with the most love in my voice! or give a little yearning plaint, "hem," with a shake of the head! and the *you* in the foto responds not!

And I'm thrown back on the wireless system! Turn from the foto-you to the Real Thing, You in Manitowoc! To you, in Manitowoc, by wireless, I send in endless waves love-looks, love-thoughts, love-words—to you, Heart! Do you feel the waves "washing on the shores of your thought"?[2]—Do you?—*You!*

(Must I give chapter & verse for "washing on the shores of your thought"—or do you remember from whom and from what I am quoting?—Oh, yes, *I can quote*, Cully!)

Just when will the Chicago Convention be? And when are you planning to go to Galesburg?—

I'm going to do what I can about getting a speech arranged—for you in Princeton! It would be great—for we would have a day together out of it anyhow!—Don't forget to write me when the Chicago Convention will be—exactly.

I've sent off the letter to W—So that's off my mind—I wrote just the fact—and a little word to show it was the Real Thing—meant everything to us—put this little word tactfully tho and simply so it wouldn't hurt. And added that *We-Two* would want his comradeship always. Which is true. He will be one of the Companions—next time we drink to our comrades we'll include him. He's a good man and does what he can in his own way for the World—Of course maybe he'll not want *us* for comrades—but I don't believe he's that kind. However I don't understand him thru & thru—so he may surprise me.

I feel that I do understand You thru & thru! That's the Wonder! That's why we're not separate atoms but a Molecule! You! You!

Civilization: its Crime and Compensation![3]—Its Crime: that you are in Manitowoc and I in Princeton.—Its Compensation: that notwithstanding we are One—One despite the miles between us!

Across the miles I kiss your good eyes! and your hair, dear! and your lips! Cully!—*old pal!*—

Liz

P.S. It isn't "Our way of Love" (is it?) to expect things from each other—each does what he likes—spontaneously—And it always arrives right! Because the Molecule is Real!

1. Liz was one of the names my father gave her.

2. "Washing on the shores of your thought" is obviously a quote from one of his letters, unfortunately missing.

3. "Civilization: Its Crime and Compensation," probably a parody on the title of his lecture, "The Blunders of Civilization: Its Three Great Crimes (War, Child Labor, and the Death Penalty)."

27.

Thursday—5:30 P.M. April 9, 1908

Dear Cully:

Just got home from school—and found your two letters and the poems—I read and read and dreamed and planned, and now I've time for only a note before mail-time. But I'll write again—*after mail-time!* This is only a "stay-bit" to keep me alive till this evening when I promise myself a very feast of writing!

You—Cully—you proud splendid Boy, You! You Glory of the

Creation! You strong and proud and wise and free! I know what it is all about now—the eternities—the infinitudes—the Milky Way! All is explained! The Cosmic—and the microcosmic! This blade of grass here! This pebble! *You* explain all. We know. We know. *You* justify all. We understand. We understand.

Listen, you Cosmic Forces! (the gray priestess speaks) You have done well! The agony of your effort was worth while. This Heart—even this proud Boy-Heart—you have achieved! It is well.

The Gray Priestess has spoken.

And now turn we from solemn apostrophes to the gods. Give Paula leave to speak to Cully! Heart to Heart!—

I am planning too for the summer! Yes, Cully—somehow, someway—we shall get to Klinger's![1] We will have our way! We must! The tocsin calls! And we are strong—alive!

Paula

1. George Klinger was a neighbor of the Steichens, on an adjoining farm.

28.

Thursday April 9—Evening

Such letters, Heart, such letters! What a Man you are! You are the Miracle that I have looked and looked for these years! The Miracle has come to pass: *You Are!*

You glorious Man! Good and clean and strong! You Miracle!

I had dimly visioned you—the counterpart of myself—*in Dreams!* (For neither in life nor in books did I catch sight of you—but *only in Dreams*—)[1] And lo—the Ideal became Real! *You to love—You to love!* That's the Great Fact: that I have *You to love*. I have found You! You Miracle! You who call forth all the Love I am capable of—and more! You infinitely lovable! "Big and looming" the future before us. Every day I shall find more and more things in you to love—I shall grow in power to love. The power to love *has been* growing in me since you came into my life. And it will keep on growing: this power to love has infinite possibilities, now that it can exercise itself on You—You, infinitely lovable!

Before you came into my life, the power to love didn't have a chance to grow in me. I had more love already than I could use—than I could find a worthy object for! And now! Now I have *You To Love!* You Miracle for whom I looked and looked these eons upon eons! You whom I can never love enough! The reach always just exceeding the grasp! You Heart! Clean and strong and free and proud! My mate!

Surely I am blest among women—having such a mate—one who calls to the highest in me, and to a something yet to be that is higher still!

You mate-man! What a challenge you are to your mate-woman! Oh Carl—Carl—Carl!

And what forces made you what you are—so that I reach and reach to love you enough—and always it is not enough! (Such a glorious feeling this—of something always Beyond. It means growth—life and more life for us!) What forces made you what you are! All those years of struggle when you were "a heart where hope fought hard for life"[2]—*You*—*You*—were in the making! You always *strong*—always *master*—always *proud!* My Wunderkind! When you told of the struggle of your young days—I understood! That boy-heart of yours undaunted, brave, heroic! and good, clean, sweet! That in spite of all and thru all you developed the genius in you, is wonderful! That you developed the heart you have—the sweetness—the hope—that is more wonderful still! You Miracle!

Such poems you send. Surpassing anything ever written to Woman! You Poet-heart, what a challenge you send to my Woman-heart! You so loved! so loved! You beautiful Voice! You Poet! Cully—Love—

And what you say about B and eugenics! All so virile! You, son of the Vikings—proud and free and strong! Every word you say is masterful! My Carl! Such fire in your words and such wisdom in your thoughts! I'm proud—proud of you—you have Viking-spirit! Such indignation—splendid! And you are right—absolutely in the right.

And election night it was "*Jesus wept*" and "*Goddam*" with you! Oh, Cully—I understand!! *You!* Pal!

(By all means send me clippings like the enclosures to-day.)
Now—it's good-night, Cully, and Love—love—love[.]

Paula

We-Two, Boy and Girl,
by the Sea together!

1. "I had dimly visioned you . . . in Dreams." See note to Letter 66.
2. This is from the poem "Paula," beginning "Woman of a million names," which follows after Letter 29.

29.

S-S

The S-S stands for two Souls. The hyphen means they have met and are.

S-S stands for *poise.*[1] It means intensity and vibration and radiation but over and beyond these it places harmony and equilibrium.

Don't ever write when you're played out or needing sleep. I get many letters from you that you haven't written from an ink-pot!—I will average about a letter (or note) to you a day. Sometimes the stress of three or four days campaigning may mean a gap—but Paula will get Sandy[2] by wireless—knowing what is what.—There will be nights when I get to my room and will not dare take a pen and talk to you—thinking, dreaming, loving, planning—because it will mean out too late in the morning for work!

On what roads we have not yet gone in our lives we must go hand in hand guiding each other. We have much to learn but such heart-companions—you supple hardy Daughter of the Regiment (Woman of a Million Names!)[3]—can learn and get joy in the learning.—All your pictures go up on shelves and tables the minute I locate in a room. You are with me always as a redeeming, transcending Presence. The intangible You floats about the room. I conjure scents of your hair (that copper gleam in the black!) (You posed for Titian—I was marauding on a Viking ship but I missed you then—that was why I kept on marauding!)—Always you are with me, giving me your smile for my failures and mistakes, accepting everything, having seen in me as I have seen in you—a something last and final of sacred resolve and consecrated desire—the something that gave us each a tint of silver in our youths—by which each interprets all that the other does—always seeing *intentions* if not accomplishments.

So you fill the room—always—you awaken all the purity and intensity of the dreamer in me—with you I am proud of all romance in my blood—you embody all the heroines of history to me—you are all the actresses and all the prima donnas—yet you are also Paula, Lilian, this figure caught on your brother's prints—an individual—the glad laughing girl and playmate with whom I built a House in the Woods—whom I carried over the bogs of marsh on high windy days—going with me on every intellectual ascent, every play of foolery, washing dishes, watching stupidities even, and getting down to the practical and work-a-day—no poems nor biographies will ever analyse or depict the S-S! Paraphrasing the exasperation of the critics who fumble in futility attempting to epitomize the meaning of Shakespeare, it will be said, "The S-S? It *was!*" And to-day: *It is!*

You are my Other Self—a complement. I might say love and kissings and everything that is fond and passionate to you. I might use all the superlatives of language and every caress that short Saxon words will carry to you. You are the most beautiful, graceful woman in the world, the most splendidly equipped of heart, intellect and feeling, in all the world.—Yet through and over all this is better and more beautiful and inspiring—some spirit of You, quiet, homely, brooding, steady, unfaltering—always, always mantling me day and night—watching incessantly—pure and near and certain—it is this that has made me sob like a foolish child—I am committed to this thing, lost and abandoned with You—the Ideal—the Woman who has lived and knows—the Woman who understands—You.

Always this glamor and glory of two high, superb selves intermingled, flits around me, a kind of atmosphere.—I have felt strange and unusual of late—neglected the more practical things—moved in sort of reckless and ecstatic moods—but mostly in a calm—bathed in contemplations and conjectures. It's some sort of gathering of forces going on—getting the latitude and longitude of these shores whereon you and I—the S-S—are sequestering.—We will sail! Ay—we will sail, you heart!—I will strike my old pace in a few days, keep up with all district correspondence, write circular letters, and socialist stuff for newspapers, work on my three economic lectures for next winter, read to keep in touch with the world-currents, hold noon and evening meetings, look up professional & business men & trade-unionists who lean our way and put the thing up to them and at least sell them a copy of Thompson's pamphlet, solicit pledges, urge the secretaries to keep dues collected, drag delinquents back into membership, get a line on the records of congressmen & legislators for use in the fall campaign, and to keep from going crazy sit by a riverside under trees and starlight and think about this wonder and glory of You—Me—the S-S.—This will all mean short notes to you, we knowing that back of the great love must be great action.—I enclose a letter from Joe,[4] the dear lad. He will always be a welcome guest. We will make him bring his violin and have him bring along the ham and fry it himself. Gee! That would be a lark for Joe, and for us.—Then there will be Rube.[5] He and his "Black Tiny" will respond to the atmosphere of our den.—What pictures we'll have on the walls! I want to crazy-plaster them, college style.—The announcement thru the district will make collections better. Why shouldn't S-S put it up to the district as S did? If they don't know a good thing we will make them see it.—One large room, a few, strong, simple things—that bridge crossed we will pass over all others we come to—when we come to them.—So much for now—Get your full share of sleep—cherish your fine health—Flying-Hair—Indian!—Always, always, you throw around me that mantle of a glory worth living in and living for—you heart.

—Love and love
from
Carl.

1. An essay on "Poise" in *Incidentals* (1907) gives more of his thoughts on this word. In part it goes:

> The men who do great things that astonish the world and work changes in its business and art and politics are generally quiet and sure and often rather

careless and easy in their ways. They do not fumble, stutter nor apologize. They know that in the long march of humanity up from the jungle into the wider lights of civilization, one man amounts to very little.

Finer and higher than anything else in human conduct is poise. He that ruleth his own spirit is greater than he who taketh a city. It does not come by magic nor purchase nor inheritance. It comes from work, sleep, and digestion, and it follows on laughter and love and good-will and belief.

Conquer the kingdom under your own hat and all the world shall be yours and look good to you. Even so.

2. Sandy had been one of his nicknames as far back as college; at *To-morrow* it became Saundy.

3. His poem "Paula," which follows, was written at this time and opened with these words. He gave her names for her various moods, Kitty, Liz, and Fanchon, among others.

4. Joe was Joseffy, a magician friend whom my father met in the days of *The Lyceumite;* he also played the violin. Joseffy had an act with a "talking skull," which he represented to be that of the necromancer Joseph Balsamo, and his letters were always signed "Mysteriously yours." My father wrote more than one article about him. Two were published in *The Billboard,* and one of these was later published by the Asgard Press in a small brown booklet (circa 1910).

5. Reuben Borough was a socialist friend whom my father met in Chicago during the days when he worked at *The Lyceumite*. Borough was also a contributor to *To-morrow* and worked at the Chicago *Daily Socialist*. My father went with him to many of the socialist meetings and lectures in Chicago.

Paula

Woman of a million names and a thousand faces,
I looked for you over the earth and under the sky.
I sought you in passing processions
On old multitudinous highways
Where mask and phantom and life go by.
In roaming and roving, from prairie to sea,
From city to wilderness, fighting and praying,
I looked.

Dusty and wayward, I was the soldier,
Long-sentinelled pacing the night,
Who heard your voice in the breeze nocturnal,
Who saw in the pine-shadows your hair,
Who touched in the flicker of vibrant stars
    Your soul!
Woman of a million names and a thousand faces.

In the hammering shops I stood,
In the noise of the mad turmoiling,
In the clanging steel and grime and smoke
And a dreariness numb of hand and brain.
To a heart where hope fought hard for life
You called from out of the years ahead,
Woman of a million names and a thousand faces.

When I saw you, I knew you as you knew me.
We knew we had known far back in the eons
When hills were a dust and the sea a mist.
And toil is a trifle and struggle a glory
With You, and ruin and death but fancies,
Woman of a million names and a thousand faces.

You are the names of all women who are and have been,
  Your face is the sum of all faces.
Tumble your hair and give us that look
And the wrongs and shames and shattered dreams
Are explained and gone like the yesterdays.

For you are the light of the world's dim dawn
And eternity speaks in the hum of your voice.
Out of days bygone rise your gesturing arms
Resplendent of poems and systems to-morrow.
You are statue and eaglet and priestess,
You are folly and beauty and laughter and wisdom,
You are the woman who understands!
Woman of a million names and a thousand faces.

30.

Friday, April 10
After School

Such letters! I didn't look for one this afternoon—but it arrived! Two yesterday afternoon—one this morning—and one now! Such lavishness! You give and give!—And we can afford to be prodigal—for a spell!—We can afford to be carried away by the Wonder and the Glory of the Achieved Fact, the Commune!—Soon we'll settle down again to Work and Rest and Exercise—and how! You'll work as you've never worked before—and you'll rest too and take care of your health as never before! So will I.—The Commune will not be found wanting in world-service.—And these days in the Clouds are needed—"it's some sort of gathering of forces"[1]—The greatest things are doing—hidden even from us—in the dark womb of Nature. What things we know not!

And when hard work recommences—and I get the short notes—and you too shorter letters or maybe notes only from me—we will both understand! *The S-S unit is.* We are *One.* I know what you are going to say before you speak. I see you and hear you and touch you all day long, all night long, everywhere and in all things.—So letters are non-essentials.

For the present tho—I've got to write—write—write. I've got to express myself that way. I've got to send you sheets & sheets of exclamation points! After a while will come a beautiful calm acceptance of the S-S—something really grander than this present exclamatory ecstasy! I've not gotten over the sheer wonderment that *we have met!* You are! Had I seen you before anywhere—*You with all your parts assembled*—the least glimpse of You—or some foot-print of You—or any token—the discovery of You would not have been such an EXCLAMATION POINT—.

Parts of you I had seen: broken fragments of you! But oh, the difference between a Man and a mere piece of a man. Genius in some direction or other I had known in men—and some one isolated virtue: purity in this man, courage in that man, and so on. But a virtue or a talent (tho inhabiting a body that walks and talks and eats) is not a Man!

You are a *Man!* All the parts assembled! You are all the separate intensities of Shelley—Bebel—Kautsky[2]—Walt Whitman—Marx—Wagner—the Vikings—Christ—Buddha—Lincoln—Heine—Browning—You are all these separate and different intensities! But *harmonized!* Brought into equilibrium! *You are Poise!*

The S-S is Poise—above all things—as you say—as you-who-is-me say!

That's why I say the world will never produce anything better than the S-S. Indeed the S-S is what the world was created for! This sounds like rank individualism—but you understand. I can say this of the S-S—not as We-Two—but as the Realization of the Ideal! I will glorify this Realization of the Ideal *impersonally*—It is no part of my religion to under-value a great Achievement because I am part of it. (I have passed that way—I was in the convent[3]—but now I am out!)

So it is that I am not so very greatly concerned about what you will *do*—what you will *accomplish*. The main thing is: *You Are*. You are yourself the *Achievement*—"a man with all the parts assembled." As for your *doings* they will be *worthy* because *you* ARE and therefore cannot do anything unworthy. We shall do the best we can to make "two blades of grass grow where now there is but one." We shall do our best *to do something*—to leave some *thing* that we have produced here on earth as a bequest! But we'll remember that *the life we live* is more important than *the works we leave*. Yes. Sometime this earth and all the works upon it will be Dust—Dust—Dust! But the S-S cannot be reduced to cosmic dust! It is a Real Fact that defies dissolution! Suns and systems may perish—but We-Two *Are*. This isn't mysticism. It is the very realist Truth—as true as that fundamental fact "I am"—which is its own proof. We met and we felt that we had known each other eons and eons and eons—and that we would know each other for eons and eons to come! This is a fact—of *Consciousness!* In one minute, consciousness can live all eternities of time—can reach all infinitudes of space! That is why such a fact of consciousness as *the S-S* transcends all things we may do—in importance in permanency.

Now of course we'll work and work to leave as much of a bequest as we can. We-Two are a social product. So we owe society a debt—which it will be our privilege to repay richly. On this we are agreed.—

But appreciation of a gift comes before repaying it. The World has created us and has brought us together: it has produced the atoms and has given them the chance to unite in the S-S molecule! Our first duty is to appreciate this gift of Nature's. It has cost eons of agony and toil and blunders to fashion and shape our two atoms. And for eons Nature has sought to bring these two atoms together—but always we just missed each other and Nature was baffled for the time! Now she has achieved her purpose: *the S-S molecule is!* Our first duty is to appreciate the molecule—to give it more and more poise—equilibrium! To give it the best chance! The best chance, Carl!

We will give the S-S the best Chance! It is in us to do this—simply because We-Two *are* what we are.

And then to do what service we can for Society! How we do not know! Whether we shall make much of a splash we don't know nor care! It will depend more on circumstances probably than on ourselves whether we do make much noise in the world. But good we will do!—all the good we have strength to do!! That we know. We will work hard and joyously and well! There will be poise in our work—as in our lives. Our work will be attuned to God's work!

What it will be we know not. In good time we shall know. (Just as we met—and knew each other—in good time!) Maybe it will be the district for a long time to come. Maybe not. Maybe you can serve the movement best as a free lance—like Robert Hunter—I mean without being an officer of the Party—just a member—working independently—contributing to different papers—speaking etc independently—agitating privately. It all depends on what sort of work you are best adapted to. We must find the job that fits us! There are plenty of different kinds of jobs—all affording a big chance for social service. We'll try and try till we find our own particular niche—the one that just fits us. Then we can do big work—when we've found ourselves—and if we don't find ourselves, then maybe it's that "the times are out of joint"—but anyway we'll try and try and try and never give up! We want to help as much as we can to up-build a better civilization for Society. We have "sacred resolve and consecrated desire"[4] in our hearts—and courage—and hope—and physical strength. "*We will do*"[5] good. Somehow. In this field or in that. Organizing—or private agitation. Editing a paper—or contributing to many papers. Poetry or the lyceum. Who knows which of these fields we will do our best work in—What things are shaping themselves in the dark womb of Nature, hidden from our eyes, we cannot know!

But whatever it is—it is good!

You—Carl—*You,* all the parts of a man assembled! You twentieth century mate for a twentieth century mate-woman! You Miracle—You!

Will I ever cease exclaiming over this miracle that *You—Are!*

You calling to the finest in me, the most spiritual (Pentecost! Pentecost!)—and calling, a Viking-son, to the most elemental in me! Such poise! Carl! Carl! What a man—all the parts assembled!

Play-mate too—Cully! Pal! Sweet Fool! Playing in the woods—playing house! "We braggarts"—paid spot cash for all our furniture (including hat-rack) no installment plan for us! Such braggarts we were!—And running down the road hand in hand—happy boy and girl!—Such fun, Cully—such fun!—Oh we know how to play—and yet I—I had not played with anyone since I was twelve—not really *played* with any one. I had played alone—but somehow I never let myself go when anyone else was near. I had played, since twelve, with the wind and with spray from the lake—with a dog too sometimes—but not with a person till you, Cully, infected me with your Gladness and Playfulness—With you I became free and natural as with the wind—I let myself go—I laughed and played and played.

Cully, that was fun—wasn't it? And won't it be fun next summer—and the next and the next. Such playing as we have ahead! Oh, Cully!

Now to sleep—Good-night! and good-night! I see you going up the narrow stairs candle in hand—saying good-night and good-night—your eyes full of love—you, Cully[.]

Ah—those days at "the farm"—Such days—Such days—

I throw a kiss to you—Good-bye—

Paula

Such a sweet kiss you threw me at the station—Cully—I've thought of that often. I thought I had the last kiss for a time when your lips were on mine—but then you threw me another! You dear—you Cully—

P.S. About the Princeton Speech![6] I have an idea. Princeton would probably take to this plan better than to what you suggest. Have the lecture at the high school or in a church. Charge admission. The money to go to some benefit—the public library fund—or a church society—anything Princeton likes! That is, all the money except what you would get as fee. We had Dr. Moulton[7] of the U. of C. Extension lecture at the high school—a course of 6 lectures—this fall. There were admission charges—

and all the receipts over and above Dr. Moulton's fee went to the Public Library Fund. I think I could get the Board to engage you for a lecture at the school—if they could make money out of it themselves *for the library of course!* There must always be some *benefit* else Princeton will not turn out—nor even open its halls I do believe! Princeton does not care for *lectures intrinsically*—it's the "*benefit*" that draws! The high school assembly room would be fully as good as any church—it seats 300—but a lecture would not draw enough to fill it—perhaps a hundred Princetonians would turn out for "the benefit"! As for Walt—he wouldn't be a drawing card! I don't believe a person in Princeton besides myself reads Whitman! There isn't a complete volume of Leaves of Grass in the Pub. Lib.—just Triggs' *Selections*[8]—and they are unread.—*Of course that makes no difference*—Princeton will listen to a talk on the text of Whitman as intelligently as to any other talk that would be worth while.—I'd laugh if you'd make a hit with them. There's no telling.—You know I made a hit *in a small way* at the "Literary" last year! I mine-self!—There's no telling.—They are amiable—*so* amiable—the dears!

Well—what say you?—answer this right off—and if you approve—I'll get right to work and try this plan. What should I say your terms would be—the lump sum you would get out of the receipts—?

It will be a lark!

1. These words are from Letter 29.

2. Karl Johann Kautsky, a German Social Democrat, was the author of *The Social Revolution* and at one time secretary to Friedrich Engels.

3. When my mother graduated from the eighth grade in Milwaukee in June 1898, she wanted to go to the public high school in September, but my grandfather, with his Catholic biases, did not consider a high school respectable for girls. So she stayed at home that year as a millinery apprentice in my grandmother's store; my grandparents hoped that she would eventually take over the business. Instead, she studied at home and in the meantime found out about a convent academy for girls, the Ursuline Academy in Chatham, Ontario, run by Ursuline nuns. Since this was satisfactory to my grandfather, she went there (September 1899–June 1900), taking fifteen subjects, including three hours of French in the morning, Latin, English grammar, American history, English, ancient and modern history, a half year of algebra, a half year of geometry, astronomy, and botany. That summer she studied for the college entrance examinations and did three years of high school work in three months; she passed and entered the University of Illinois in the fall of 1900. She chose the University of

Illinois as it had a library science school, but found out later that a college degree was a prerequisite for taking the library science courses.

4. This is another reference to Letter 29.

5. "We will do"—From "You."

6. My father had suggested giving a lecture on Walt Whitman at Princeton.

7. Dr. Richard Green Moulton, M.A. (Cambridge) and Ph.D. (Pennsylvania), was a professor of English literature and of theory and interpretation at the University of Chicago; lecturer to Cambridge University (extension) and to the London and American Societies for the Extension of University Teaching; author of *A Short Introduction to the Literature of the Bible* (1901), which my mother acquired in 1903, the *Literary Study of the Bible, The Moral System of Shakespeare* (1903), and *Shakespeare as a Dramatic Thinker* (1906). He was also editor of *The Modern Reader's Bible,* in which each book was printed separately. My mother had a few of these, principally the books of poetry, Psalms, Proverbs, and Job.

8. Oscar Lovell Triggs, author of *Browning and Whitman* and editor of *Selections from Whitman,* was a professor of English at the University of Chicago when my mother was there; she had courses under him and considered him brilliant. Later he was editor of *To-morrow* at the Spencer-Whitman Center in Chicago, at which time he accepted some of my father's early poems for publication, almost the first that had been accepted for publication anywhere, except, of course, for the *Lombard Review* and the Asgard Press.

31.

[April 10, 1908]

O hyo! One of the Samurai to submit a poem begs of the Celestial Cherry Blossom! Cherry Blossom have sit so sweet under the high tree and at the long shadow looked so fine imperturbable and loving of beauty, she make son of Nippon, brother of the chrysanthemum, glad in his heart. Something smiles on us O Cherry Blossom! It is Fujiyama, the great shining Fujiyama! Let us climb up to Fuji's peak, O Blossom, and lay there a lotus of white petals, kissed with the colors of the rising sun.

32.

April 11th

Have played all day—Went to the woods at nine this morning with a flock of children—little girls, preps and freshmen—about a dozen. Stayed till five in the evening. We picked flowers—mostly hepaticas (I inclose a few—pressed)—we romped—we played ball—ate our dinner—gathered more flowers—ran up hill and down—jumped across the brook—and babbled nonsense and exclamation points!

I had your colleen-gossoon letter with me[1]—it came with the morning delivery just as I was leaving the house to go to our meeting-place—I was a little late so couldn't stop to read it. Else I would have got there too late to make the street-car, as planned. So Kitty read your letter in the woods, Micky! It mixed well with the babble and laughter of the youngsters. What with the wind and our running my hair was tumbled enough—if only Micky had helped muss it! Oh Micky—it's a foolish fond Kitty that likes to have her gossoon tumble her hair—and—tells him so!—Foolish fond Kitty! I made believe your fingers were in my hair—mussing it—stroking it! And I made believe I was tumbling your hair—you Micky—my gossoon!

Oh, it was a day! Such adventures! We fell in with a bunch of small boys—fine chaps—reckless daring—such leaps over the brook and back—and jumps from high promontories!—and such tree climbings! Fine reckless little fellows—with glad mischievous frank eyes! I saw You, Cully, in the lights in their eyes—so free and gay and good! The "baddest boy" in the lot of course had the *best* eyes! As I always expect—I know—the "bad" boy is the boy with the fun and love in his eyes! Nathan Gray (What's in a name—forsooth!) was the "awful" boy in this lot—even my dear little girls spoke that way of him. But such a lad! Such eyes! Such gayety! Such teasing! Such human nature! Such kindliness! Such love!—And only a Boy!

I called him Cully just for fun! and because I saw somewhat of Cully in him! somewhat of the comedian—K.M.—Cully!

If we had had a woods like this at the farm—and such weather as this—my God!—it would have been something all but "beyond human power"—Bryant's Woods[2] is a winding ravine—a stream meandering thru the bottom—with side-ravines and tributory brooks branching off—the banks of the ravines very high and finely wooded with beautiful old trees and young ones scattered between and lots of underbrush—the banks sloping gradually sometimes, but mostly sheer and steep, or terraced. Imagine there winding ravines flooded with sunshine—swept by strong yet sun-warmed winds—fragrant with spring-odors of earth and flowers. Hear now the poignant call of a bird from the shadows of some side-ravine—or now the tinkle of the brook clear and sweet below.—Oh heart—heart—heart!

Sometime we must pitch our tent in some sweet sunny spot like this!—in Spring!—And be wild things together—we-two! Even the tent had better be a figure of speech!—Sleep together under the stars! no other canopy!—Cook our food over the camp-fire: bacon and beans or something else that's most plain.—Live—live poignantly—keen for the beauty around us and within us—the undefiled, clean, elemental beauty of the place and of ourselves!—

A Retreat—Carl—Heart—you understand?—a religious retreat from the vanities of the World—where we could "devote ourselves to God alone" for a little time!

This afternoon's delivery brought me another letter from you—a short letter but all the Wonder of our Love in it. You Carl! You!—You Miracle of a Man—such a heart you have! Oh, *You-to-Love! YOU*—to Love! Yes. This is Consecration.

The same mail brought me this little note from Whitnall—in response to my letter informing him of "the fact" definitely—that we-two had made up our minds and would "marry"—I put it simply in the common lingo—

The note is very characteristic. He is anything but flowing on paper. There is reserve and repression in every word. You will hardly appreciate that—not knowing his style of writing. It is more the style of primitive picture writing than of language. Or it is the style of ballad poetry—with gaps—. omissions—abrupt transitions.—It was long before I learned to read and understand his occasional letters to me.

You notice the stilted "I am not acquainted with Comrade S" and you notice the calm of the man in what follows: "I will trust in your conclusions." There's a sweetness in that "I will trust in your conclusions" (what an awkward word—*"conclusions"*!)

I am glad I told him. He is good—very good—you will love him. It's true his goodness is in some ways narrow—so much so that he may not be [able] to understand you (tho I know he'll like you)—in fact he *surely* will not be able to understand you any more than he is able to understand me. But We-Two can understand him—and *appreciate* him (I was going to say "pity" but I changed it to "appreciate").

You need not return W's note. Destroy it, please.

If for any reason we can't arrange the Whitman lecture here—I believe I'll come to Chicago for the Sat. & Sun. of Convention week—and see you there—so we'll see each other about May 17th in any case! And you'll stroke my hair—and I'll h'm h'm and say "*Cully*"!

I'm addressing this to New Holstein. By this evening's mail I sent a letter written yesterday evening to the Oshkosh address—hope you got it before leaving there. I should have mailed it this morning—but it slipped my mind in the rush of getting off to the Picnic—the children kept telephoning me until I became infected with their childish excitement—and forgot! until I was on the car! Too late! You would probably have gotten the letter Sunday had I mailed it Saturday morning—or don't you get mail Sundays? I get mail here Sundays—call for it.

About how long it takes your letters to reach me: Letters mailed by you in the evening stamped 9 P.M., I get the next afternoon. Letters stamped 10 A.M. in your district, I get here the following morning.

I enjoyed Joseffy's letter—there's a *real individual* in it. Which is saying a lot for "Mysteriously yours, Joseffy"—and for his gift to put himself in his letter. Won't it be fun when Joseffy comes to see us with ham that he'll fry! Himself—Joseffy the Mysterious!—And then that other Joseffy of the Violin! the Violin!—What a sweet boy he is!

No more to-night. I must make up sleep—I'm recovering my equilibrium again in the matter of taking care of my health—I hope you are, too, dear. I think we-two are the sort who will do our best work between forty and sixty—if we don't spend our strength recklessly—we-two have good constitutions and fairly good physical-culture habits as a basis for a long life. I said long *life*—not merely long *existence*. We have kept our childhood long—we should keep our prime long—

So I'm going to do the right thing about going to bed in good time. You try to, too.

Goodnight and love—love—love—Cully!

from Paula

P.S. Did you notice that the Vanguard prints your paper on The Sordid[3] in this month's issue? It's great stuff—really great—compressed. A thing *really done!*

1. The "colleen gossoon letter" is among those missing. She was the colleen, "Kitty Malone," he the gossoon, "Mickey Malone," the names they gave each other for their gay and mischievous moods.

2. Bryant's Woods was on land originally owned by John Howard Bryant, a brother of William Cullen Bryant, the poet. Three other Bryant brothers, Arthur, Cyrus, and Austin, also made their homes in Princeton, and the poet visited his brothers there, though he lived in New York City. There is little left now of the Bryant's Woods of which my mother writes, for after more than seventy-five years the realtors have had their way with it, and it is now a housing area. But the ravine and some of the woods are still there.

3. See Appendix B for this article.

33.

[April 11, 1908]
Saturday—Enroute Oshkosh

It's yesterday morning since I heard from you.—What you have sent to Sheb. will be forwarded, reaching me tomorrow or Monday. But I'm getting you by wireless—You're a Great Soul—a Wonder Girl! How we rushed together! What a flaming mad glad glory of a folly it has been & is & will be! You dare-devil stuff of impetuosity—You! Where did you get this heart that so goes with me on such chances? Such a mad woman for a mad trooper!

We stand with a choice of forty roads. We pick one, saying, "This is the way and the only." It is a winding road into an untravelled country. It is a road we can learn only by touching the dust of it. We know a thousand forces of unknown dangers will hover around us. Powers & influences beyond our control will gamble for us. But at this one road we stand, & say, "This is the way & the only way. Down this way we go. If hell waits for us, we're ready for hell. If mountains & valleys of poetry & dreams-come-true look for our coming, we are coming! This is the way & the only way."

Good-bye—Paula—My Girl—My Dream-Girl-come-true-(and surpassing)-My Wonder Girl—

Carl

34.

Saturday Night

Nor have I worked it out—thought my way thru this thing of death—there's something running thru life now I never knew before. I'm not afraid of it—but I don't understand it—and it's some new filament of power, a new Chance I've never seen at work.—

—The coincidence of our ideas and plans and whims is something I would not have believed till—the Wonder Woman came!

Can't you find some mystically beautiful name in German to match Wunderkind? There must be something—to describe the girl-goddess to whose heart the Wunderkind's heart always beats—it's up to me, I know, to find it, but I can't get one tts[1] adequate.

To that poem I sent the other day, let's add this line:[2]

1. tts—that's. My father here used "tts" in abbreviating that's as a part of his simple shorthand, which eliminated vowels.

2. The line mentioned in the last sentence is not with the letter.

35.

[April 12, 1908]
In the Woods—Sunday afternoon

Am playing again to-day. Came out to the woods this morning after getting the mail (a letter from mother and two from you: the Cherry Blossom letter and the letter with the "*Important*" Portrait of an—yes!—an Important Person).[1] And am here for the day. Have been drinking in the beauty of this warm sun-bathed April day. And have dreamed. And played. And gathered hepaticas with many a "H'm!" and "Oh!" at finding such a variety of hues in them—some deep purple, some white with a spirit of a purple tint just suggested—some pale pink—some lavender—some blue and more blue—some purest white. And all these hues fresh and lovely and glistening! And such texture in the petals! And such fragrance—not heavy and voluptuous—but hardy and bitter-sweet with all the vigor of March winds and the strong tang of a succulent green thing that has sprouted in forest mold! No pampered hot-house flower—this child of March winds and April sun-shine!

So the morning passed—dreaming and playing and enjoying beauty—and in all this you were present and near to me, Love. Always fellow-dreamer—play-mate—comrade-poet—fellow-worshiper of Beauty—you Breath of my Breath—Soul of my Soul—Heart of my Heart—you, other atom of the S-S!

And you had dinner with me too! Yes, Cully. We had our second meal together in the woods to-day! We had each an orange and as many egg-sandwiches as he wanted! And it was a good dinner. We enjoyed each mouthful—masticating thoroly in true Fletcher[2] style! (not that we did it for Fletcher's sake or for Christ's sake—no—we did it for our sakes because we enjoyed our fare)[.]

And after dinner—reading S-D-H[3] etc.—

And I wrote mother a good long letter. Her letter this morning told me that she is sick—has been very sick in bed for a few days—feels better now tho—is able to be up again. Poor mother, she is worn out, mostly from too hard work and the load of responsibility she had to bear—but partly too from her intense emotions, mother always took things hard—and there have been many agonies in her life. She had a splendid peasant constitution to start with—else she couldn't have lived thru it. It was work and work, early and late. In Hancock mother had the store, trimmed the hats herself and sold them, often staying up till 2 and 3 o'clock in the morning trimming hats, and then she'd get up again at 6 to do the washing or scrub the kitchen floor and get the other housework out of the way before 8 when she opened the store. Of course those were the days of hardest work—father was working in the mine and later as clerk in a general store, and mother had no help of any sort in the store and in the house. And Ed was a little kid and I a baby.—Since then mother hasn't worked quite that hard—After a while father quit working (he wasn't earning much and mother's store was paying well) and took charge of the house—cooked and washed and scrubbed—did everything about the house. So mother had that worry off her mind. But father was always around and interfered in business matters that he didn't understand and couldn't understand—for millinery is a *woman's* business besides father was old-fashioned in his business ideas as he is in other things. So there was new worry and anxiety for mother—And every change to a larger store mother made, always met with father's opposition. Father simply represented so much friction to be overcome, in mother's life. And I can't remember his ever showing any affection for her. He used even to be harsh when she was sick and exhausted. The last years in the store it was the regular thing for mother to be so tired that she spent most of Sunday in bed with headache or fever. And father had no sympathy for suffering—never having known any himself and being too unimaginative to understand it without having had the actual experience.—Of late years he is better—he has had a few little aches and pains himself and mother nursed him so kindly so faithfully, it seems to have touched him a little. Besides he feels happier on the farm—he always wanted to be on the farm—it's his element—I feel sorry for father—mother was too much his superior in every way. He didn't have a chance to express himself. He would have been happy with a good stupid obedient wife of the old school—a wife who would have accepted a gentle beating from her lord and master every now and then! And he should have had children who feared and obeyed the master of the house—That would have been a life worth living—for father! Then he could have had "self-expression." Poor father! His children, rebellious, self-willed, with strange incomprehensible (to him) ambitions! His wife always standing by the children—backing them up—finally taking the reins out of his hands so as to help the boy and girl realize their ambitions! Hard lines for a man who cherishes the old old German ideal of the father as master of the house and of the wife and of the children. Yes. It's really a pity. Father had possibilities in him. Maybe if he'd had a chance to domineer over us to his heart's content, he might have found out that there is no real satisfaction in lording it over one's family—And so he might have grown thru experience—as Goethe's Faust did! But he didn't have a chance. Not ours the fault, nor his! It was a mismating, that's all.[4]

How did I get to talking—or philosophizing about father! O yes—I was telling about mother's being worn-out from a hard hard life—business work & worry—and father's opposition and harshness—and the separation from her children (hard for such an intensely maternal woman who has no other channel for the love in her—if father had been affectionate she would not have clung so desperately to us)—then the tragedies in Ed's life—and my extremist ideas: apostasy from Catholicism—nay, atheism!—and my socialism—and vegetarianism![5] Yes even my vegetarianism was a tragedy—for at first mother thought I would die sure if I ate no meat.

And now mother is a broken wreck when she should still be in her prime—for she's only about 55. She can look so well one day—and the next she's all in.—This short visit from Ed upset her—and she is worried about his health and his happiness—and the new baby.[6]—It's no use. I tell mother to let us children bear the burden of our own cares—but she's gotten so used to shouldering responsibilities that she can't help it. So she worries on Ed's account. Useless—but natural. I understand dear mother—dear, dear, good mother—the loyal comrade-mother!—thru thick and thin she's backed us up.—And now she understands me—understands that we are happy and that We-Two are One. And she knows that that's the best thing in life. She's very happy over it.

In mother's letter that I got today she mentions something that B. said at that dinner to the effect that we ought to wait a number of years, not only that then our growth would be finished and so we could perhaps choose mates that would be endurable for life, but also that you might work up to a securer position by that time. And mother adds: "But I don't agree with him. B means well giving you this fatherly advice (you see the good mother is a simple soul in some things: "fatherly advice"! Ye gods and little fishes!)—but I think he's wrong. It doesn't matter much about 'securer positions'—if Carl is 'good to you'[7] that's what counts." Mother wrote in German as she usually does—but the foregoing is the substance of it. "Good to you" I translated literally—you get the meaning thru the homely wording? I myself shouldn't have used that expression—it belongs to the angle of vision of the older generation—mother's generation, not ours.—But even so much of love as that expression "good to you" implies mother never had from father, unless maybe the first years—Edward's earliest recollection is seeing father strike mother—he was not older than 3 years—but he can still see the whole scene—a kind of visual memory of a thing that startled and terrified him at the time. Father never tried to do it again after that—for mother would not suffer it—she had too much self-respect.—Anyway you see it means something to mother—this phrase, "good to you." "If only he is 'good to you'—the rest is of little account." Mother has a feeling for essentials. Browning words it somewhat differently: "Love is best—leave unto the world the rest."[8] "Being good to one" is the old-world phrase for "love." Love has a different meaning for us—we can't stand for the suggestion of patronage in "being good to one." But mother *is* of the old-world—and for an old-worlder she reaches wonderfully *near* where we kids stand.

By the way, at that dinner Miss T—in retracting her race-suicide theory which she at first advanced, said: "For myself I could not be more wretched than I now am, if I were most wretchedly married." Afterward she wanted to unsay this awful confession. But it did reveal an agony of emptiness in her life—cold and loveless—Poor little woman! She has womanly possibilities in her too—a kindliness and warmth of soul—but so hidden and overwhelmed by a mingled mass of busy-work &

scholastician or what-not—Her confession was of course exaggerated—but there is a truth in it: the story of a life "hanging patchy and scrappy"—"unfulfilled"![9]

It is late—(I'm finishing the letter at home in my room) so I'll stop tho I want to go on and on—rambling thru all sorts of subjects—No matter. You'll get to know me more and more, so.

Now for rest, so I'll be on deck for work to-morrow!

Do you know, Carl, I'm all expectation looking forward to that other "Unimportant Portrait" of Me—which you'll write for Rube and Joe and me to see—(and Ed? and Elsie[10]??)—in *The shack in the woods!*[11] Oh! Oh! Oh! What fun it will be for Kitty & Micky alias Sandy and Snooks alias Pal and Pete alias Cully K.M. and Liz D.W. alias Carl & Paula alias Charles & Lilian alias Wunderkind and Thaumaturgist et cetera! ad infinitum!!! In the shack in the woods together!

"Turning pages in a big book"[12]—Oh life and life and life—"a glorious splendid thing"—we-two turning the pages together!

Good-night, Cully! Good-night! My Poet!

Lilian

Mother sends Greetings—and your postal pleased her so. Says: She "will keep it"—

1. The "Important Portrait of an Important Person," obviously one of her, and the letter with it are missing and probably were lost or accidently destroyed long ago.

2. Horace Fletcher (1849–1919), a writer and lecturer on nutrition, attributed his recovery from illness and indigestion to the simple process of chewing food thoroughly. His principles were to eat only when genuinely hungry and when free from anxiety or depression. This came to be called "fletcherizing," and my mother and father firmly believed in it.

3. The *Social-Democratic Herald.*

4. My grandmother, on the other hand, thought her love very romantic because she had married out of the peasant class, a Steichen, who was then, she said, "a very handsome young man." Her family opposed the marriage because my grandfather was not healthy and predicted that he would die in a couple of years, but opposition only added spice to their romance. He was not a good businessman, but this had nothing to do with love, and although he was not demonstrative, he gave my grandmother as a love-token a diamond ring. To me he never seemed quick-tempered; rather, his objections seemed to take the form of teasing or grumbling.

5. My mother's vegetarianism began when as a child my grandfather insisted

that she eat the fat along with the lean, which she refused to do, and after that would eat no meat, which worried my grandmother. As an adult she found moral reasons for not eating meat, along with some other socialists, such as Edward Carpenter and George Bernard Shaw.

6. The expected Steichen baby became Kate Rodina Steichen.

7. I think that when my grandmother wrote "if Carl is good to you," she had in mind her sister Greta, of whose goodness and patience she often spoke, but whose marriage was very unhappy, since her husband was *not* good to her: he drank too much and sometimes beat her. Eventually Greta became blind.

8. "Love is best." Robert Browning used this phrase more than once, in "Easter Day" and in "Love among the Ruins." But I cannot find "leave unto the world the rest" in any of his poems. The nearest I could come are the lines "ask only love, and leave the rest" from "In a Balcony."

9. The quoted phrases "hanging patchy and scrappy" and "unfulfilled" are from Robert Browning's "Youth and Art":

> Each life unfulfilled you see;
> It hangs still, patchy and scrappy:
> We have not sighed deep, laughed free,
> Starved, feasted, despaired, been happy.

10. Elsie Stern, an English teacher at Princeton, was my mother's best friend there. Elsie was gay and amusing, but slight and delicate, not a very healthy person. My mother, though small, radiated good health to such an extent that Elsie nicknamed her "Little Brother." At Christmas Elsie had married H. Lacey Caskey, and they soon after moved to Athens, Greece.

11. The phrase "the shack in the woods" refers to Letter 29.

12. A line from the poem "Careless Hearts," below.

Careless Hearts

Careless hearts
Under the high tree
Where the long blue shadow
Lengthens and changes
Under the moving sun,
We sit turning pages in a big book,
Laughing and learning big lessons,
Forgetting it all and learning it over again,
Careless hearts under the high tree
Where the long blue shadow lengthens.

36.

April 13 Monday afternoon

So the S-S starts its fund to-day! Watch it grow! And then for a roof—four walls of a room—three chairs (one for You and one for me and one for Company—Joseffy or Rube or some other of our Camerados)—also a hat-rack!—and a bread-box!—and an ash-tray!—and some bowl or glass for wild flowers! Oh—and of course—a coffee-pot!!

And do you mean it Cully—that you think we'll probably decide that it will be wise for us to register the S-S *this summer* and to begin a home together? And if so where do you think would be the best place for our home—"the farm" or Milwaukee or some central town in the district? I don't believe "the farm" would be a good place—for many reasons. Milwaukee has its advantages—a good library, so that I could gather data for you from government reports etc. And as I'm acquainted in Mil. I could get private pupils more easily—to help for the commune fund. On the other hand if we made Oshkosh our headquarters, you could probably spend more time at home—and I could enter more into the life of the district, be identified with the movement there, perhaps be a factor worth while myself, a helper on the field (there would be ways in which a woman could be a helper on the field—without being the less a woman for it—rather fulfilling her woman-nature). I could go with you on short trips sometimes when I would be of use to the cause. I could talk to woman's clubs—maybe make a hit as I did here in Princeton, and in Valley City too![1] I would feel nearer you and your work—and you know we want above all things to share all our experiences good and bad as absolutely as possible! Giving the S-S molecule the best Chance! I want the hardships of the pioneer work in the district to hit me as hard as you! I want to be at your side so that I'll feel the knocks as keenly as you. It was lucky for me that I happened to have "experiences as deep and somber as your own," out of which this stuff of me came to be your Mate-Woman. It was *lucky chance*—that I "ascended the same spiral of experience"[2] as you! But the last year or two my life has been too sheltered—and I'm afraid Milwaukee would mean too sheltered a place. Perhaps. You will know best. I could get into the thick of it in Milwaukee too (?) And you will know whether I could keep as closely in touch with your work from there. In a way Mil. is general headquarters for the State—you know to what extent—I don't. Here's where the Sandburg-atom must judge for the molecule!

Very likely I could get pupils in Oshkosh too—to eke out what income we got from the movement. But the ideal thing would be if I could help swell the income from the work in the movement, so I wouldn't have to do any or not much tutoring—for tutoring is mere money-getting like stereopticon-selling—not work, service. We would live ever so plainly. I'd rather subsist on the barest necessities and give all our energies to work that is worth while—work for the Cause—or work that tends in that direction—I'd rather live most plainly so that we could devote ourselves wholly to developing the movement and to developing ourselves, the S-S, for future service in the movement—I'd rather be *most* poor so we gave the S-S the best Chance—than live comfortably but at the risk of the highest development of the S-S in love and service.

More anon—Carl—(It's hurry—to make the mail now.)

1. From 1904–6 my mother taught at the North Dakota State Normal School in Valley City, North Dakota.

2. The phrases "experiences as deep and somber as your own" and "ascended the same spiral of experience" are apparently quotes from a letter to her from my father in which my father suggested that they get married the next summer; the letter is unfortunately among the missing.

37.

[April 14, 1908]
Tuesday morning

I'm all ready to start to school—and it is time for me too—but I want to add a word for you to get in Kiel with my letters of yesterday—In those letters I asked you to weigh and balance & consider what we had better decide about the *when* of our marriage—But I put only one side of the case. Now I haven't time this morning to put the other side—I've got to be off in a minute. It will be enough if I say that I do *see* the other side, sometimes very strongly. If we waited till a year from this summer we could have a Big Fund to start with—and that would mean more untrammeled work for the Cause—and security from "the sordid"—no matter what turned up.—I should hate to think that we might *possibly* make too large demands on the movement. I mean in case everything else should turn against us. I fear I'm not making a strong case for "the other side"—you know best if I am in the foregoing particular. But it is a fact that we could plunge into the movement more recklessly if we had a $1000 more or less to back us up—instead of a few hundred. It's a great advantage to be *really* independent financially—and an economic base to fall back on gives that feeling of independence.

Besides the summer would pass well with a few visits at "the farm"—and next year visits Thanksgiving—Xmas (2 weeks if you could spare the time) and Spring vacation. And the letters. The letters—such as You write!—We can live eons and eons even so—Time hardly counts—We'll be young next year yet! We have poise. We know that the Important Thing is that we have met—and we must give the S-S the Best Chance.

So take this side into consideration—you are a good advocate—be its advocate—I took the role of advocate for the other side—then step out of your role as advocate—

Be a judge & judge—with Poise![1]

Lilian

1. In Letter 29, he had written, "The S-S stands for Poise."

38.

[April 14, 1908]
Tuesday afternoon

I feel like a wild thing—what with the spring day without and the buoyant health within me! What a day it is—sweet and brooding and throbbing too! Oh, love, I want to play in the woods with you—to run up hills and down, hand in hand—then stand together and look and listen.—And I want to rest my head on your breast and feel your arms folding me, Cully, Heart!—

And I must cover your hair and your sweet eyes with kisses—Love! You are so good! so good!

I'm off for the woods—to play that you are with me! It will be part make-believe (for I won't really hear your beautiful resonant voice—nor feel the touch of your fingers clasping mine!) but mostly it will be the very truth. You Presence, you! Breath of my breath!

I'm off now—the wind shall tumble my hair (the dear gossoon helping!)—for it's a wild day in spring! Something throbs and throbs in my heart—something throbs and throbs without, in the warm sweet air and in the song of birds!

Something throbs and throbs.

Heart—we are off now—into this sun-bathed World of Spring!

39.

April 14—Night

I made a start on "Woman and Socialism"[1] this evening. Just sketched it out. Had to stop because my brain got tired—I've been keeping late hours—burning the mid-night oil over school work and letters to you! Tonight I must get to bed early. Then when I'm rested I'll attack "*Socialism & woman*" again. I enjoyed sketching the thing out this evening. Together we ought to make something really worth while. You'll have to blue-pencil generously—for you know I *will* say "arduous labors" for "hard work." I've explained why—so you understand. My vocabulary is bookish—more or less. I'll learn from you—learn to "speak your speech, love." That will be one of the many many gains I'll get from living with you. I may develop under your influence to the point where I can speak the vernacular so as to reach working-women. I don't know how much fluency in the use of a language one can acquire at twenty-five! It seems late in life to begin to learn to speak!—But maybe, maybe!—What if the S-S should achieve that!

I'll be sending you a first draft soon—how soon will depend on a variety of circumstances—among them the amount of work I'll have to put on the Sophomore Contest[2] that comes off next week and the Freshman-Prep contests of this week!—I want to write the paper as soon as possible tho. You would like to use it soon, wouldn't you?—Besides I like my sketch—so I'm anxious to work it up.

By the way—in your Sunday letter you wrote that you were sending me "quite a bunch of Mss"—Nothing has come yet—I hope this doesn't mean that anything has got lost in the mail! Let me know whether you sent the Mss or not.

I must to bed now—no matter how much I want to stay up and write you.

But one thing more. You suggested running out to the farm while you are in the neighborhood giving your talk at Hartford[.] Mother would so much enjoy it—father too in his way. Except that this cousin of father's is there now—from Luxembourg (You remember the folks got the letter telling that the cousin was on his way to visit them)—so maybe that would sort of spoil your visit. Still maybe on the other hand it would be fun! A sort of Stuttgart Congress with speeches in two languages!—Then mother isn't quite well yet—she writes she is able to be up a good part of the day now tho—from about 10 AM to 4 or 5 PM. It's just weakness now—and she's regaining strength steadily she writes. The dear good mother!

Now to bed! Or I'll never get my brain good and clear to write the *W. & Soc.* paper.

Goodnight! A kiss, Cully, and Good-night!

1. "Woman and Socialism," an article he had suggested that she write. She gave it up finally, but my father wrote one, which had many things she mentioned to him in her letters.

2. An elocution contest.

40.

[April 15, 1908]
Wednesday—evening

Dear Heart:

Today you are in Kiel—I suppose this minute you're holding forth from the rostrum!—With four love-letters in your breast-pocket!—one from Paula, one from Lilian, one from Kitty, and one from Liz! Aren't you ashamed of yourself, you, Cully? You! Isn't one sweet-heart enough? Must you have a black-haired girl, and a red-headed girl and a gray-haired girl—and—and—Cully, Cully—aren't you ashamed?!!

I suppose I ought to be ashamed of myself! To send you four letters in twenty-four hours! (and some among them letters with double-yells! Shameless me!) But I couldn't resist. I'm going to try to be more moderate from now on tho. I find I'm neglecting my school work and losing sleep. The latter I certainly can't afford to do.

Have spoken to Mr. Magill[1] about arranging for your lecture. I think probably it will go through. I suggested $25 and you pay expenses (Rail & hotel). Perhaps $25 and expenses would have gone just as easily. But I was afraid of scaring Mr. M. off. Maybe it was tact—maybe it was poor business. I know I'm not good at driving a bargain. No business intuitions in me.—To-morrow I'm going to hand Mr. M. your circulars. Then he'll weigh and balance for a time (he's that kind) and perhaps by next week we'll know what he thinks—his conclusions!—Then it will be up to the board!—

If this plan fails—I'll try to get the Woman's Club interested.

If Magill is very favorably impressed by the circulars, I might make a stand for *$25 & expenses!* What do you say? Or should I let it go at plain $25?

"Letting it go" doesn't sound aggressive enough—Somehow! Besides every little counts toward the goal—the commune-roof! Watch the S-S shelter fund grow!

Isn't it fun to be making plans! And isn't it fun to build castles, not in the air, but on solid earth! You! Carl August!

Here's to the S-S! Give a rouse!!!

You splendid Boy! Dauntless spirit! So you got your crowd together at New Holstein—rounding them up yourself! Bravo! I'm beginning to have an idea of the varied activity of an organizer!

Did you notice that Gaylord got nearly as many votes as Berger for alderman-at-large.[2] Both ran ahead of the ticket.

Berger 21, 543
Gaylord 21,460

The next highest vote polled by an S.D.P. candidate for alderman-at-large was 20,724 (Handley). Seidel as mayoralty candidate got 20,907. Gaylord's showing is fine—he has made Milwaukee sit up! and take notice!—And he probably didn't get all the boosting he might have had from headquarters either! Here's to Gaylord! Give a rouse!

Cully, are you taking care of your health?—You must! Cully you're such a Beaute when you're not looking worn-out, dead-tired! It's a fact. And it's worth while. When you look fresh and strong, you can inspire hope and splendid discontent! But a worn-out face can't radiate hope! (All it can do is to preach self-sacrifice! And that isn't a final thing—an end!) As Cully—the one-time baseball player—you can bring such hope into the movement! With that health and vigor and freshness radiating hope from your face! You know what dear old Walt says:

"Is reform needed? is it thru you?
The greater the reform needed, the greater the personality
you need to accomplish it.
You! do you not see how it would serve to have eyes, blood,
complexion, clean and sweet?
Do you not see how it would serve to have such a body and
soul that when you enter the crowd an atmosphere of
desire and command enters with you, and everyone
is impressed with your Personality?
O the magnet! the flesh over and over!"

Thus old Walt "To A Pupil!"[3]

And he's right.

Now as for soul, there's no need of mentioning *that* to you—You have *that* fast for keeps! But your body—such a fine athletic body it is—I'm afraid you don't fully appreciate it. Take Walt's words to heart. I can't forget how old and tired you looked March 27! I couldn't help feeling a kind of pity for you then—which *you* don't want me to feel, nor do *I* want to feel. And then after two or three days of rest, what a change! You looked the boy—you looked the Cully! You were ten years younger *at least!* How you must have worked to have looked so worn-out, when you have such a splendid constitution that a few days comparative rest fixed you up, tho we kept very late hours those days—very late hours! You revived under the regime of late hours! You with your iron constitution!—What hours you must have kept working and working to have brought yourself to that worn-out state by March 27th.—You! Criminal, You!

Promise to be a Better Boy hereafter!

Oh of course—once in a while—you may go off on a drunk! *[4] Work and work for nights and nights if you will!—But not as a general thing.

And I suppose you have been taking care of your health as a general thing. I suppose your worn-out condition March 27th was the exception—the occasional drunk! Else you couldn't have recuperated so fast and have been the Beaute you were, Cully, after a couple of days at "the farm."

I hope you have your fine fresh strength *now*—in your campaigning—It will tell in gains for the movement.

Take rest and save your strength and freshness for the Cause—and for the S-S!

And I'll do likewise. Is it a go?

Goodnight now. Heart, I love you and love you and love you! Cully! You! A kiss! And Good-night!

*In fact—You ought to go off "on a drunk" every now and then! And get your fill of work!—Now that I know it's only a drunk—not a chronic condition—I'll not pity you for it. *You! Cully!*

1. Hugh S. Magill, principal of Princeton Township High School.

2. Winfield Gaylord and Victor Berger were not running against each other but were two of eleven Social-Democrats running for the office of alderman-at-large.

3. Walt Whitman's "To a Pupil" from *Leaves of Grass* (1860).

4. That is, be intemperate about work, and work too hard.

Carl Sandburg, 1906, "alone in the armchair with hat & coat" (Letter 26).

THE world goes forward by personalities.

A suit of clothes can't talk with you nor shake hands nor touch your heart into new beauty and joy and knowledge. But what touching, tangible, beautiful things have been done by suits of clothes with men inside!

Books are but empty nothings compared with living, pulsing men and women. Life is stranger and greater than anything ever written about it.

CHARLES SANDBURG

LECTURER : ORATOR

Address care of THE LYCEUMITE,
Steinway Hall,
Chicago, Illinois.

Folder for the Walt Whitman lecture, "An American Vagabond."

Milwaukee Socialists

Victor Berger (Steichen photograph, 1907).

Carl D. Thompson (Milwaukee County Historical Society).

C. B. Whitnall (Milwaukee County Historical Society).

Emil Seidel (Milwaukee County Historical Society).

Carl Sandburg, 1908, by Edward Steichen (above and on following two pages).

41.

[April 15, 1908]
Wednesday night

You mischievous, ubiquitous Imp! I have just come back from a long walk—and you were everywhere—a mystic booger of a shadow-woman playing tag with me all 'round—Fanchon with her flying-hair. Was out of the town a way and one slope of land made me think of the House in the Woods. Do you remember the House in the Woods, Paula?—how the reprimanding winds and the sullen clouds tried to scare us how we were too warm to be frozen out—how the S-S molecule-commune looked at its watch and at 6:10 regularly scampered toward the sunset! How you had the impertinence to call me "Fool" and I resented it with wild circling motions!—The Molecule-Commune!—that's the worst yet.—There's a twist of the way you say Cully that you don't get into writing. The "Hm" with your own peculiar staccato I am getting down pat.

I hope you are doing well under those bundles of "lithrachoor" I sent you. All sorts of scraps but some day this I that is you and me will use them.—There's no figuring on the future with any certainty as to where we'll be. We'll always keep up this fight for better living conditions and a greater civilization but how long we'll be organizing we don't know. Speaking and writing is the work I love best—may be editing a paper—if the situation were a bit different at Appleton now, I would start a labor paper there, for the Fox River unionists, the A.S.E.s and the S.D.s.[1] All sorts of things in the air.—We may decide that I play the lyceum game, when I have ripened some. If I can't give socialist lectures regularly, Whitman and the religion of democracy, the breezy Great Wide Way, &c. are big stuff, and between evening stunts I can write and privately agitate, &c.—I would say the gods are good to us only we constitute a god ourselves, the two of us.—Have you seen Us on a pedestal?—One not deriving income from the party movement is in a better way to influence & criticize and aid party tactics.—Gaylord was very unfairly treated. He is supersensitive, but he was not given a square deal.—So while the probabilities are that I will be in this district indefinitely (possibly till we get some men in the legislature and a congressman!) there's no certainty.—If you can get any kind of an opening in a Princeton church, arrange for the Whitman lecture on May 17, 18, or 19. I can come down from the national convention. Make the proposition that I pay all my expenses, but will take a collection after the lecture. The latter non-partisan and unbiased. You needn't say that it leads people to say, "I guess I'll have to read that Leaves of Grass!" Do you see, Kid?

You woman of a million names—from Sappho to Lena Ashwell, you are all! All of them! You copper-haired glory—you radium.—

—A long kiss, love—and good night—and good night.

1. S.D. refers to Social-Democrats. At a guess I would think that the A.S.E. stood for Appleton Social Educators.

42.

April 17th 1 A.M.

Have just finished correcting a batch of themes! I began late after writing a few long letters—among them one to Mother and one to Elsie (The Maid—no—The Matron—no The Mate [Caskey's Mate] of Athens!)

The themes simply *had* to be done.

But I want *to write to you* (I wrote enough *about* you in my letters! Wait till Elsie's reply comes: that will be worth reading!)

But at this hour! I know, "my lord" (?!?!?! etc), you are ordering me to bed! And you're right. I need rest and rest. And didn't I lecture you on health but yesterday! So you're loaded!

So I'm off to bed—like the good sensible girl I am! Obeying "my Lord"! (?)

Goodnight! Cully! Pal!

This is just to send you love and love. And to kiss your lips—You Breath of my breath! Carl—Good-night!

Lilian

43.

April 17—1908

It's leap and plunge!

Of Course!

"Look before you leap," says the old saw.

Well, we've looked! I should say!—How many pages were there in all of "*looking*" in those "Look-Before-You-Leap" letters to Kiel? Say, how many? I guess we've squared it with the old saw all right! Well I guess!

Enough of "looking"!

Now for the *leap!*

And your pictures came today—(And I should not leap! Jupiter Stator! I should not leap!!!!) The one with the bare neck[1] is really *you,* Cully—all but the eyes. (Paul, Paul,[2] how could you so spoil Cully's dear eyes! You shall answer for it, Paul—according to the old dispensation—an eye for an eye! Paul!) Now at last I have a picture that's really *You!* Don't I want to throw my arms around that neck of yours, Cully! You! (And I should not leap! Jupiter Ammon! I should not leap!!!!)

It's to be this summer then—unless the Heavens fall—and if the Heavens fall!—why—THEN IT SHALL BE THIS SUMMER ANYWAY.

How airily you refused the office of *Advocatus Diaboli* which I passed on to you! Good for you, Carl—we are God's advocates, the pair of us! Avant Sathanas!

Let there be no more talk of weighing and balancing and prudence and rainy day funds!

We have looked!

Each understands—and each feels equal to it—to the hazard and the chance of it! to the glory of it! to the effort!

"We will do—we will live!"[3]

We'll have leaps to take in future—with ten thousand times the hazard of this leap—doubtless! And we'll make it without a doubt! We'll make it!

Isn't it?

Everytime we'll make it!

We're equal to all things!

We—two—pals—
Side by each!

You, Micky, what do you mean with your blarney—Do you think for that I'll let you muss my hair this way and that!—Oh, you do, do you? Then take this and this and this—see how I've mussed your hair now! Micky! Now will you be good? Will you? Won't you? Will you? Won't you?

Oh Cully!

And we love our room in Oshkosh already! Allah is Great! And we are his prophets! What a life together of work and play ahead of us! We will live!

You—*You Are*—You Heart—You to love *unreservedly!* no excuses! no reservations! You—who are *All!* My Love and My Love! Carl!

I kiss you long and long—You, my splendid poet—my blessed rebel—my glorious Mate-Man! "*The Man who understands!*"

Good-bye—for a little time—to speaking to you on paper—The wireless talk goes on! *Always!*

Paula

1. The reference to "the one with the bare neck" has puzzled me, because I know of only one photograph that answers this description, one by Walter B. Loomis, a Galesburg photographer.
2. Paul Fournier, a Chicago photographer.
3. "We will do—we will live." From "You."

44.

[April 17, 1908]
Friday—5 P.M.

It's settled. I wrote you that this noon, but I want to repeat. I have just gotten your Manitowoc letter.[1] The last faintest shadow of an IF has vanished. I see there is an abundance of resources. I see that We-Two can chance it as far as we are concerned and as far as the "one-chance-in-ten-thousand" of having a baby is concerned. We-Two can chance it *without an economic base to fall back on!* We have our brains to fall back on!

So if Ed can't do his part this year—nay, if the worst comes to the worst and he can do absolutely nothing this year and next too—still mother can be secured from financial worry! (I see we don't need a baby-fund.) There are the $400 I've saved. That would tide the folks thru this year and next, even tho Ed didn't contribute a cent.

I received a gratulatory note from dear Edward to-day. I inclose it!—How I wish Ed could have seen more and more of you—the Cully in you! The time was too short. We are going to have great times together yet!—So much and so much before us!

You notice the reference to "Pa." Heretofore Mother always had to "break the news to father" and bear the brunt of his opposition—for of course he is always "The opposition." I tell you that was mighty hard on mother. But from the time when we were little kiddies she shielded us in big things and small things from father's anger, by *secrecy*. It was hard on mother and bad for father. So Ed is glad the news won't have to be broken again by mother. I told father. He grumbles and acquiesces—It's different from what it used to be—before he knew he was beaten. Now father knows it's no use. Of course he thinks we ought to wait and wait and wait—until the coal-cellar is filled with fuel, and the larder with food, and the money-bag with shekels!—But I put it to Pa kindly but firmly that *that* was our business. So he acquiesces—cheerfully rather! And personally he really likes you! You have tact, man! And that's the way—Pa has his points and I want him to be as happy over my forth-going as can be! I had to be *firm* for once. That settled it for good and all—There would be no quarrelling with mother over it—and I showed there was no use quarrelling with me. I knew what was what—that this was matter for C.S. & L.S. to decide. But I'm glad he likes you—for if there is one person in the world pa loves—it's "Lil." He is very fond of me—and that's sad too—it makes him jealous of the real big love and understanding between mother and me—something he's shut out of—Poor father—so misplaced! He might have had a little girl—a pocket-edition of himself—they could have been such chums! As it is he hasn't a little girl in that sense (just as I haven't a comrade-father!)

Now I've written Ed just to-day that we have decided to have the marriage this summer. And I've asked him how about finances?—Now we'll wait and sip our cofffee the while!

Nothing depends.

The marriage comes off anyway—

If Ed can't help out the finances[2]—my little hoard of $400 more or less will be devoted to that end. To make it dead sure—secure mother against the chance of this hoard being lost in a busting bank—I could put it in postal money orders in the box mother and I have in a Safety Deposit Vault in Milwaukee! We could marry with clear conscience—with mother provided for for this year and next—She wouldn't be involved in our risk.

It's all so clear! Now I know that you know what you can do *alone* if need be—that is—

Pshaw! It's so dead easy!—But I didn't realize before that you had enough resources to cope with the baby-possibility within the year.—But you can—It's all right—Old pal!—

My I'm happy! For I *don't want to wait!*

LIZ

P.S. I wrote Miss T in reply to her letter I sent to you inclosed in my Hartford letter. I told her that I could not apply for the position in a Wis. school that she suggested—I said I would retain my position here "*if I taught another year. I might go into journalism, frinstance.*" That is vague enough. I thought best not to say anything about *our* decision for the summer. As far as I'm concerned I don't care whether they know. But I don't see any reason for telling them yet. Do you? If you do, tell them.—I'm writing this so you'll know how much I've told.—In Mil. I told Miss T. our marriage would probably come off a year from this summer.—

I sent you a photo addressed Hartford. Did you get it?

1. The Manitowoc letter mentioned here is missing.

2. My uncle wrote in answer:

You are evidently in a bad way as far as being in love is concerned.—Prosit. Do just as your heart dictates if your good sense will permit you, and then it is sure to be all right. At any rate you have only yourself to be responsible for.—Of course I will always be on hand when I possibly can to fill in the cash account on the farm. Your reducing the whole thing to an even 300 is a demonstration of your impracticalness.—Have they ever done it for a year on anything like that.—The exhibition was more of a success than I had hoped and I can see my way clear for another year and of course that means that I can also take care of Ma & Pa.—I am sending Ma a check for $200.00 now.—

As for all the rest that will be taken care of.—I had planned to have you and Ma come over to Paris for the vacation weeks but your wedding changes that.—And I am sure you will all have a full summer with *that*.—I am glad for you Paus'l and *hope* it will turn out right—hope oh so hard—and love you.—Ed.

45.

[April 18, 1908]
Saturday afternoon

Dear Carl:

Just received your letter of Friday evening—thanking me for my health-admonishings—and telling your idea about The Woman & socialism leaflet. I'm glad there's no pressing need for hurry. I want to write it *now*—but my time seems more than taken up with school work etc. I'm still back on a few sets of themes. And I'll have to help those Sophomore boys a lot next week. It just happens that these weeks are the busiest in the whole school year for me. This sophomore contest is the only "big event" I've had a hand in this year (I managed to evade the Jr. Contest and the Sr. play). Then the two Prep-Freshman debates—one came off Thursday—the other will come off next Tuesday.

Today I cleaned house! I don't mean scrubbing etc. but making order among my papers—clippings—etc—and in my clothes-closet, bureau drawers etc. I had not got settled yet since my return here.—It gives me a good feeling to see everything in order about me! I feel now I'll get the work I want to do planned and done! First catch up with correcting papers and "do up" the prep-freshman fray and the Sophomore dramatics. All this will be out of the way by next Friday evening. Then I'll be able to do justice to the leaflet. There'll be good time. All my classes are well started in the classics they'll use to the end of the school year—the work is planned out. And there'll be no extras.

Good! The plan of the work to come is in excellent order—like my room!

It was a good job this house-cleaning!

"Maybe you'll be L.S.S. and I C.S.S. in sixty days"!! That sounds great! Oh, Cully! We two working together and playing together—the S-S! In sixty days!—And from then on and on for all days—forever!

To come down from poetry to mathematics (Math. is fun too—don't you think so, Micky?)—the 60 days will have to be stretched a little L.S. thinks—and so does C.S. or will shortly—Mother will want me for a little while anyway as plain L.S.!—Say we allow two weeks after I get home before the marriage. Then Carl D. could do the hocus-pocus for us about June 26th![1] How does this strike C.S.? (Will it fit in with your *work*?)

And what is your idea of the ceremonial occasion anyway! I've always abhorred the idea of weddings—used to say I'd make the least possible noise about it—if I got married, that I'd go to a justice of the peace (a street-car our conveyance) and register (since Society demands *that formality* before a marriage of hearts becomes a marriage of bodies as well)[.]

It shows that our civilization has not risen above the level of the beast, when such a fuss is made over the ceremony which sanctions the physical union. As if *that* were *the* important thing!

Of course a wedding festival might mean something else—celebrating not *what is to come*—but *what is*—not the union of bodies which is now (forsooth!) sanctified—but the union of souls which *is, was and shall be*. Two souls have discovered their identity—and they take this moment of registration as a convenient moment for calling their friends together to rejoice with them in their happiness in The Real Thing—the great fact that the two souls are One.

There are these two possible interpretations of the Wedding Idea. I do believe most weddings are of the disgusting sort—based on the principal that the physical union is *the* great important thing. I suppose that's no reason against a wedding festival in the *right spirit* with the *right people* participating.

Wouldn't we both like an S-S festival (not a registration-of-the-body festival)—and Rube and Joseffy and your Mother should be there—and my Mother and Ed and Elsie & Lacey Caskey and—yes, and Wagner and Robert & Elizabeth Browning and Edward Carpenter and Ibsen and Shaw and poor old Walt—all these should be there as well! On further thought we could add to the list! (Of course Gaylord[2] and Carl D. are present!)

But such a festival is impracticable! So maybe the best thing to do would be to have Carl D. and Gaylord and [half page missing]

Have just Gaylord and Thompson or Thompson only if Gaylord was out of town—and have it all simple and sweet—*un*ceremonial.

What say you?

I think it is fun to talk over these little non-essentials! Don't you, Cully?

But I've got to stop right *short* to make the mail now.

Love from
the Colleen

1. Carl D. Thompson.
2. Winfield Gaylord.

46.

[April 19, 1908]
Sunday Night

Your "Thoughts about Art" is splendid! It's what only a Wunderkind could write! So proud and daring and so big-hearted!—The thoughts are my thoughts (Another case where the still small voice of my heart and brain find utterance thru you with your Organ-Voice, O Wunderkind!)

"The hell with art till the people have time to wipe the sweat from their faces and rest a little from their labors"—Great! and great! and great!—You, Heart!—To burn with such godly wrath, such a white fire of indignation! You big-hearted Carl you!—

When your Voice shall thunder forth to the World your "Thoughts about Art"—shall we find so much as a grease spot left of the esthetes who babble about "Art for Art's Sake"—If we do, I have a recipe for removing grease spots: not even *so* much must be left of them!

Liz is fierce to-night! Will fight, as Sandy's second—to a finish!

But I'm to be critical you say. Goodbye Liz!—Enter Lilian.

Lilian thinks the introduction is needlessly self-assertive. No use announcing you are going to do bold things. Let the reader find that out for himself. It will flatter him—to make this discovery *all by himself.* And why spoil this harmless little joy in the reader's bosom!! Gratify him!—You see my idea? If you tell the reader you are going to be bold, he, being a timid man himself, will suspect that if you are so conscious of your boldness, you must be *too too* bold.—And you needn't ask him to take your word for it ("believe me") that there's good sense in the "Thoughts." The "Thoughts" speak for themselves.—The minute you launch into your subject (after the Pending "Believe me")—you are great. You soar. Never once do your wings trail the ground. It's real inspiration—something last and final—every objection vanishes, slinks away ashamed and is no more!

One trifle—I believe I wouldn't say "*handsome* buildings." I'd substitute "grand" or something of that sort suggesting the big simplicity of great architecture ("handsome" isn't a big enough word to describe the really great in building—say, the Parthenon or a grand cathedral).

I'm almost ashamed of mentioning such trifles.[1] I do think this is one of the best things you've written—strong—virile—keen-edged—Such a blow from such a Sword! Is it "Balmung"?[2] You—young Siegfried![3] You!

And these thoughts we shall live! Our service shall be in the world of action—rather than in that of art (Art shall be something added, for good measure! But our *big service* to the people shall be to help them get for themselves "a little rest from their labors"! Ain't it, Cully? Paula helping! The Double-Ess present in person!)

Now I'm going to say Good-night—I'm resolved to be good and not stay up late nights any more. In the name of the Ess-Ess, Good-Night! (You do your part, mind Carl! In the name of the health and the power and the long-life of the Ess-Ess!)

Good-night!
Love and love
from
Lilian

1. This letter is a perfect example of how tactful my mother was with any criticism—and she was generally right.

2. Balmung was the sword of Siegfried.

3. At this time Siegfried was a favorite hero not only with the Germans and lovers of Richard Wagner, but also with many socialists. In George Bernard Shaw's essay "The Perfect Wagnerite," he tries to show Wagner's revolutionary tendencies in *The Ring,* in which Wotan represents monarchy; Alberic, the dwarf, capitalism; and Siegfried, anarchism. It would be interesting to know if my mother had ever read this essay by Shaw.

47.

4/19/1908
2 Rivers, Wis.
9 P.M.

Just had a five-mile hike—over sandy hills wild & wind-beaten—and into pine woods along the lake shore. Grand somber glooms under wide branches, thickets & pools, & all the weird orchestration of frogs, crickets, night-birds, & whatnots with tongues & throats & voices—A bog kept me from reaching the shore—I could hear the surge—it was like Freedom—"Ever beyond!" So I took a seat (nobody asked me, Kitty, I wanted it & just took it—that's the way with S-S!) yes, I took a seat on a mossy, big log and lit a cigar. I read out loud to the tintinabulation of the frogs some lyrics to you. Some were original and some not so original but they were all lyrics! I spoke them to you—the "rythmic [*sic*] time of the metronome of want" was in them—the Want of YOU to be there—warm hand & wild hair and good face—The shadows had come a-creepin', slow and quiet but sure as shadows. The dusk had fallen all around when I was getting the last puffs on the cigar. I looked up at the sky and startlingly near, thru the green-black boughs of a massive pine was a burning, glowing star, a glittering, melting, concentred flame seen thru this one hole in the roof of the forest. I called out to the Booger-Man, "You know the name o' that star?" "No," said the Booger-Man. "Well," I said, "you Ignorance! you, if anybody asks you, the name o' that star is *Paula!*" And the Booger-Man mumbled something and took hisself back where he come from. Wouldn't talk no more! Whatdye think o' that? The Duke sends love to the Duchess—gee! such a duchess!—and says to himself, "Hard lines" but is comforted with the Duchess saying, "God rest you, merry gentleman!" adding sotto voce "Sweet fool!" Wasn't that a trick of Fate to send your letters to Hartford when I'm in Two Rivers? I feel sorry for Fate—poor thing—using such a cheap stratagem to keep us from wigwagging our love-signals—Fate has a lot to learn yet!—

Good-night, Paula, my great-heart—like the pines & stars I worshipped with to-night—Good-night, Paula—I kiss your grand face—it's a night of grandeurs—and you are its star—Paula! I kiss you as the last glory of this night of glories.—Carl.

48.

April 20—1908

Got your Saturday Night letter just now with the Sunday note telling that the Hartford date is postponed. I sent you a letter and a photo of me (by Ed) to Hartford. A letter to 344 Sixth St had already gone off too!—You'll have to send stamps I guess to have the photo forwarded from Hartford—4 cents.

My! I'd like to have seen Thompson's smile—when he read about the leap and the flipping of coins! A broad big-human smile from his good big heart.—I know it was! He'll give us his blessin' and mean it—and be glad and glad with us!

Do you think the knot had better be tied in Milwaukee? Mil. would be more convenient for Gaylord & Thompson. But maybe they'd enjoy a day at the farm? I don't know which would be better. We might leave it to Gaylord & Thompson to decide!! That would be original! Or we might flip coins again!—Anyway wherever it comes off, it will be as informal as possible. And you must wear a soft blue shirt—the one you wore at the farm—(If we had the knot-tying at the farm you could even roll your sleeves up! if the day was hot!)

Here's my picture of the "nuptial rites solemnized" at the farm—Gaylord and Thompson arrive about 11 P.M.[1]—driving all the way from Mil. or part by Rail—as far as Menomonee Falls, then drive to farm. (We-Two would have been up early—washed up breakfast dishes (Fun! and fun! and fun!)—helped mother get a nice simple farm-dinner ready). Gaylord & Thompson received with glad gay shouts—rah-rahing etc!—trumpets—Yawps!—"any noise good or bad"—Then maybe we'd all take a look at Pa's corn and potatoes—see how they're doing—discuss whether it's a good potato year or not!!—too wet or too dry!! etc! etc!!! Then dinner. (We'd have to forego the splendid fun of dish-washing for the time being—out of consideration for the darn guests!). Then a walk thru Zimmer's orchard[2]—Thompson would be moved to talk about the farmer question—agrarianism—and we could give him a pointer or so—we who carried on such a fast campaign in the county this spring!—And when Thompson & Gaylord felt they had enough of tramping—were ready for work—back we'd hike to the dear little old little white farmhouse! And under our own apple trees maybe—or in the arbor—with as much despatch as pleases the "holy man" who officiates, the knot should be tied! You in your blue shirt, sleeves rolled up—Kitty dressed ready for a romp over the hills the same as Micky—which romp over the hills we'd take after the "ceremony," provided Thompson & Gaylord felt equal to it!

Now draw or paint us a picture of "nuptial rites" in Milwaukee! Then we'll compare! See which will be the most fun and the least bother all 'round.

I confess it would be a lark too to just go to Milwaukee offhand and do the thing up still more simply—if possible—It has its points. You embellish it! And we'll see! You suggested it—what was the idea??

By the way is there *any reason* why I shouldn't write Miss T. that it is to be this summer already? I would a little rather that she heard it from me before hearing it from others—or soon after anyway. You know people like to be told. And she's honestly fond of me—it might hurt her if I didn't tell her myself—that is if there's no real object in keeping it secret. What do you say?

And for the district, if only I can make good, Cully! As a speaker, I mean! That would be great—great GREAT[.] And we'll try and try to make it go. It's *just* what I'd like most to do—it would satisfy the big ambition I've always had to do some real Service for the Cause! We'll work to make it go. More of this later.

As for household goods—I say: *as little as possible!* I like the way the Japs have!—I have such supreme contempt for even the better class of furniture produced by our Occidental Civilization, that it will be no deprivation for me if we never *never* own a piece of it!!—When the time comes that we feel we *have* to own a few things why "all right"—"What must be, must" you know!—But neither of us has a hankering after the stuff!

I have a way of comparing frescoed ceilings with the sky set with stars—Orion & the rest—that always nips in the bud any possible infringement on my part on the 10th commandment "Thou shalt not covet thy neighbor's goods!" The sky is the big arched ceiling—the only one in the world big enough for us anyway—(we who strike the very stars with our sublime heads!!)—the sky is the really beautiful ceiling that's ours for the looking, since we have eyes that see—With such eyes as we have our only difficulty will be not being able to enter into possession of all the things that *are* really ours—ours for the mere looking—We won't have time enough to walk over all the land we really *own* (because we have power to appreciate it!)—we won't have time to walk to the ends of our domain—says the Duchess to her Lord, the Duke of Buckingham-and-eggs!

Good-bye—now or I won't make the mail!

I kiss you long and long—Heart!—Love!—my Carl!—Breath of my breath—

Paula

1. A.M. This must be a mistake by my mother, for although she wrote "P.M.," it is obvious that A.M. was intended.

2. Across the road from the Steichen's Little Farm, Henry Zimmer had a large farm of about seventy acres, with an orchard. They were good friends and neighbors to the Steichens, and when Henry Zimmer heard, two months later, of the wedding, he organized a shivaree, but instead of beer they got a lecture on socialism from my father.

49.

[April 20, 1908]
Monday

The Duke sleeps so sound last night and so long that he uses cold water before rough-towelling this morning. From 11:00 P.M.

till 7:30—the longest sleep in weeks—Good Sweet Duchess—you are a good coach!

Have just finished 9 letters—S. D. Herald correspondence—a bunch of paragraphs titled Short Ones for the International Soc. Review, good-naturedly side-swiping the catastrophists—form letters for district secretaries, &c. &c.

The pencil is on the go and I must give you a message. I have imagined You in the other corner of the room—working with your work—talking to you at intervals—sometimes just looking—one look doing for a thousand words!—Paula! you great deep Heart! You!

Item on Lilians vocabulary: You're a Teacher too—do you know?—Besides Pal, in the woods—and Coach, on fletcherism, sleep, &c.—and Mate, companion, sublime woman inducing poetry & interpreting big things by look and gesture—besides these, you're Teacher. "Forth-going," "under-song," Wunderkind, weltanschauung, "play-fellow," you put these in my head for keeps. You're a literary stylist and a pundit! While we sit idly looking on landscapes and seascapes, I shall pump you for facts—quiz you and quiz you—draw fundamentals of science & art, stray incidents, from the repository back of your forehead into mine—the yellow pages of forgotten lore illumined by the gleam of your eye—you the pundit—me the pundit—boy and girl pooling all their powers—never grad-grinds!—but someway always having their fingers on the essentials of life—thoroughbreds!—proud and strong and knowing—eaglets—from their eyrie scenting the dangers before they arrive and then being ready with defense and reprisal—nestling many a day on the crag and enjoying the overlook on the blue sea and the horizon's peace—Eaglets, I said, Paula!

All the big people are simple—they relish a subtlety but they don't explain it—and these lives that long biographies expatiate on, they weren't near as long nor involved as the biographies are! Life is a river on which we drift down down thru an unexplored country. What rapids or calms or shallows are around the next curve, nobody knows. Columbus sails for the Indies and bumps into North America. Balboa goes sight-seeing in California and tumbles head first into the Pacific. To say what you'll find down the river of life is folly. To say you'll not baby if you're spilled out of your boat, to say you'll keep your head when you come to rapids, to say you'll stand uncovered in the hush of a clear-breaking dawn and greet with song and laughter every beautiful day—that's possible!

All the big people are simple, as simple as the unexplored wilderness. They love the universal things that are free to everybody. Light and air and food and love and some work are enough. In the varying phases of these cheap and common things, the great lives have found their joy.

Hist! Paula—O Duchess—the Duke is preaching—let him babble!

The point is: We're such compounds of health and power that we're indomitable. We may find what we're not looking for but we will either go around it or it will get out of our way. This S-S unit hopes to live so to bless and benefit. It wants to work for socialism and help usher in the New Civilization. Let the world and destiny behave and not by any circumstance so distract us from this work for we will become marauders if we need the money.—Ain't it?—Yes, so simple we are, so little we want, we are wise and will get what we want. The S-S so announces!

—Maybe sometime while I'm on the road you will find time in Oshkosh to gather a lot of these philosophizings into an MSS for a book. The good-cheer cult is having a big vogue—the world has never had too much Hope nor enough Love. And it might be a gamble worth while to try the whole publishing world on the proposition—give them all a chance. There are a lot of details to the whole scheme, but it's a good deal less hopeless than Carlyle's Sartor Resartus or Stevenson's stuff and others, in beginning. What with the poems, the paragraphic essays ("Intuitions" "Short Ones") and stuff like that Thoughts on Art, and The Sordid, which after this we'll try on the Craftsman, The Independent, the new mag. Hunter is working on—there may be results. To put some of your stuff in the paragraphic essays, put it out as from the two of us, with a Steichen print of the two of us facing the eternities—we've got a great fighting chance. And if we ring the bull's eye on the target of public favor, with a book, there will be calls for us to lecture.—The S-S is glad for whatever there is around the next curve.—Adios now, you big fine girl-heart—I tumble your hair again & it falls down all around your good

head—and we whisper things we learned way back in the eons.—
Adios—Paula—Sixty days—sixty days—

—On the way eternal we go out, afoot and light-hearted, healthy, free, the world before us, the long brown path leading wherever we choose.

P.S.—About that Whitman lecture—it was built to please agreeably souse and shock—Princeton will sit up bewildered a little, amused slightly, but thrilled and pleased more—for I glorify whatever is human and Princeton being human will enjoy the glorification and chortle with your own self "Ya —— yep!!"—
Am I voluble to-night or are you looking at me with some rarely luring look of yours?—You mischievous Suffragette! You plotter! You exclamative punctuationist!— Ain't it lovely scenery from the car-window, Kid?—

Cully

50.

To his Nibs the Duke of Buckingham-and-eggs:

Greetings! Likewise admonishings (most lady-like, most duchess-like admonishings) lest his lordship neglect to do his little stunts, tumblings, punchings and the like grave duties of his office,

from her Nibs,
The Duchess.

April 21,
A.D. 1908

51.

Tuesday April 21, 1908

The malevolent Fate plotted darkly, but Paula was too quick.—
First, some other Fate mixed up with Fate No. 1 and your letter

of the 18th which should have reached me Sunday, was given me yesterday.—And this morning at 8:30 I get one that left your dear hands only yesterday afternoon. You've got *despatch*—momentum—go—and yet you're not a hurrying hustler—You're a Wonder! my Thaumaturgist!

About the non-essentials—I like your picture of the wedding doings at the farm—it would please your mother better probably than any other plan. I had thought of our taking a car out to Thompson or Gaylord—get the knot tied much as we might wash our hands at a wayside hotel—a few minutes chat—a stop and chat at T. or G., whichever lost the toss (!), attend to business and greetings at headquarters and then ho! northward!—But the farm picture is a lark, and so simply gay—that may be best—I leave that with you and the dear Mother.—If Joseffy has no Chatauqua dates then, I will have him on hand, with the skull of Balsamo, and the violin.—

My folks I shall calmly inform when it is all over. Merely more of the unexpected which they regularly expect! Charlie has been so queer in his tastes. They will look so and so at you when we go to Galesburg one day! Gee! that will be fun—and downtown and at the college they will look and they will find you baffling and only sense something of power and beauty & wisdom & love—something as far-off and cross-textured as my poetry and warm and open as myself. They won't understand you any more than me—but they will love you—yes, you will be good for them! A few, a precious few, homely and yearning—O so yearning—will understand. My mother out of her big, yearning, hungry heart will hug you before you leave and with a crystal of tears will find the soul of you. Mary & Esther and Martha[1] will all like you deep—but they have not starved so hard nor prayed so vainly—they will get only sides of you. We should have a whole day with Wright (The Dreamer) of Asgard[2]—he will do us a poem!

I shall save Green Bay and Marinette and Sturgeon Bay for The Honeymoon. Inasmuch as we recognize some spectral validity in a wedding we must also concede a period of time immediately following a wedding known as a honeymoon. It is a shooting the chutes and at the bottom is The First Disgust. At the end of the honeymoon, they have found out which is absolute and to be obeyed. One subtly or outrightly domineers, the other similarly and synchronously submits.—Or, there are sweeping northwesterly winds and storms in which this and that is torn up or broken down and flung windward while the wind whistles like anguish, despair and foiled hope. This condition, commonly known as hell, is followed by drought, monotony, a little dreariness, and then a capitulation to breakfast, dinner & supper. Smiles are put on and taken off like wearing apparell. The hell-fires of revolt freeze over into strange, smooth, stupid satisfaction. Once a year on some wild night, the lurking rat of regret gnaws a hole into a calloused heart and tremulous lips give a cry, "Life cheated us! Life cheated us! Something is lost! something precious and wonderful is gone and will never come back!" But a little sleep, a little slumber, and a breakfast of buckwheat cakes and pork sausages and greenish coffee—and the gnawing is quiet for another year. The consolation is, "What does it matter? Everybody does it!"—Yes, we will call it a honeymoon and then we will have done with concessions to society. We will do our own christening & baptizing & if it ever comes to funerals we're likely to call in Clarence Darrow the Agnostic or Father Vaughn the gentle priest who is bigger than the Catholic Church or a Xtian Scientist friend or just read a few lines of Whitman ourselves and let it go at that—living the calm and simple—

The district has so much of natural beauty, Lilian. That was one of the things attracted me up here. All nationalities are represented in it. You will find wilderness unspoiled in Oconto. You will find civilization at its best and worst along the Fox River—black, choking industrialism, and libraries, concerts, women's clubs and art from Schuman-Heink to 5¢ vaudeville. All big, pulsing, turbulent, panoramic! I have for it all the passion & enthusiasm Walt had for

> "Proud, mad city! my city!
> O Manahatta! My Manahatta!"

And all our efforts, dear will be cumulative—the more we do the more we can do along any line. Our income will always be on the increase. Continued agitation and organization will familiarize us intimately with the various situations making us increasingly competent to advise, guide & direct the comrades. Loyal, whole-hearted friends, like bitter, implacable enemies, will constantly multiply.—Such a trip as it will be, dear love-pal—Mate-Woman!—Sweetheart!—proud, beautiful Lilian!

[Written on back of last page of letter:] Yes! write Miss Th.

1. Mary, Esther, and Martha were his sisters.
2. Philip Green Wright.

52.

April 21—Night

Paula is the gay-heart again (the same as Kitty)—

After writing the afternoon letter (the corners of her mouth woefully down) Paula went out into the woods—and

> "The little gray leaves were kind to her
> The little green things had a mind to her
> When into the woods she came."

(adapted from Sidney Lanier) [1]

All the tiny green buds reached out to comfort me—and I was happy. Spring in my heart responded to the Spring in the buds and the little first-leaves.

And the peach trees—all pink and sweet and delicate—such wisps of trees—young things happy to be alive! I was happy.

Next spring, Carl, we'll be together and see this wonder of little gray leaves—and little green things—and blossoms a-blow—and wind-flowers—and violets—and warm balmy spring nights—and stars—and surge—and glooms of pine-forests! We-Two together!

Carl! and Carl! and Carl! A long long kiss—My Love—My Heart—You—Sweet!—A long long kiss—We-Two who are One!

Lilian

1. Adapted from Sidney Lanier's poem "A Ballad of Trees and The Master" (1880):

> The olives they were not blind to Him,
> The little gray leaves were kind to Him,
> The thorn-tree had a mind to Him
> When into the woods He came.

53.

[Two Rivers, Wis., April 21, 1908]
Tuesday Night—10 P.M.

Back from a long hike again—sand and shore, night and stars and this restless inland sea[1]—Plunging white horses in a forever recoiling Pickett's Charge at Gettysburg—On the left a ridge of jaggedly outlined pines, their zig-zag jutting up into a steel-grey sky—under me and ahead a long brown swath of sand—to the right the ever-repelled but incessantly charging white horses and beyond an expanse of dark but over all, sweeping platoons of unguessable stars! Stars everywhere! Blinking, shy-hiding gleams—blazing, effulgent beacons—an infinite, travelling caravanserie—going somewhere! "Hail!" I called, "Hail! do you know? do you know? You veering cotillions of worlds beyond this world—you marching—imperturbable splendors—you serene, everlasting spectators—where are we going? do you know?" And the answer came back, "No, we don't know and what's more, we don't care!" And I called, "You answer well. For you are time and space—you are tomb and cradle. Forever you renew your own origin, shatter to-day and reshape to-morrow, in a perpetual poem of transformations, knowing no goal, expecting no climax, looking forward to no end, indulging in no conception of a finale, content to move in the eternal drama on which no curtain will be rung. You answer well. I salute you to-night. I will see you again and when I do again I will salute you for you are sincere. I believe you O stars! and I know you! We have met before and met many times. We will meet again and meet many times."—All this time I was striding along at a fast pace, to the music of the merry-men. The merry-men, I forgot to explain, ride the white horses and it is the merry-men who give voice to the extasy [*sic*] and anger and varying humor of the sea. The tumultuous rythms [*sic*] of the merry-men and a steady, ozone-laden wind led me to walk fast and when I turned from the sea, there burst on my vision, the garish arc-lamps of the municipality of Two Rivers. So I turned to the sky and said, "Good-by, sweet stars! I have had good companionship with you to-night but now I must leave star-land, and enter the corporation limits of Two Rivers town. Remember me

O stars! and remember Paula down in Princeton, Illinois! and if any agitators appear in star-land, let them agitate—it will be good for them and for all the little stars." And as I plodded down a narrow street just past the hovels of fishermen and the tenements of factory workers, I quoted from the bare-footed, immortal Athenian, "The gods are on high Olympus—let them stay there." Yes, let the gods who are on high Olympus stay where they belong. And let us turn to the business of rearing on earth a race of gods.

There—it's out of me, Pal. It was a glorious hike. I shall sleep and sleep to-night. And you are near to-night—so near and so dear—a good-night kiss to you—great-heart—good lips—and good eyes—My Lilian—

Carl

P.S.: P.S.S!—No, I will never get The Letter written & finished. It will always need postscripts. I end one and six minutes after have to send more. All my life I must write at this Letter—this Letter of Love to the Great Woman Who Came and Knew and Loved. All my life this must go on! The Idea and the Emotion are so vast it will be years and years in issuing. Ten thousand love-birds, sweet throated and red-plumed, were in my Soul, in the garden of my under-life. There on ten thousand branches they slept as in night-time. You came and they awoke. For a moment they fluttered distractedly in joy at stars and odors and breezes. And a dawn burst on them—a long night was ended. God! how they sang. God! the music of those throats—such dulcets and diapasons of song as they sang! I hear them & I know them. These birds want freedom. These imprisoned songsters are all to be loosed. But I can let out only one at a time. Each letter, then, is some joy till now jailed—but now sent flying—and flying and flying!—at the touch of release, called out by the Woman Who Came.

So Paula, you have letters and letters to come—and we will send birds, love-birds with love-songs, flying out over the world. We cannot live the Sheltered Life, with any bars up. It is us for The Open Road—loosing the birds!—loosing the birds! Jesus wept, Voltaire smiled, William Morris worked, the S-S flung the world twenty-thousand beautiful, vibrating, fleering,[2] indomitable, happy love-birds singing love-songs swelling the world's joy. Even so.

1. Here, as in all his early poems referring to the sea, he means Lake Michigan.
2. "Fleering" is obsolete now; it meant fleeing.

Back to the Beach

Now with the long, loud stormbeat
Gone now and outswept
  Elsewhere,
The sea is at peace today.

The heart of peace is here
And gives soft breath
On the sea's face today.
Slow lines of wave
Mingle their murmur
With a low wind moving.
A few cries of white birds
Come across on the levels
Of creeping surge and winding drift
And they all go back
To the Great Mother at peace today.

I will sleep to-night
And remember you,
You and your wide murmur of peace,
White bird, low wind and soft wave,
  I will sleep
And my heart shall remember
The look of your face today.

Two Rivers in 1908[1]

1. This poem is included here because my father wrote at the bottom "Two Rivers in 1908," and also because it seems to fit the mood of the letter. This does not mean that it was sent with this letter, although I think it would be a good guess that it was.

54.

[April 22, 1908]
Wednesday afternoon

I like the idea of the Mil. wedding—it is breezy—has vim and go—However, as you say, mother may like the farm wedding much better. We'll put it up to her.—As for a lark at the farm with Gaylord & Thompson—we could have that later in the summer. We'll have to come back to the farm later and live in the tent in the orchard for a week! Maybe we could do that in July or August—when you have to come to Mil. anyway. We could have some fun haying then!

I know the district will be great in every way—wild natural beauty—and the teeming life of cities—both!

What a honeymoon it will be! In the far-north—Oconto—Green Bay—etc. Will we go by lake?—Anyway when we get there, we can walk (day or twilight or night—any time we please!) down to the shore and hear the surge! The Sea! The Sea! We-Two together, pals, lovers, comrades! What a honeymoon it will be!

Sixty days! Sixty days! Then for the deep sea! The S-S ship fairly launched!

How the Sea calls and calls!—You, gray old Sea with your Challenge—listen!—we will come—we will come! We are climbing down the bank, we-two together, as fast as we can! We will arrive—we will reach the shore—old Sea—(and sail!) In Sixty days! Sixty days!

How the Sea calls and calls! Carl! Carl! We-Two, proud seamen, unafraid, impatient to leave the solid land, bold rovers—what a voyage before us! The beauty—the storms—the work—the joy—of the Sea. The Sea!

I am thinking of the Sea—and the Voyage—and the S-S Ship!—Carl and Paula together!

55.

April 22—Night

Have just finished a letter to Miss Thomas—telling her that we launch the S-S this summer, and that she's to sing out "Bon Voyage" when we hoist anchor!

I wonder what C.D.T. will say when he has the talk with you on things "further than that" relative to the leap. Surely C.D.T. won't turn out to be "pusillanimous"—I mean *timorsome* about "ventures"!—If you do, O Carl D., so much the worse for you! The S-S are reckless bold sailors—and have no use for considerations and hesitations and "ifs" and "buts"!!—Have a care, Carl D.T., lest you be weighed in the S-S balance and found wanting!

That Galesburg trip is something to look forward to! I suppose we'll see some eyes as big as saucers, will we?! What fun! What fun!—And they won't understand Charlie's other self any more than the original Charlie! Rather the puzzle will now be a genuine prodigy!—Charlie was baffling enough, but lo now a duplicate—Charlie, a woman to match Charlie: ye gods, a Prodigy! a Prodigy!

So much for the town.

But the Mother—that will be different. I love her, flesh of your flesh, Cully—heart of your heart! The mother who bore the Wunderkind! I will find *You* in the Mother, Carl—*You* not yet unfolded—yet still *You!* all the possibilities of *You* in the embryo!—I love and love the Mother—and I know she will love me.

The girls I don't see so distinctly yet—but I'll love them and Mart[1] too—there will be *something* of Cully or Carl or Sandy or Micky in each of them, surely! Or if not, at least they are wrapped in the glory of having lived years and years with you "seeing Shelly [*sic*] plain" all the while! "How strange it seems and new"![2]—

Why I'll *love* the very town where Cully was one of de dirty dozen! Galesburg! Galesburg! Old town, I love you—because Cully played on your streets—and suffered—and hungered with the heart's hunger—and struggled—and won out achieving *HIMSELF*—so that now CULLY IS!

My heart will go out to everything and everybody in Galesburg that meant or means anything to *You!* Cully!

Maybe we'll make that Galesburg trip a year from this summer! No matter *when,* tho.

Good-night. It's 11:30. Have practised the whole evening with those sophs[3]—fun too in a way—only I'd rather spend the time talking to you!

Good-night! And kisses to you, my Cully!

And says the Duchess to His Nibs, the Duke of Buckingham-and-Eggs—says, she:

> My lord, right nobly did your worship acquit himself Sunday Night. Such hours of sleep are much to be commended, dear my lord—

Says the Duchess, says she! And makes a handsome courtly bow—and Exit Duchess!

P.S. Did you happen to save Ed's letter. If so, return it to me and I'll send it on to mother. I referred to it in my letter home, and mamma asks to see it.—You know how it is with Ed. He writes so little.—But it's no great matter if you haven't kept the letter. It would give mother some pleasure to read it tho.—So if you have it, send it.[4]

1. His brother, Martin Godfrey Sandburg.

2. From Robert Browning's "Memorabilia":

> Ah, did you once see Shelley plain,
> And did he stop and speak to you
> And did you speak to him again?
> How strange it seems and new!

3. The sophomore play was called *The Mistakes of the Night,* adapted from Oliver Goldsmith's *She Stoops To Conquer.*

4. My grandmother saved every letter she had from my uncle and every printed article about him that she saw.

56.

ESS-ESS 23 SKIDDOO IX * * * *

The dook is hereby solemnly and publicly reprimanded for going off on drunks and midnight debauches when he'd promised not to.

As we go to press, we receive an eleventh hour communication from His Nibs, in which he confesses to a second drunken debauch prolonged far into the Night. The dook's guilt is therefore multiplied by TWO.

In order to make the punishment correspond to the offence—that is, in order to multiply by TWO the solemnity and publicity of this reprimand—we shall mail our subscribers TWO copies of this IX number of the ESS-ESS.

We have observed that slight penalties make no impression upon those IN HIGH PLACES. Hence the severity of this punishment. Even a DOOK cannot fail to be impressed by this TWICE solemn and TWICE publicit REPRIMAND!

That his Nibs will speedily mend his ways is the hope of

The Editor

IMPRINTED ON
THE 23RD DAY
OF THE MONTH
OF SKIDDOO

Written in pencil in his hand on the reverse of Paula's letter:

> You were mad—mad as the maddest boy tt[1] ever flung
> away his life on a bloody rampart.
> You were gay—gay as the gayest sailor tt ever went down
> in a rotten boat on a tossing sea.
> You were wild—wild as the wildest mountaineer tt ever
> obeyed the lure of a lone tall peak.
> You were mad, you were gay, you were wild,
> You may have lost, you may have won, I do not know.
> But this I know: The ramparts, storms and peaks of life you
> touched and knew and thrilled to.

Star-eyed girl of the heart that
knows,
Where did you come by your eyes
that see,
Where did you get your heart
that knows.

You were mad, you were gay, you
were wild,
You may have lost, you may have
won, I do not know.

But this I know: The ramparts,
storms and peaks of life
you touched and knew and
thrilled to.

Part of the poem that accompanies Letter 56.

Star-eyed girl of the heart that knows,
Where did you come by your eyes that see,
Where did you get your heart that knows.[2]

1. That.

2. The poem that follows is placed here because it was apparently developed from this poem.

Paula

Star-eyed girl of the heart that knows
Where did you come by your eyes that see?
Where did you get your heart that knows?
What passing ghost of silver breath
Blew on your hair that breath of white?

You tell me of dreams, sea-tinted, sky-fashioned,
You pour out sweet thoughts like baskets of flowers,
You scatter me whimsies, wide-handedly tossing.
Tree-top anthems, smell of the rain, and shy wood-blooms,
The wind that goes winding the sunset trail,
The mud and the bugs, the red spring wonders,
You know them all and you pass them along!

Where did you come from?
Where are you going?
And what are you going to do when you get there.

57.

Thursday [April 23, 1908]

I'm in the thick of work—all sorts—getting stage properties together—writing the program-copy with synopsis of scenes etc.—spurring on the vocal music teacher to coach the boys more on their song—lastly coaching the boys myself for the play, morning, noon and night—Tomorrow evening it comes off—and I'll be free to enjoy these beautiful beautiful spring days. To-day we've had spring showers—you know what that means—a freshness and a fragrance over everything! Oh, I get glimpses!—Everything is budding out! bursting into life!—And to-day all the young green is so fresh, so glad, so fragrant with the sweet warm rains.

I've written mother a long letter—telling her all our plans—also putting it up to her to decide whether it shall be a Mil. or a farm wedding. I argued in favor of the Mil. wedding—tying the knot with absolutely *no* fuss or ceremony—but left it to mother to decide. I have thought of several further considerations in favor of Mil. Mother wants to please all her friends. If we have a farm wedding, that will be impossible; they'll feel hurt not to be asked—at least a few of the most intimate old friends will. But if it were explained that we just went to the minister's house and had the knot tied in haste, why no-one could feel hurt. See! Maybe that argument will appeal to mother. Anyway it makes little difference either way. In either case there will be a minimum of ceremony. Mil. or the farm. It's up to mother.

I have heard from mother in reply to my letter telling her we have fixed the date for *this* summer instead of next.—Mother is sensible. Doesn't doubt that we know our minds—doesn't urge delay. How could she indeed? Mother has always been a man of despatch herself—acting as quick as thought. All her business moves were precipitate.—So she understands our haste! Good for her!—Oh of course mother writes that she feels that she is losing her little girl etc etc etc!—That's where the dear mother falls short of being a perfectly healthy minded woman. Nursing griefs—some imaginary—Still the prevailing note is Gladness. Mother has *sensed* it—the Big Thing—that *we-two* are a Rarely mated pair! That it is a great glory that we met, found each other.

I'll miss the mail if I don't run!

Love and love
Paula

58.

[April 23, 1908]
Thursday Night

Just back from a *short* walk (after a *long* rehearsal—) (the last dress rehearsal!) A dark night with a high wind and now and

Thursday Night

Just back from a *short* walk
(after a *long* rehearsal —)
(the last dress rehearsal!)
A dark night with a
high wind and now and then
flashes of lightning. A
wild night. A night for
the Poet and Fanchon!
We walk, our arms
around each other —
Fanchon throws her head
back and the Poet's lips
are on hers. Against

Part of Letter 58.

then flashes of lightning. A wild night. A night for the Poet and Fanchon! We walk, our arms around each other—Fanchon throws her head back and the Poet's lips are on hers. Against the background of the dark wild sky, the swirling black clouds lit up with flashes of lightning—Fanchon sees the face of her Poet, a proud noble face! and daring! Fanchon draws the face to her—and covers it with kisses—and the wind blows wildly—and the lightning flashes! And still Fanchon covers her Poet's lips and eyes and cheeks and hair with warm kisses!

Sweet, we are so near to-night—as we pace our beat—soldiers on sentinel-duty—soldiers—two arms around each other—one coat wrapping us-two—so near together! We think of that last glorious night on the farm—we-two so happy under the eternal silent Skies!

O you Heart!

You to love and love, and it will not be enough! You to worship, as I look into your good good eyes, Sweet! You to worship and worship—and it will never be enough! Always You are—Beyond!—

Cully, I love you and love you. I kiss you—your dear lips and eyes and hair all covered with warm tender kisses, and I can't kiss you enough. Always this unsatisfied yearning to give more and more love and more and more kisses. Sweet! So good! So good! You to call out all the love in me—and it is not enough! I can feel the Soul of me growing and growing—there is that love-for-you within it expanding and expanding, pressing on all sides upon the walls of my Soul—and so these walls are biggening! The Soul of me growing and growing as my love for you grows and grows and grows! Oh, Life and Life!—I must look long and long at the stars, and turn my face to the wind and the rain beating down hard on me, and listen to the rushing of winds and waves and the deep rumble of thunder, proud, solemn music—that so my Soul may biggen and the Love within have a better chance to grow as it so yearns to! The love for you fills my Soul to bursting now! I feel the Love pounding and throbbing and pressing and yearning and hammering against all the walls of my soul!

And you Heart! *You are!* You whom I can never love enough! Whom I love unreservedly to the full capacity of my soul—and then it is not enough! You, Heart, for whom I must biggen my soul—always expanding and expanding—and it will never be enough!—Such a life of growth for love's sake—you give me—you Heart—Oh Carl! and Carl!

So good you are! So big! So sweet! So clean!—What a Man to love and love!—No, I shall never give you enough love—but I give you all and all, every power of my soul loving you—loving you!—and reaching and pushing out to become more a power for loving you! for loving you!

And that is the great thing—that transcends infinitely anything I ever *dreamed* of, before *You* appeared and I saw and knew and loved *You!* That is the great thing—that *You are the Man who cannot be loved Enough!*—It will never end. "The letter will never be written."[1] Always there will be growth! More and more love! And still something Beyond! Something to yearn toward! And never quite reach!

Such a love-life we have before us. Oh, Carl! My love and my love! I kiss you a thousand thousand times! It is not enough—still I withhold my lips from more and more kisses. A million million kisses would not be enough either. So there is a poised restraint. But never satiety. Our love is infinite. It knows no bottom. It *is*—and it *grows forever.*

My Love and my Love,
Good-night!

1. The phrase "The letter will never be written" is from Letter 52.

59.[1]

The *contest* is over and done with! At last! The Play was a brilliant success!—Also I made an after-dinner speech which was applauded and applauded and applauded. (The speech was all blarney—tho I meant what I said too—I like the Sophs here—they have vim and push and go. They are a lot of Johnnies on the spot! Very good—[*as far as it goes*]!) Well, my speech *arrived* all right—this pleased me for I've never tried this sort of thing before—and didn't know if I could "make a hit" with it.—Of course it didn't amount to anything in itself—but who knows?—maybe I *can* do things that will amount to something in the ten minute speech line *and that will make a hit too!*—H'm, Carl?

The contest is over. It kept me up till midnight yesterday—(and a busy day it was). This morning I slept late and then went to school to help straighten up—see that stage properties etc. were returned. Then this note—which I must mail right *now* to make the A.M. mail.—

This afternoon I shall take time to write all the things that have accumulated in my mind these days of short letters.—

Love from Kitty and from the Duchess and from Lilian & Paula etc.

1. This letter was written on the back of the program for the contest and the play.

60.

[April 25, 1908]

To her girl, the Golden Girl,[1] the dear mother is beginning to cry "So Long!"?—

Wonderful Mother—and Wonderful Daughter.

It's a rare thing—so deep and close a chumminess—with such a foundation in the things that are everlasting.

She was one of the factors in That Week at "the dear little, white little house"—as unique in her way as you.—I said to you, "She's Whitmanic." And she is. Nothing but the Limit, the farthest and highest, for her boy and girl. Nothing but the Limit for herself, working in the scope of her chances. A rapt enthusiast, giving all, risking all, and no surety of returns.

What a Life! If there's anything in the story that a Recording Angel puts down all the "good" and all the "bad" we do, how easily and calmly she could look that R.A. in the eyes!

Thinking, reasoning, logic, can't find its way into and understand this between You and Me, Paula. But *love* can. *Heart* and *yearning* can. And that's why the Mother will understand clearer and more finely than any. She may say the "So long!" with a

To her girl, the Golden Girl, the dear mother is beginning to cry "So Long!"? -

Wonderful Mother - and Wonderful Daughter -

It's a rare thing - so deep and close a chumminess - with such
a foundation in the things that are everlasting.

She was one of the factors in That Week at "the dear
little, white little house" - as unique in her way as
you. - I said to you, "She's Whitmanic". And she
is. Nothing but the Limit, the farthest and highest,
for her boy and girl. Nothing but the Limit for herself, working in the scope of her chances. A rapt

Part of Letter 60.

heavy ache in her heart. But she loves you and I think her mother-heart sensed it that I'm the kind of a boy the girl she reared ought to have. I know her. I had that wave of feeling toward her and I believe she's toward me as I am toward her. So that she knows the S-S is wise, that else is impossible.

And this in the long run may be true too: That she not only not loses her Golden Girl but is gainer by an attachment, a companion piece which goes with the Golden Girl! She not only keeps Lily, the choicest book in her library of life, but she gets a Volume Two!—Not a whole Volume maybe, but a kind of glossary, something that will show her new meanings in Lily, the G.G.!

All this in the long run, by the big way, the far look! She will understand if the love for her girl is as big as the wide fine life she has lived. Even so.

1. My mother was far from looking like a Golden Girl, having black hair with a few copper strands left from the early days. But starting in the 1890s and for some time after the turn of the century, this expression stood for beauty, grace, radiance, and other lovely attributes to Woman. Richard Le Gallienne, in his novel *The Quest of the Golden Girl* (1896), wrote, "How is it that I, a not unpresentable young man, a man not without accomplishments or experience, should have gone all these years without finding that

> 'Not impossible she
> Who shall command my heart and me'—

Without meeting at some turning of the way the mystical Golden Girl—without, in short, finding a wife?"

61.

[April 25, 1908]
Saturday afternoon

Oh, yes—I'm in training too. Started afresh 2 hours ago (after the debauch of this past week's work on the Sophomores). And lo—Results! Already! You ask for proof? Good—here 'tis. Just before sitting down to write I picked up my watch from the dresser. A button-hook caught on the chain. I carried watch & chain half way across the room before I noticed the extra weight. Then when I did notice it and looked down and saw the old button-hook—such a laugh! Kitty was tickled to death! And all over this whimsical play of the old button-hook! Plain fun tastes good when you're in training! (tho it's been only for two hours!).

And now Kitty's going to keep on training! Be sure when we meet next I won't be fragile and breakable! I'll dare you to crush or crunch me! You, Cully! Do your best! And I'll say "More!—More!" I want you to crush me hard! And then I'll throw my arms around your neck and squeeze you so—you'll know then that Kitty is in "baseball form" herself! And I'll bite you too—wouldn't I like to eat you up tho—you Cully—You, my gos-soon—You—bad Mick you!

Do you know, Cully, Monday will be the menseversary of our Great Ride Together from Brookfield to the farm in storm and wind and lightning and black night! Such a ride! "We have lived." How the elements love us, Carl—to come so close to us; one might almost say, to butt in on us! We didn't beg the wind and the lightning and the thunder and the rain—we didn't beg them to give us their company! It wasn't a ceremonial "call"—we hadn't given out that we would be "at home." Out of sheer love for us, they *intruded* their presences upon us—slapped us in the face with love's abandon—pulled and tugged at us—and kissed us with rough hard kisses—the impetuous elements! And didn't we shout back tho! And didn't we give these rough old intruders to understand that we love their sort—love them hard—for their lusty mad gayety and their free common ways! And didn't they give us to understand that they would butt in on us again and often again.—when we least expected them—for we were their sort, they said (the mad, bad, glad elements *said* so!)

Oh—we're *in* for it, Carl! We're going to be together in all kinds of Mud and Rain and Wind! And then we'll quote from your *fine fine* "A Yawp" : "Gee! Ain't We glad We're here."

(By the way—that yawp is great stuff—it's Cully—I feel like saying "It's the best yet"—More Whitman than Whitman himself. Really *common*-big-human!—Maybe you'll do more in that vein some day! In the Shack in the Woods! Liz along!)

But "you and me" Cully—we *are* going to mix a lot with the elements!—We must camp out some time in our old pine forests to the North. Sometime. This summer with the presidential election on I suppose we won't have much time—but maybe next summer we can! Such play as we'd have! If Rain and Mud butted in, we'd know how to play with them too! Wouldn't we tho! Or if it was Wind and Sunshine instead—all right, we'd play with them.

You, old elements, you know it but I want to tell you again: "The S-S hasn't any calling cards with 'At Home—Wednesdays—Four to Six' printed in the corner. But you—old elements—you will always be welcome guests! Come any old time, unannounced, and we'll play with you. You are like Joseffy—you can come *any* time!"

Now, Cully, I'm off for a long walk—out on some country road—You'll be along by virtue of a splendid "Make-Believe." In sixty days—our being together won't be make-believe, thank God! My patience with Make-believe will last that long. But no longer, Cully—*Positively no longer!*

Here are wireless-kisses—Cully! I love to send them—but soon I want to kiss your warm living lips—and have done with Make-believe and long distance communication!!!

Kitty is in training!—and you see the result!!! She makes demands on Life!—So it is, Cully. The healthier you are, the more you insist that Life shall satisfy your Wants!

Good-bye—I'm off into the country—

Menseversary corresponds to anniversary, March 27—April 27. Paula's Dictionary

---

62.

[April 26, 1908]
Sunday

A "trifle" of FIVE (5) letters from you to-day, Sandy! And such letters! The beautiful lyric P.S.: P.S.: P.S.S.—about loosing the love-birds—and the big hearted letter about mother from Carl *who understands*—and your proud "But me no buts" letter—and the Commune Manifesto letter (reminiscent of the Communist Manifesto) "L.S. and C.S., Unite![1] You have nothing to lose but your chains—You have a World to gain. The history of the world is not only a history of class struggles but of marriages!"

Good! This afternoon I shall put on my hat (I always do that on solemn occasions here in Princeton—but not otherwise! When Elsie Stern and I went to Mr. Magill's house last October to bring the word that she would break her contract and marry at Xmas and he'd have to look for another teacher—why, we both got our hats out of our trunks [we hadn't worn them all fall]—and put on fresh shirt-waists and our good skirts—and oh! Cully, it was so *funny*—so funny—at Mr. Magill's, at *the most solemn moment of all,* I looked down and saw that my old tan linen skirt showed a good half inch all around from under my good black skirt!! We had so much fun over the mock-solemn ritual of changing dresses that we never noticed that I had somehow forgotten to take off the old skirt—and so I went in both—the old skirt showing under the Sunday-go-to-meetin' ceremonial skirt—Elsie noticed the deficiency in my dress-up about the same time I did. And we chortled across the room at each other—startling poor Mr. Magill nearly out of his wits—we had been so solemn almost funereal up to the minute we burst into mad gay chortling!!!—That was a gay night—Cully!—Micky should have been there to see the fun! It was metropolitan opera-bouffe!—You'll remember the other elements in this vaudeville performance—Mr. Magill, the Man, *de*-lighted to be rid of that obsession, the inexplicable Miss Stern!—while Mr. Magill, the Moralist, tried hard to feel the regret he knew he ought to feel at losing a teacher who could not be replaced!—As for the whimsical play of that old tan linen skirt [bedraggled at that—I had worn it that afternoon on a ramble in the woods—and the grass was wet and the paths muddy!]—Mr. Magill and his wife affected not to notice it, out of stiff politeness, tho I knew they were fairly busting to laugh at the ludicrous sight of *me with my dress-up hat on* [me who never wore any sort of hat!] and *with a bedraggled tan skirt showing under my good dress-up skirt* [me who am ordinarily neat enough!]—Such gayety! that is, for Elsie & Kitty Malone! *Not* for the Magills!)

(Oh, no, no—Kitty hasn't lost the Art of the Parenthetical!)

But to get back to where I was when I started off on this Model of an Extended Parenthesis:

This afternoon I shall put on my hat (Maybe a fresh shirt-waist and a good skirt too—We shall see! We shall see! I feel in a mood for a lark!) and go to present Mr. Magill with an *expurgated copy* of "The Commune Manifesto"—That is I shall tell him the facts—marriage this summer—so he can begin to cast about for a new teacher.

This afternoon then—with the Manifesto in our pockets ("You have nothing to lose but your chains! You have a world to gain!") we shall cross the Rubicon! Burn our bridges behind us! And press on—to—Rome! City of Dreams-to-be-Realized! Rome! Rome! Out of the ruins that You have left in Rome—O Time and Change!—we (aye, *we,* "love-crazy, life-intoxicated fools—going Somewhere")—even *we* shall upbuild you, out of your *ruins of mystic dreams,*—A CITY WONDERFUL OF REALITIES! O Time and Change, others have gone to Rome before the S.S.—we know it! Some of them have lived there till death, content with the ruins they found there for their habitations. Others have lived in those beautiful ruins of mystic dreams awhile, and growing weary of them because they were but *ruins* and ruins of *dreams* only, left Rome to search elsewhere for the City Wonderful of Love. Some (who had it in them to be *builders* not *tenants* merely) tried before us to do what we shall try to do and succeed in doing: they tried to upbuild a Real City out of the Ruins of Dreams they found—and failed. Their failure shall not discourage You, O Time and Change, nor shall it discourage us, the Wunder-kind-Thaumaturgist builders—The Master-Builders!—Oh, we know—too that there are some (builders, at that) who never came on to Rome because they heard of its lying in ruins. They were impatient to build and thought the old ruins would be in the way;—not having seen these ruins they did not know the elements of beauty and of strength in them! They were sure no good could come of *ruins!* Or Maybe they had passed thru Rome and had looked upon these ruins *with eyes that saw not.* And so whether they passed thru Rome or not, they are now looking for a different site on which to build the City of Love, or they have found a site for it on what they think new ground, but it is the old site of Sodom or of Gomorrah (which were burned to the ground)—what a site for a *City Wonderful of Love!* Alas!

But Ess-Ess knows that *Rome* is the site for the City Wonderful. The Ess-Ess knows the elements worth while in the old ruins. The Ess-Ess will build you such a City out of your old ruins, O

Time and Change—such a *City of Realities!* out of the *Ruins* of your *Mystic Dreams!* that—you'll sing us a few *Hosannahs*—Ya!—Yep!—You will!—You Old-Time and Change will sing Hosannahs to Us-Kids!

As for Your Boy in the Rain—it's a Steichen print and something more added—it's a Steichen print and a Whitman poem combined—the *art* of a Steichen print and the *heart* of a Whitman poem.—Ed has a big heart himself but he doesn't let it speak enough as yet in his work—tho he is planning work for the future that will be Heart as well as Art! He has the *Conceptions* (you remember how he talked of the workmen who build the sky-scrapers) but the Whitmanic prints are *yet to be done!*

Yes, Carl we'll discuss what you call your "gang-folly" etc. I see your point. I appreciate the need for "the man on the box frantically gesturing"—there are times when he must be called in. And we'll discuss the question of whether this or that occasion *is* a time when *he is needed*. And there are other things—myriads of other things—to discuss.—I remember your saying some words of praise about Shaw's "The Education of Children." We must discuss it. I think it unworthy of Shaw. The truths in it are truisms—impractical truisms[2] (paradoxical?) at that! Very tame.—And what he says against Darwinism[3] strikes me as pure and simple *rot*. I could almost believe he tried to write the worst rottenest rot he could—to see how the public would take it, perhaps—he's devil enough to do that! But if that were so I'd expect to see some sardonic leer between the lines! But I don't see any.—I give it up.—Maybe Shaw was on the drunk when he wrote that about Darwinism.—He seems to see Darwinism pitted against Socialism—as if Enrico Ferri's Socialism & Modern Science[4] hadn't answered that charge (made by the "Darwinians pure & simple"! And now Shaw must come and make the charge on behalf of the "pure & simple socialists.") That last paragraph especially I call mystic & Utopian—Mrs. Eddy might do as well![5] Or some Utopian impossibilist!—However, I'm not afraid of it. We expect the unexpected from Shaw. He has a right to babble a little if he so pleases—and it won't hurt him nor us nor socialism nor Darwinism. When Shaw talks sense (as he does most of the time, directly or indirectly, straight from the shoulder or by indirection of irony)—when Shaw talks sense, he's G.B.S. a man who counts in the growth of the World. When Shaw babbles like a New-Thoughter (like poor Murray Schloss[6] for example) why he's just Mr. George Shaw, a private person whom nobody knows or cares about—he doesn't count for good or for ill.—Nothing formidable about the mystic babbler! Ho! Ho!

We must discuss it some day with the paper by Shaw before us. Maybe you'll make me see it in a different light—as you made me see the Present and Future of Poetry in a different light (tho you remember how positive I was at the start). Perhaps. Or perhaps this time I'll be the one to show you.—Anyway we'll have a good discussion! We know how! It won't be rag-chewing. We'll get somewhere. We know how to give and take!

Another thing. You must tell me about Ellis Jones[7] and Lyman Chandler.[8] I don't know them.

Isn't it fine that we have been treasure-hunting in different countries and parts! So we have *new* things to show each other! Not simply *duplicates!* Isn't it fine that we are such splendid complements of each other—not mere copies!

Such a give-and-take as our life together will be! We-Two Comrades! Comrade-Lovers!

I went to bed at 9 last night and slept till 6!—Nine hours! That's my time. I'm in training! I told you yesterday how I was beginning to show the effects. The same to-day, only more so. I feel very happy and sassy—glad to cross Rubicons—eager—impatient—My patience will last nine weeks! Not a day longer!

Good-bye—

Love and Love from the throbbing yearning heart of

Paula

1. The "But me no buts" letter and the one with the parody on the *Communist Manifesto* are not with the other letters and must have been lost.

2. This essay, written when George Bernard Shaw was fifty, was critical of the British system of education, but offered no solutions that were not impractical. And my mother put it in a nutshell in saying that "the truths in it are truisms—impractical truisms."

3. Shaw described himself as a "Neo-Lamarchist" at one time, and he took the viewpoint of Rudolf Virchow, a German pathologist and member of the "progressive" parliamentary party who disliked new theories in both politics and science. A few days after the Congress of Naturalists met at Munich on September 18, 1877, Virchow said that "Darwinism leads directly to socialism." The German biologist and philosopher Ernst Haeckel replied, "There is no scientific

doctrine which proclaims more openly than the theory of descent that equality of individuals, toward which socialism tends, is an impossibility; that this chimerical equality is in absolute contradition with the necessary and, in fact, universal inequality of individuals. Socialism demands for all citizens equal enjoyments; the theory of descent establishes, on the contrary, that the realization of these hopes is purely simply impossible; that, in human societies, as in animal societies, neither the rights, nor the duties, nor the possessions, nor the enjoyments of all the members of a society are or ever can be equal."

4. In *Socialism and Modern Science,* Enrico Ferri did his best to refute the idea that socialists are naive. "We know, as well as our opponents, that all men cannot perform the same kind and amount of labor—now, when social inequalities are added to the inequalities of natural origin—and that they will still be unable to do it under a socialist regime—when the social organization will tend to reduce the effect of congenital inequalities. There will always be some people whose brains or muscular systems will be better adapted for scientific work or for artistic work, while others will be more fit for manual labor, or for work requiring mechanical precision, etc. What ought not to be, and what will not be—is that there should be some men who do not work at all, and others who work too much or receive too little for their toil."

5. Mary Baker Eddy, the founder of Christian Science.

6. Murray Schloss, a businessman, publisher of *Wayside Magazine.*

7. Ellis Jones, one of the old *Life Magazine* co-editors, spoke at the "Socialist Symposium" in the Roycroft Chapel at East Aurora, New York, July 13, 1907. Other speakers were Lyman Chandler, Sadakachi, and Charles Sandburg. My father was there to give his lecture "Civilization and the Mob." He probably met Ellis Jones at the Roycroft Inn, earlier.

8. Lyman Chandler, formerly Elbert Hubbard's private secretary, had left him in 1903 to work for socialism, then joined *Wilshire's Magazine.* He was with Hubbard when my father came to the Roycroft Inn as a guest, and gave the Whitman lecture, "The Poet of Democracy," on July 5, 1907. After meeting Chandler, my father wrote to Philip Green Wright to pass along a compliment: "Lyman Chandler, who is artist, connoisseur & business man, & hasn't much to say, thinks *The Dreamer* par exellence" (July 6, 1907).

63.

Sunday night

All rested—all pink and gay and ready for anything, hither & yon or whithersoever—

—Such a girl you are—such a soul you are—just as I swing back into irreproachable health, comes your benediction on all my follies & lapses—so free a girl, so big—human—such "pilgrimages to the white birches, listening for the fall of a dewdrop"[1] you have made.

Poet you are too—you blow blossom-odors on your letter-pages—sweet-breathed girl.

—I love your breath—

Had a Bohemian dinner this noon—really Bohemian—the comrade's name is *Kratochvil*—is tt Bohemain enuff. Doughballs, roast pork with carroway *[sic]* seed & black gravvy *[sic]*, sour cabbage, a bottle of beer, coffee-cake and black coffee—a symposium right from Prague itself—the stuff they build *Kubeliks*[2] of—you vegetarian!—Then I walked two hours in the sun & wind, took a bath & slept an hour—and now I'm ready for anything!

Almost Mickey-like to-night, Kitty—"could eat all the elephants in Hindustan & pick my teeth with spires of Strassburg cathedral!"

Fagged and worn, I *knew*. Pink and gay, I *know*.

We're going somewhere!

The S-S! Lilian & Carl! Facing the Eternities.

I kiss you—You, the Ineffable—You, the Wonder-Woman.

On the paper here—the foolish paper tt tries to receive my message & take it to you—on the paper I say "Good-night"—but it is not goodnight—waking & sleeping, you are the great thought—the other Me—and you are here—your other Self—your other Me—My Love—Good-night, Lilian—good-night!

Carl

1. "Pilgrimages to the white birches" was a quote from her Letter 5.

2. Jan Kubelik (1880–1940), a Czech violinist and composer of violin concertos. My father was enthusiastic about his music and wrote a poem about his playing the violin, "Jan Kubelik," which was later published in *Chicago Poems* (1916).

64.

[April 26, 1908]
Sunday Night

The Rubicon is crossed! Kitty didn't wear her hat—for it rained!—Anyway Lilian had the Whitman lecture in mind, and so restrained Kitty and made her behave herself!—And Mr Magill was genuinely pleased to see me happy—and he didn't have to conceal his real feelings. I always told Elsie that she was too hard on the poor man. She would say and do all sorts of contradictory things and then enjoy his bewilderment. Poor fellow, he hadn't brains enough to realize that she was only playing with him! I used to tell Elsie that when you have dealings with an honest weakling like Mr M. it's your duty (if you are a strong person yourself) to supply him with "an interpretation" of yourself—not a true interpretation of yourself as you are, *that* he couldn't understand—but an interpretation that will serve him as a practical working hypothesis for explaining to himself your actions. I supplied Mr M. with such a working hypothesis—it's not *Me*—but it's a *Near-Me* that he can understand and that he thinks is me. It serves. Mr M. is happy. And I can do as I please because he trusts me.—It isn't as gay as Elsie's method, but it has the advantage of being practical and big-human, kindly at the same time.—Elsie admitted all this and more—but she said she had to have a scapegoat—there was nothing else in Princeton to exercise her wit on—he must suffer!—I would remonstrate and protect the poor little man sometimes—and then again I'd be carried away by the gayety of it all and help bewilder and confound him!

Today I told the fact to him simply so he would understand (tho Kitty did feel tempted to tell it in a devilish way—to startle and confound him—but Kitty was suppressed by Paus'l) and Mr M said that when he read your circulars the thought came to him that you would be just the right man for me—and he suspected how matters stood! (Isn't it a wonderful little man? Isn't it?)

We didn't say anything about the lecture. I believe tho that that is as good as settled. We can count on it—or very nearly so. I want him to bring the subject up himself. That will give me an advantage.—Of course if he doesn't say something definite about it soon I'll have to jog him up. I'll give him a few days more time to think over the news I gave him to-day. Then, Mr M., Sir, we'll have to talk business—settle on the date etc.!

But we can count on it! I do believe. We may have to come down a little on the price. We shall see. I'm just saying "We *may*." But we can count on the main thing. Your visit.

And I'll be glad to have you incidentally see Princeton (aside from the *main* thing—*our seeing each other*)—. For I know the beauty-spots—and you must see them. Bryant's Woods is as lovely as any woods can be—I've told you about its ravines with wooded slopes and the little brook winding thru the bottom with little rapids and falls.

Yes, we'll count on the visit.

23 Skiddoo!

We're getting there all right—We'll *"skiddoo"* out of bachelordom all right! In Nine Weeks we'll SKIDDOO! For the North! For the Life-Together! We-Two!
IX

Kitty and Micky!
23
SKIDDOO

65.

Monday—the 27th

A fitting menseversary of the Great Ride Together—a mad moody night!—I have just had a hike along the Fox River and Lake Winnebago—a mad moody night!—the wind and air changes its mind every two minutes like a distracted bourgeois woman who can't decide whether to marry for love or money. Snow and sleet & hail—I got all warm walking & took off my hat to the pushing waves & blowing swirls—and paid my worshipping wonder to You—YOU—of a month ago—and of years back—and of *now*—One month!—Such a night as it was, slashing rain & a wind tt almost took the carriage off its braces—our hands talking louder than the howling gale—(And Paula pipes

Monday – The 27th

A fitting anniversary of the Great Ride Together – a mad moody night! – I have just had a hike along the Fox River and Lake Winnebago – a mad moody night! – the wind and air changes its mind every two minutes like a distracted bourgeois woman who can't decide whether to marry for love or money – Snow and sleet & hail – I got all warm walking & took off my hat to the pushing waves & blowing swirls – and paid my worshipping wonder

Part of Letter 65.

up, "How much of the distance is remaining?")—Foolish girl! foolish question! for nobody knows how far we've got to go nor where we're going!

It all seemed as tho it had to be—all imperially natural—We-Two out of a world-stress like that surging between sky & land—finding ourselves—not each other, but our*selves*—

We left the Sea of Dreams that night—I knew you for the Lily Lock Girl—the Lost Continent Girl. All others of men & women were "They" and "Them"—You knew me for the Thirty Mile Ride Boy—the Brushwood Boy who had to find the girl up that slope from the Sea of Dreams and past the tunnell [*sic*] and the railroad house splashed with roses![1]

That night and that week were like the calm surety of Hamlet saying, "If it is to be it will be. Let be."[2] Strange, halcyon days calm with the gestation of new life-forces. The Inexpressible was in and around us.

And to-night—I want you! I want You!—Always the Brushwood Boy and the Lost Continent Girl should be together—planning & struggling & loving together—up the slope from the Sea of Dreams—on Lost Continent helping "They" and "Them."

Sixty days—sixty days—then we start on the Long Ride Together, across Lost Continent—by cities, flocks and pastures—never in all our roaming finding aught more wonderful than this magical air & forked lightning & sky-crescendo that forever plays back & forth btw [between] & in We-Two!—Sixty days? No—Fifty Eight days—the days are getting longer but they're getting less—they're getting less!

Paula—Heart!

Carl

1. The "Sea of Dreams," the "Lily Lock Girl," the "Lost Continent Girl," "They," and "Them," the "Thirty Mile Ride Boy," the "Brushwood Boy," and the "railroad house splashed with roses" are all in Rudyard Kipling's story, "The Brushwood Boy," in which a boy and girl dream about each other—have dream-adventures before they meet as adults—and fall in love. My father drew a parallel because she had written him that only in dreams had she seen someone like him, while he wrote her that she was his Dream Girl come true and more. (See letters 28 and 33.) In the dreams of the Brushwood Boy and the Lily Lock Girl, however, "They" and "Them" were feared, but in his letter here he has turned them into people who need to be helped, probably meaning on the road to socialism.

2. "If it is to be it will be. Let be." This is not an exact quote, but rather his own condensation of the meaning of Hamlet's words to Horatio before the fencing scence (Act 5, scene 2): "If it be now, 'tis not to come; if it be not to come, it will be now; if it be not now, yet it will come: the readiness is all; since no man of ought he leaves knows what is't to leave betimes, let be."

66.

[April 27]
Monday Afternoon

You don't think I was rash in "crossing the Rubicon" yesterday—do you? I don't see any element that could enter into our decision that we haven't considered.—I know there's no possibility of anything turning up in my individual sphere (my family etc). And YOU are just as sure—aren't you? You don't think that Carl D. Thompson could say anything to make us feel we ought to wait another year? Do you?—If you do, tell me so, for as yet there's time to recross the Rubicon—turning our backs for the time being on—Rome!—I could tell Mr. M. to keep this position (for next year) open for me, say for two weeks longer. By that time you would have seen Thompson in Milwaukee. And it wouldn't be so late but what the school could get a good teacher in my place. So it would be all fair and square to everyone concerned.

I didn't see any possibility of anything turning up to make us hesitate—that was what made me tell Mr. M. yesterday. I like to treat people fair.

And it seemed unfair not to tell Mr. M. when our minds were so definitely made up to the leap this summer. The best teachers are usually engaged—contracts signed up—by the middle of May at the latest. So from the standpoint of the school it was important that Mr. M. should know, and begin to cast about for a new teacher.

However, it will be no hardship for him to have to suspend final decision for two weeks. He can be getting applications, have interviews with candidates etc—all this preliminary work will take two weeks very likely—and then when the 2 weeks are up, and you have seen Thompson, and we know for sure whether I won't want this position next year—then I can resign definitely and he elect some one else, or I can keep the job myself, as the case may be.

It's up to *you,* now. From my angle of vision I see no IF that would make advisable this holding on to the option of my job here for another two weeks. And you, Carl, haven't hinted that you saw any IF from your own angle of vision.—But it just occurred to me that maybe on second thought "what Thompson might say" would prove an IF from your angle of vision—the District etc.—which I don't understand as well as you—not yet! So I'm just askin'.

Shall I ask for two weeks extension of time on the option of this Princeton job for L.S.?

L.S. hates to think that there's an IF!! Still L.S. is a sensible girl—and if the *IF* is valid, why L.S. will swallow the pill and—[I give it up! you know what I mean—I needn't try to straighten out this mixed metaphor of a *valid pill!!!*]—Lilian can wait for Sandy—if Sandy says so—just as Lilian can leap with Sandy if Sandy says *so!*—Sandy has said the same thing to Lilian—now Lilian says it back to him!—Lilian and Sandy are such pals!

From Ed I haven't heard since I wrote him that the marriage was to be this summer. I don't even know whether he's still in N.Y. or whether he has sailed! Maybe my letter didn't reach him in N.Y. and so was forwarded to Paris—and I'll have to wait to hear from him from Paris! Maybe he got my letter, was busy, and is putting off answering—as usual! I've told you about his cussedness about writing letters!—Anyway I'm not "anxiously awaiting his reply"—whatever it is, it won't make any difference in the plans of the Ess-Ess!—So Ed can be as cussed as he pleases about delaying his answer—Paus'l is serenely patient! Nothing matters much to Paus'l these days—*"Carl is!"* and that's the main thing. "In IX weeks the Ess-Ess will put an end to the *lie* of living apart!" and nothing else counts.

In IX weeks the love-life together—actually *together*—begins! *Unless* there's a little IF attached? Is there, Carl?

Oh I wish there weren't! Let's tell Carl D. to go to Vaudeville! if he urges delay! Shall we? Shall we, Cully? We were Man and

Woman eons and eons ago—long before the district was! long and long before the district was!

And anyway we-two *will* make good in the district, whether Carl D. sees it that way or not. We *will* make good!

But that is aside from the Big Point: That even if there were some slight drawback from the standpoint of the district (tho I can't conceive such a thing) still—We *should* marry this summer—because—Eons and Eons before the district was, we-two were Man & Woman—our souls and our bodies consecrated to each other—

(But we will make good. My voice *is* pretty strong *when I use it*—pretty strong for a woman's voice, untrained at that—I haven't it in me to be a writer or an orator of any account—but I can learn to give good talks, Cully helping, my Coach!—And then we ask for so little of the things that cost money. We have your room now. I have clothes to last awhile. And I can live and *thrive* on a diet of bread and peanuts and walks and fresh air!—Surely I'll be able to do enough for the district to compensate it for at least enough bread & peanuts and water and fresh air to sustain life in me!—To say nothing of the gain there'll be to the district in Cully's work when Lilian is there in presence to inspire!—Oh—we can't miss making good with the district!! And *more* than making good!)

I wish I were there to help land Mrs Hicks! So I do!—There's no use talking, the district can't get along without the Double-Ess present in person!

The Dutch-Ess will work up a little 10-minute German talk to warm the hearts of the clamorous Dutchmen who want a German organizer! Ya! Ya!

We're the "Internationale" allright! When you get your Swede talk ready—and I my German talk—we can give them a sort of club-sandwich—the Swede & German talks sandwiched in between Your English Oratory and Mine!—Great!—

I'll stop on IX—the mystic symbol! Love and love

from
Paula

If you're going to cross
the Rubicon, cross it!
Don't stop in the middle—
you'll only catch hell from
both sides. Keep your head
in the air. Get into the dust of the
road. And if you want to sing
—why, sing! sing!

Letter 67.

67.

If you're going to cross the Rubican, cross it! Don't stop in the middle—you'll only catch hell from both sides. Keep your head in the air. Get into the dust of the road. And if you want to sing—why, sing! sing!

Ain't it? Pal?[1]

1. My father wrote this short note in very large letters, and deep black ink, crosswise on the paper, as if to emphasize every word, particularly the idea of "crossing the Rubicon." Then he turned the page around and wrote the last three words—Ain't it? Pal?—from the corner of the letter in much smaller script.

68.

[April 29, 1908]
Wed. Afternoon

Just got your letter saying It's VIII now. The S-S wireless again! Yesterday evening I wrote you: it's VIII now! And now this afternoon the same message from you.

And this morning came your letter saying "There's nothing left to consider"—and yesterday evening Paula wrote "it would *have* to be a go." "I *can't* wait and *won't* wait"—Paula needs Cully desperately!

I haven't told mother yet that we are planning to be married so early this summer. I had a letter from her to-day in which she speaks of some sewing that she and I could do toward the trousseau!!—I see I'll have to do some explanationing! What do *we-two* want with a *trousseau!* Ain't it?—No—nothing of that conventional sort of us! I don't believe I need anything at all in the way of new dresses.—Unless there's something you particularly want me to have—something you have a particular fancy for—If so, let me know *now*—and I'll have it made here—I want to cut the wait at home as short as possible—and dress-making then is out of the question. For the wait is simply to allow a reasonable time for mother to visit with me—Your suggestion to have the knot-tying about June 15–20—and then stay on at the farm—has its points! We'll think it over and find out what mother would like best.

Maybe this would be a good arrangement: Let mother have me all to herself from June 14 to June 20 (It will be hard on *me* not to have you—but I know mother will want me all to herself awhile. When you are there you monopolize my attention! Mother will want to be the center of my attention for a little space) [.] Then June 20—the marriage rites—you arriving at the farm the day before—Then another week at the farm—all together—About June 27—Northward, Ho!

How do you like it?

It seems good to me.

Our symbol would now be VII instead of VIII! And mother would have me all to herself for *one* week—and she'd have the two-of-us for another week! I don't believe that plan could be improved upon! for an *all-around* happy plan!

Good-bye—I run to make the mail again!

It's no joke about my running to make that early evening mail. Yes, I have to *run* often! and as fast as I can go! And then I only make the mail "by the skin of my teeth"—

Father's Luxembourger cousin is gone—and mother's on her feet again—and anxious and eager to see you. I hope you'll run out to the farm for a visit when you give your lecture at Hartford—When will that be?—You can telephone to the farm from Milwaukee (probably from Hartford too)—or a letter mailed in Mil. before 6 P.M. reaches the farm the following noon. Let mother know when to expect you—It will be a happy day for mother and Paula will be with you both—over the miles—

Glad to get to know Edson[1] & Parlette[2] by letter. Splendid comrades—both—They must come to the shack, Edson and his girl—and Parlette—and all the cameradoes. Such doin's as there'll be!

Ho! Ho!

Shall it be VII?[3] (I must write mother and get her viewpoint—soon.)

Lilian

1. Charles L. Edson was an old friend going back to the days when my father was managing editor of the *Lombard Review* at Lombard College, and Edson was editor of the college monthly at Kansas State University. At this time they began their correspondence, and when he was through at the university, Edson settled on a farm in Arkansas. This man should not be confused with Charles Farwell Edson, the musician who later composed for *The American Songbag*.

2. My father met Ralph Parlette at the Lyceumite office and had just received an excited complimentary letter about *Incidentals*. He once wrote of him "Ralph Parlette is one of those pale, frail creatures who exist by a silken strength of spirit. Put the ordinary soul, that of Smith across the street or Jones around the corner, each of whom never makes use of his imagination, in the lean body of Parlette and it would wither and blow away into nothing. Parlette has a fancy as active as a minnow, free as a sunbeam, varied as the colors of the rainbow. The worse things are with him the better. He finds a silver lining in every cloud."

3. The wedding as planned was for the last week in June (the 27th), and their numerals counting the weeks go by that. But here she suggests a week earlier. Actually, they were married on June 15.

69.

[April 29, 1908]
Wednesday Night

I'm done with foolishness. You won't hear Paula asking again whether maybe the Rubicon was crossed prematurely—whether we ought not to ask for 2 weeks extension of my option on this Princeton job. No, I've done with all such foolishness—It's settled & settled! In nine weeks—no—by George—in *eight* weeks (for this week is nearly over—We're counting on about June 26—eight weeks from this Friday—date not *fixed*, but thereabouts).

In eight weeks then!

Paula is willing to starve—to take in washing, if need be! But Paula is *not* willing to live the lie of separation a day longer than these eight weeks! The daughter of the Regiment will be along! Privation and toil—*anything*—she's equal to, only she must be *along!*

Can't stand it! *Won't* stand it! this being away from you, Cully—cut off from the "Me" I love the best, the *"Me"* that's in our home in Oshkosh now!—I get so tired of this old *L.S. Me* that's always present, hanging 'round all the time when it's the *C.S. Me* I want and want!

You, Cully, *You*—I want and want!

> It flashes on me with the rising sun
> It creeps on me when the day is done
> It hammers at my heart the whole night thru
> This want of you—
> This want of you—[1]

I've done with foolishness.

The Rubicon *is* crossed. Paula has done with every last shadow of a But or an If.

Paula means business.

Paula *must* be with Cully. If it's only to glance up from my work and see you at work in another corner of the room. We-Two must have each other's presence. We must talk together about big things—and babble about little things—and drink coffee together—and play together—and walk together—and tumble each other's hair—and cover each other with kisses. We need each other in a thousand thousand ways.

We have a world to gain! Nothing but heart-ache to lose!

Paula is in a mood like Sandy *"Enroute Oshkosh."* Paula is "scorn—supreme disdainful scorn telling the butters and iffers to stand aside—to go to hell—to vaudeville—anywhere—but away! away!"—

"So fine and pure at the last and deepest is this S-S fabric, interwoven of hope and love"—[2]

> That's the whole thing in a nut-shell.
> And it's settled now.
> The last faintest shadow of an IF vanished forevermore.
> It's the marriage in VIII weeks—VIII!!
> That's the symbol now: VIII!

So let 'em all stand aside! The butters and the iffers—unless they're looking for trouble! The Ess-Ess means business and won't stand for any foolin'. So.

It's dead-sure—VIII!

Paula has been walking in the rain again to-night—bare-headed—little rivulets running down her cheeks—Paula well-pleased thereat. And wind and rain have quickened the throb of Paula's heart—beating and beating with yearning love for Cully—Paula has been at the old play—turning her face up to be kissed by the wind and the fresh sweet rain—but making-believe that really it was Cully whose lips were on Paula's warm and near (instead of April wind & rain!)

Now Paula says Good-night—wishing so much, so hard, to be near Cully, whether he's strong and alive or all fagged-out and done-for. Whatever his mood—he is always *Cully—all-the-world,* ALL-THE-WORLD to
his Paula—

Wednesday Night

P.S. I finish one letter and send it and then I want to start another. This time it's on the pretext of sending back these notes and papers that you ask me to return. Of course I must write a few words along. It *shall* be only a few words, for it's bed-time and I'm getting to bed nights *about* ten o'clock now regularly. Oh yes, Paus'l is a good girl! Yep!

Good that you sent me these papers. So I get to know you and know you better—which spells—to love and love you more and always more! You Wunderkind whom I worship with all my heart and with all my brain! My Wunderkind!

The mother I love—and want to kiss—my heart will beat to hers when we meet!—dear, yearning, mother-heart! I love her! I want to put my arms around her—and she will feel how I love her because she is Charlie's mother—and she'll know then *how* I must love *you,* and how happy we are! She'll know it's something worth while—and it will gladden her mother-heart! The dear mother—I want to kiss her.

Lilian

1. Although Ivan Leonard Wright is now almost forgotten, at the turn of the century and for some time after, lovers of poetry were familiar with his poem "The Want of You." My mother's memory was not entirely correct, in this quote from the second verse, though I think hers an improvement. The original goes:

> It flashes on me with the waking sun;
> It creeps upon me when the day is done;

It hammers at my heart the long night through
This want of you.

2. This quote and the lines in the previous paragraph are evidently from another letter of his that was written "Enroute Oshkosh" (not Letter 33) but that is missing.

70.

[April 30, 1908]
Thursday

You fit into the part, Paula—a frail hectic Ethel Barrymore wouldn't look right on the job—But you look the part!—you will be reason for admiration oftener than anything else.—It will be fun experimenting with park meetings this summer, on evenings & Sunday afternoons—There's so much work, too, that can be divided between us—correspondence, interviewing prospects, writing press-stuff, selling literature.—And you're such a devil, regular she-devil of a socialist; and then such an individual, artist (Miss L.S.), wild girl (Fanchon), merry girl (Kitty), sweet woman (Flavia), whatever there may be of privation in material living (knocking around barnstorming as Minnie Maddern, Bernhardt, Maude Adams & all the stars did), won't equal the deprivation, the want of avenues for expression, in your life should you teach another year.—And I, I know I'll NEVER be any better prepared to live the Life-with-You than NOW. I burn up vitality & live intensely—so the longer we wait, the poorer prepared I am!—And You—You see these things—It's the biggest, most promising experiment we ever started in the laboratory of life.—We can't help but win in the end. We, the S-S, are so made! We can't help but win, eventually.—But who was ever better equipped with youth & health & ardor than we? We-Two!

You're the finest soul, the wonderfulest heart—ever—ever—ever———VII!—One finger less each week!—Then the leap! Then the scramble up the bank of the other side of the Rubicon, marching in dust and sun, loafing in blue twilights and sleeping under the trees & stars, skirmishings, wounds in the rain, rest after battle.—You Woman of Romance! You're the Soul of All

Great Romance or you wouldn't dare!—I've only aimed to present you the facts tt give me my viewpoint. What I've expressed to you has been myself, what I see & feel from where I'm looking. I haven't tried to give you, in a way, enthusiasm or daring. I've only spoken myself, feeling tt what I uttered was yourself.—I learned in the Great Week that you're absolutely fearless to obey your heart-promptings, that you're hardy. The Soul of You, all that Sea of Surging Thought & Tinted Dreams tt is in you, all the sky of love and earth of beauty in you, I knew from your letters—You the Supreme Soul-Mate!—In The Great Week, I learned all the rest, found you The Daughter of the Regiment, fresh as all youth, gay as all holidays, mad as the maddest soldier tt ever flung away his life on a bloody rampart![1] glorying in The Last Ditch if in The Last Ditch there was Love and the Ideal! My Heart! My Heart—Paula—it is wet eyes I have for the gladness of it! that it happened! that you came!—I kiss you a long long kiss for love, for love—the love of You—Lilian—the miracle—

Carl

1. Note the similarity between "mad as the maddest soldier tt ever flung away his life on a bloody rampart" and the first line of the poem written on the back of Letter 56.

71.

Thursday afternoon

You are getting badder all the time, Cully. I see I'll have to come and take charge of you! *I'll* send you off to bed in time! I'll see that you train! You, fraud you!—Is this the way to get into baseball form?? Oh, you need Paula! (I waive the point Edson makes about a woman's civilizing influence)—You need me as your physical director—to see to it that you do your stunts and that you get enough sleep—You!—That's what you need—a Physical Director!

I'm trying to be good myself. But somehow with tests and themes—and grades—I seem to keep rather late hours myself. But the worst is I don't get in enough walks—a few hours' more or less sleep don't matter so much, for I get seven hours' sleep anyway on the average (eight or nine hours is the ideal plan for me). But walks—that's what I've been neglecting lately. The trouble is when I'm thru with school work, I want to write you—and usually do. After finishing up my work at school in the late afternoon I come home to my room and write you—instead of taking a walk. Then after supper, I'm more than likely at my table again *writing you!* So it goes! And I never get the half of what I want to say written anyway! It's unsatisfactory business—this of being some 300 miles away from the person to whom one wants to talk all the time. I used to get a lot of satisfaction out of the companionship of my own soul—It was enough if I told myself my thoughts.—But now it's different. *Cully is the Self* I want to think aloud to. It's Cully's companionship I want—and want! I'm tired of Paula and Paula and always Paula! and never Cully! But the days—thank God—go by and go by!

I'm off for a walk now—I'm feeling tired to-day and I know it's oxygen I need and exercise! You be good too! And take time for the sleep you need! So we'll both have a lot of health and strength accumulated by this summer—

—Says Paula, throwing Cully a thousand kisses! Good-bye!

72.

April 30—11:30 P.M.

Saw "The Lion and the Mouse"[1] this evening. I don't know what made me go to the play.—Was it that I wanted to match your Wednesday Night's dissipation—Vaudeville, band etc?! Or did I go because everyone told me it was "a political play—all about Capital & Labor" and I ought to go therefore? Anyway I'm glad I went. A good play in parts. Like the Sea-Wolf[2] in some respects. The Octopus part (corresponding to the Wolf Larsen part) is strong—the love part is weak again like that part in Sea-Wolf. You know "The Lion & The Mouse" of course. If you happen not to know it, I'll give you the story of it sometime when we take a hike together this summer. A good play—there are going to be more of that trend. And the people like it—showing that it isn't true that erotic plays are the only kind that take with the people. Yes, the people like it—just as they like Ida Tarbell's exposure of Standard Oil.[3] This is the day of the People's Awakening—the wheels are beginning to go 'round in our heads! Erotic stories—erotic plays—must make room for graft exposures and problem plays. I don't mean that "The Lion & the Mouse" is anything last & final in itself. But it's good. And it points in the right direction.

Now it's late, Charles—and I'm not going to match your badness of Wednesday night by staying up till 1 A.M. No, I'm off to bed now—tho I want to sit and talk with you awhile.—At the play I kept thinking of you—and how it would have been really worth while seeing it, if you had been along. I wanted to talk to you between Acts and hear what you had to say about it.—It's an exasperation to see a thing and *you not along*. It's an exasperation to see a thing and feel all the while that you are only *one third* on the spot—the better & bigger part of you is 300 miles away, and can't see the thing. What's the use having one third of you see it—and two-thirds of you not see it.—The one-third will have to explain and make the other two-thirds see it in imagination. Then we'll feel *at one* with ourselves! This summer!

VII more weeks to live this separate (and yet not separate) life. VII more weeks of The Lie!

And we'll be going to plays together—and it will be fun! It won't be so hard keeping within the limits of our purse—for there aren't many plays good enough so we'll care much about seeing them. I've been to but two plays in Princeton this year—and if I had been flush of money I wouldn't have cared to see any more—these two were the only ones worth while presented here.—And it was gallery both times.—I guess we'll be able to see a few plays each season all right! And we won't envy the plutes down-stairs. "We would rather sit in the gallery with perception and ability to appreciate than to sit in the dress circle fat and unimpressionable."[4]

(Oh yes—Lilian can quote!!)

Now Good-night! It's a little after twelve—I close this letter to Carl on May first—the International Labor Day—my birthday! Twenty-five to-day! But that doesn't mean anything. I didn't really live till we discovered the S-S! *Now* the years will count! May the S-S be many many years together.—It's a solemn thought—the thought of death. It never used to worry me. While I was alone, a single separate person, I laughed at death—so genuinely careless that I couldn't even *understand* the common human cry, the yearning for immortality. I was impatient with people for not laughing up at death as I did myself, careless, almost challenging!—Now it's different.—I haven't thought it out to the end yet from the new viewpoint of hyphened Double Ess!—Someday I'll feel a need for thinking it out to the end, maybe—and then I will—and I suppose it will spell *PEACE*—Peace—when it is thought out to the very end.—But now I see only that it is *a solemn thought*—that I cling to Life with a new tenacity—because *you* are *of Life*. Before I knew you, Life & Death were indifferent things—I felt equal to meet both, gayly unconcerned about them. I could live. I could die. I cared not.—But now I want *Life*—Life is so precious with *You* added.—But without You—what were Life? Would it be Death-in-Life? Or what?—Death-in-Life—likely—Death-in-Life!—No, I haven't thought this thing out to the end—yet.—

Good-night—My Love—My Love.—Paula kisses you long and long, her arms clinging close—My Love—My Love! Good-night!

1. A play by Charles Klein.

2. Jack London's *The Sea Wolf* (1904). Socialists took a different view of this novel, regarding it as an allegory in which the Sea-Wolf, Wolf Larsen, the brutal captain who dominates all, was the capitalist system incarnate, dying in the end of a slow, pathetic paralysis. This was my father's view, according to the article on Jack London that he wrote for *To-morrow*.

3. Ida Tarbell's *A History of the Standard Oil Company*. (1905).

4. From *Incidentals*, pp. 12, 13.

73.

Friday Night [ca. May 1, 1908]

My walk this afternoon was under a sky of storm clouds. I was out on a country road where I could see the full sweep of sky—get all the changing cloud effects of this lovely showery May day. Now the sun would be hid behind massive lowering clouds—

now it would shine thru a rift in the sky flooding orchard and pasture and roadway in a fresh golden light. The odor of apple blossoms freshened with light spring showers was on the air—Toward sunset when the sun again broke thru the clouds suffusing everything in a mellow glow, I threw myself on a bank of lush grass by the roadside and watched the lengthening shadows of trees and of the cattle—Or I looked up into the arching boughs of great shade trees overhead—and watched the great clouds sailing and sailing past—All the while little gray and brown birds in the hedges were shaking the sweetest warbles from their little throats—and the fragrance of apple-blossoms was wafted to me from the orchard, all pink-and-white, across the road.

A day for lovers—and you were near and near, Cully. I felt your warm breath on my cheek—and my lips found yours, Love, in a long kiss.

Here back in my room, I'm all vibrant with yearning love for my Mate-Man—sweet and clean and strong—my Carl!

All the skies of wildish loving
All the seas and earth of love
Are ours [1]—

1. Lines from an untitled poem of his that he sent to her.

The world was made for loving, so they say,
And the world was made for warring and for war,
So of warring and of war, we've tasted,
And of loving and of love, we know.

Sun and dust and murk and mire,
Blown-driven things on starless nights,
And blood and tears and sweat and toil
We know.
So the pity of the warring and the glory of the war
Is ours.

Loafing in the twilight,
On the grass and in the dew,
Golden lights and cool and gloaming,
Wonder-sounds upon the pines,
All the talk of looks and lips,
All the sleeping under stars,
We know.

All the skies of wildish loving,
All the seas and earth of love,
Are ours.

74.

Friday May 1, 1908

Paula dear—

I'm going to send you clippings like these from time to time—facts, jokes, plays of wit, short things notable for the simple and direct &c—put 'em all by—use 'em as you can.—An incident, a little story, here & there in a speech, rest both audience & speaker.

I go to Appleton tonight & give my "The Poet of Democracy"[1] to a literary society out on the edge of Appleton—about 30 people of all sorts—mostly indecisive types, "sober & industrious"—the kind the local newspaper says of, when they die, "He was respected in the community and loved by all who knew him. He was kind to his mother."—A sort of deviltry possesses me at times among these—to talk their slangiest slang, speak their homely, beautiful home-speech about all the common things—suddenly run a knife into their snobbery—then swing out into a crag-land of granite & azure where they can't follow but sit motionless following my flight with their eyes.—It will be fun at Princeton—I know the stuff will hit Magill—He will bat his eyes once in a while but he will keep awake!—listening to the man just suited to You!!

I've a lot more of [Bernard] Shaw than [Robert] Blatchford in me. S. is for the centuries, will be remembered with Diogenes and Epictetus. B. is for the decades, will be remembered as a mellower William Lloyd Garrison[2] who fought a good fight and uttered for the average.

And Paula sweet, while the M.A.S. (Mutual Admiration Scty) is in session—S. stands to B. as you stand to May Wood Simons.[3] —The S-S is hill-born, knowing not only all the crops, seasons, & flowers of the valley, but things higher up—stars out on the horizon-rim not seen from the valley.—The S-S is hill-born.

We will both change, and change mightily as the years pass, but all these "assembled parts" of ours that are so much alike will only forever go forward in ever better team-work and—play.

I must catch a car!

Love and love—"I throw you a thousand kisses"—

Carl

1. "The Poet of Democracy" was the Whitman lecture, which was also billed as "An American Vagabond."

2. William Lloyd Garrison (1805–79), the American abolitionist who founded the *Liberator,* the famous antislavery journal, leader of the fanatical abolitionists, and founder of the American Antislavery Society.

3. May Wood Simons, the wife of Algie M. Simons, editor of the *International Socialist Review.* She often wrote articles for socialist magazines, and my father, who knew Simons, probably was well acquainted with her work. One of May Wood Simons's early contributions was *Women and the Social Problem,* which was widely distributed. She took part in the socialist battles, joined her husband on the party's National Educational Committee, and was a lecturer for the National Socialist Lyceum Bureau. Like my mother, she had taken her Ph.B. at the University of Chicago. Both were firm suporters of woman's suffrage and were influenced by John Dewey and Maria Montessori, though in very different ways.

75.

[May 2, 1908]
Saturday

It's all right, Carl. It's all right!—Regular hours of sleep etc. are well enough for smug conventional folks. For us gay vagabonds *irregular* hours of sleep, meals everything! We're not tied down by laws of man or nature! We—blue-blood anarchists of the original Lucifer-type—are a law unto themselves! We go to sleep when we feel like it! We take our meals when we feel like it!—When we're in a mood to write letters or poems, we'll not stop because it's sleep-time or meal-time!

The hell with the laws of so-called hygiene! Yes, there's
a time to sleep
And a time to wake
A time to eat
And a time to refrain from eating.[1]

We agree with the old Preacher in Ecclesiastes—that fine pagan sinner of a Preacher—But we don't agree with the M.D. who says the clock knows better than our instincts when the time to sleep or to wake or to fast, has come! Such poems as you send me, Carl. No—no—we have no compunction about the lateness of the hour! We live as we can live! For seven weeks more I suppose it will be reckless living—burning up vitality—and all that. And it's all right. This is the time for burning up vitality. When the seven weeks are over—we will have lived!—Oh, we *might* have vegetated—we didn't tho!

Maybe when the life together begins it will be different. Maybe we'll live more normally—play more—rest more—sleep more. There won't be this restless unsatisfied yearning for each other—that makes us live so intensely that we forget to get sleepy!—

Maybe we'll live more regularly—but it won't be because the book says so—it will be (if it is at all) because we naturally fall into a more regular way of living.

And it's possible that we'll be as irregular as ever—only worse! We don't know where we're going to—nor what we'll do when we get there. But we'll do what we want to do, that's sure.

—And the more I think on't the more likely it seems that the S-S will turn night into day quite as much after we are together and we do now while we're apart. We're not creatures of habit—but of inspiration. And the night-hours are the witching hours for play, for work, for love. We'll often be out at night wandering under the stars, by the lake, hearing the "wash wash" of the waves as we look out into the night of stars.—And there'll be nights by the lake in storms with the roar of thunder and the flash of lighting—our grand-opera nights with full orchestra!—And moonlight nights in woods too.—

No, no—we'll never order our lives according to books of hygiene. The book we'll go by will be "Poems by Carl and Lilian"—the volume that's locked up in the throbbing S-S heart!

Such a love-life it will be! Such glorious "wildish loving"[2]—reminiscent of eons and eons ago—and anticipating eons and eons to come! The Past & Future focused in the S-S of To-day.

I love you and love you—my Poet, my Wunderkind! you Miracle-come-true! You Glory, and Power, and Heart, and Man!—Wunderkind! Wunderkind! Paula loves you and loves you. The Blessing that we met! We met! *The Poet-Lover* (no poet has ever before sung so well—no lover has ever before loved so well)—and *the Woman* who understands the poems and who loves the Poet as no man has ever before been loved of women—tho, even so, "it is not enough," the Woman knows, "and it will be more," the love of this Woman for her Poet-Lover will be always and always more! but never "enough"!

1. Paula's parody of Ecclesiastes 3:1–8.
2. A reaffirmation of what she had written in Letter 58.

76.

[May 2, 1908]
Saturday

Paula—if you are asked "What is Circumstance?" tell them it's a laundry catching fire of a night and your losing your three best shirts—first time I've been stung that way. Snow on the 1st of May & such a wind as brought out only a wee 10 of us to the schoolhouse last night—that was Circumstance, but an Old One. So we called off the Lecture and I took a chair and told them about socialism for 40 minutes & there was a cross-fire of questions & answers & they made me feel just a bit sorry for writing to you so about them yesterday. Real souls!

I told Comrade Fox,[1] aside, tt one of the Three Great Facts of Life was to happen to me this summer, apprising him that aforesaid Facts are: Birth, Marriage, Death. He said he knew I had been born & also tt I was not going to die. Then, "Go on, Sandburg, I didn't see how I was going to make it when Hope and I started but when you begin, everything comes around allright." They have a beautiful little home—an extraordinary pair. He's a mail-carrier. I make my home with them when in Appleton.

At the house—Fox speaks of a sudden, "Hopie, do you know, there's going to be a Mrs. Sandburg this summer." "Good!" was the instant rejoinder. "And she's a school-teacher, too," whereat he went on in further description of You, whom he has never seen.—This little group (they are three) have a tent in the orchard in summer—they live on the edge of the town. So we will live out-doors, and work up the Appleton local for a week or more this summer.—Lynn Joseph, a young lawyer at Green Bay, married before he began his law-course at the U. of W.—took bigger chances than we are—so the Green Bay movement will say, "Hurrah!" and Wright[2] of the *Manitowoc Tribune* hasn't turned 25 yet and has been married 2 years. And James Larsen, a Whitmanic old sea-captain at Marinette, the leader there, once a populist member of the legislature, is tt combination of poet-philosopher I know will give us blessin'. This beforehand. Afterward, they'll all just smile and say, "No wonder they put out to sea, in such a boat!"

—Just saw The Sordid to-day—a trifle too abstruse for Vanguard readers—nothing about "the means of production & distribution"!—no defiance. The Socialists are too prone to like a man who makes them ejaculate, "Don't he give it to 'em, though?" Uncork the invective!

Paula—I would have liked to have been with you between acts. We would have analysed Shirley and her "My father's honor—won't you save my father's honor?"[3]

And Paula—on the trolley between here and Appleton I want You—You—to love the purple hills with. They stand up from the shore of Lake Winnebago, hazy & blue-misted—the deeps of me vibrate tremendously to the filmy beauty of it—and I want You—just to "H'm" with about it—so—

Good for Ed!—and good for the S-S! The S-S has pictures too[4]————how will our exhibition come out?—We'll see—we'll see!—

Will you send your April Vanguard to Joseffy, 16 Center *Ave.*, Chicago? I'm sending the lone copy I have to Parlette—the copies are all gone at the office.

A few more weeks of The Lie—and then!

I'm sending a five with this—it leaves me broke—but I can't raise money when I *have* money—and I'm going to try to have $50 or more for starting.—We'll make a compact tt all money from literature sales will go into the Baby-Fund—it should range around $15 or $20 a month & increase at that—I'll turn over some dust to you every once in a while if not twice, all tt there is to spare over our material needs—if we ever save anything, ever have a good bank account or not—that's up to you, after the stuff is once in—and the stuff will come in, eventually—we are about where Gaesjack was the day before he sauntered into Stieglitz office the first time—so.[5]

I now have a "Paula" envelope—all sorts of clippings on Woman & Economics &c, going into it—to be used as you see how.

Plant that fund of yours where it's absolutely safe—and it's not to be thought of except for last & unforseen contingencies—call it the Desperation-Fund.—The Baby-Fund will grow—and such a Baby! such a Baby as it will be—such a reckless cub—never to hear a "Don't"—learning fire by getting burnt—getting religion & ethics & love-powers from our kiss-microbes—never knowing *he's* or *she's* being educated—just living & unfolding—such a cub!

Goodbye—a kiss—for now—Paula

VII!!!—one by one the fingers go down—

Carl

1. George Fox, an Appleton socialist, became a good friend of my father, as Hope Fox, his wife, was in time very dear to my mother. It was through their help that the S-S later found the rooms in Appleton that became their first home. Of the "group of three," the third was their daughter, Ramona, then about two years old.

2. Chester Wright, editor of the Manitowoc *Daily Tribune*, was my father's first real friend in Wisconsin. By this time they were very close to each other, and later Laura Wright and my mother became very good friends.

3. Shirley, in *The Lion and the Mouse*.

4. The S-S pictures are the ones they have drawn for each other with words, about their life together.

5. Edward Steichen ("Gaesjack")'s luck seemed to turn in 1900, when Clarence White praised his work, and especially after he went to the New York Camera Club to meet Alfred Stieglitz, who White said was the leader in the struggle for recognition of pictorial photography as an art. At the time Stieglitz was putting up photographs for an exhibition, but he gave him an hour, during which my uncle showed him examples of his photographs and some paintings. Stieglitz later recalled that he was amazed at "the variety and vigor of artistic intention," and he bought three prints for five dollars apiece, saying, "I am robbing you at that."

77.

Saturday Night—May 2, 1908

You send me clippings—"good stories" this time—"they rest both speaker and audience"—
Do you know, Carl, I've never once told "a good story"? Never once!—Not even in conversation, I mean.—Now, *are* you disillusioned? What hopes are there on the platform for one who can't tell a good story!! I'll try to learn tho, Cully—Yep—Ya—I'll try! I know it's worth while—I know the good story is part of the platform game. Paula will try—Kitty helping!—Cully pointing the way!

You have but little idea of my limitations, Carl! Wait and see!

But it's not my fault that you will persist in thinking I have real abilities. Didn't I protest at the very start that I was no woman-genius, but a mere-woman! And in today's letter you put me 'way ahead of May Wood Simons who is something of a woman-genius I suppose! And you do it in such a way I know you don't mean (what I would assent to) that a genuine Woman—tho but a *mere-*woman—*is* 'way ahead of a sort of genius in skirts. It's a lesser achievement I believe, under present-day conditions, for a woman to develop into a second-rate genius than to realize a genuine all 'round womanhood. I've met second-rate geniuses of the Petticoat sex, enough and to spare. (I don't think they count for much—they are simply second-rate or fourth-rate *men* in petticoats.) But of genuine *women* I've met hardly more than two or so. By genuine Women I mean—women who can *love*—women who have it in them to be mates and mothers—hardy enough, intelligent enough, emotional enough to be real mates and real mothers. Women are physiologically, I believe, constituted to excel in power to *love*—while man is physiologically constituted to excel in power to *work*. A woman's physical organism is two-thirds destined for motherhood and matehood. During pregnancy and while she is suckling her child, the mother gives a considerable share of her vitality and nervous force to the child. But it's not only while a woman is with child that her vitality for *work* is partly spent in the motherhood-function. There's a week in every month when a woman's vitality is at its ebb—because of the functioning of motherhood-organs. One-fourth of the time! (think what it means in the aggregate:—if these weeks that are "wasted"—from the standpoint of work, that is—could accumulate so that one year in every four could be put down as a year of arrested mental development! Think what it would mean if every doctor had to stop intense work and rest one year in four—if every author had to take a vacation from *writing his best* for one year in every four!)—Of course a woman can think, can work, during pregnancy, during menstruation etc—she *can* think, work—but the point is that part of her vital force is *drained away from thinking, working*. She's at a disadvantage compared with men. And that's the reason, I believe, why, on the average and in the large, women will never equal men in any field of *Work*. That's not saying that the sex is inferior. It's simply saying that man is specialized for *work;* woman for *motherhood*. To say that woman is inferior to man because she can't *work* as well, is as absurd as to say that man is inferior to woman because he can't *bear and suckle children*. And people do make this latter claim! Yes! They try to prove that man is woman's inferior ("morally," they stick in—just as the champions of man's superiority stick in "mentally") by citing that he doesn't have the agonies of child-birth to suffer. As if "poor" man could help that! "Woman makes so many sacrifices"—yes, but she has the chances! Nature assigned her tasks that call for so-called sacrifices (of a special sort)! It's not man's fault that he can't die in travail!—We really had an argument on this very question at a faculty luncheon, and every member of the faculty, but myself, held that Woman was Man's superior morally for the reason given above. They couldn't see that man and woman are *different*—no, they had to rank them first and second. When they spoke of woman's *Private* virtues, I answered them by referring to man's *Public* virtues. On the average man will "sacrifice" more for some public cause, for his country (in the old days), for his class (now)—while woman will make more "sacrifices" for her children. Etc. Etc.

I say all this talk about inequality of man & woman is due to muddled brains—lack of clear thinking. Man and Woman are unlike, so you can't rank them first and second—they can't be reduced to a common denominator, that's the reason. Man and Woman are complements—one excells in power to *work* (man who is naturally fitted to get a larger share of the food for the young)—the other excells in power to *love* (woman who is constituted to bear and suckle the young).

Now of course this specialization is not carried to the same extreme in man as in the lower organisms. The higher you get in the scale of evolution the more each sex helps the other in that other's *special* function. I don't know much of biology but I remember hearing a lecture on evolution in which it was said that among some of the lowest forms of animal life the female was very like a vegetable organism, not moving about, just assimilating food and reproducing the species—while the male was active, moving about (probably developing mental superiority by contact with the outside world!!), hustling for food etc. In these cases the lecturer said the female and male organisms were very unlike: the female large—all stomach or at least abdomen, so to speak! the male small of body, all legs and arms and head!

Well *that* isn't my idea of the specialization of function in the human species. We have gotten away from that *exaggerated* specialization. (But we haven't gotten away *entirely* from the fact of specialization—nor ever will!) Man and woman approximate each other. Put it mathematically, woman is one-third man—and man is one-third woman.

There are 2 big truths that people need to know before they can get thru with the sex question: *1st* that man & woman are specialized each in his own direction—they can't be ranked first & second therefore; 2nd that while specialization is a fact, so is mutual help a fact—man must help woman more in her special function, and woman must help man more.

There will be more happiness in the world when man does more of woman's special function—when he approximates her *private* virtues, her power *to love with abandon*. And there will be more happiness in the world when woman learns to do more of man's special function—when she acquires his *public* virtues, when she learns that politics has *everything* to do with the good of her family, when she gets a *social* conscience, class-consciousness—and in short joins the S.D. Party!!

That's it. Woman must labor with man—else she will never understand him—she must be his comrade in work. Then he will *love* her loyally too.—It's the only way to have a lasting love between man & woman. Woman must work with man—think with him—venture with him. Then there's comradeship and the basis for a deep and lasting love *of souls* as well as bodies.—But it isn't necessary for this comradeship that a woman should actually achieve *as much as* a man.—There is still the fact of specialization and so, in the large, women will not achieve as much *in work* as men; while men will not achieve as much *in love* as women.—If an individual woman actually achieved as much in work as her mate—I should say the two were ill-mated, that she was his superior (provided she was a *real* woman as well, *excelling in love*). For we say the two are equal in the *work* they do; but she still excells in loving. He gives all his vitality to work—she gives part of hers to work, and the rest to child-bearing etc. And the *fraction* of her vitality that she gives to work equals the *total* of his vitality! She is his superior!

Paula is delivering a lecture—and she's felt stupid and tired too for some time. But once on the subject, Paula felt she had to carry it thru to its finish! Cully should know why Paula was satisfied that he should be a better orator, talker, writer etc than she—a better runner, base-ball player, heavy-weight lifter etc than she! Cully should know that the S-S can realize and *does realize* the ideal of Equality and Comradeship between man & woman, even tho Paula knows she is not Cully's equal in brain-power—she makes up for this short-coming in heart-power. We're equal, Pal! Do you hear? Equal even tho I can't write poems? Some day I'll give you a demonstration of heart-power—there will be times to test my woman's soul—I suppose you hold this view of the sex-question yourself—this is the view you seem to express in that Suffrage editorial of yours.[1] But it was worth while for me to explain my faith in detail anyway—so you'd know it was *my* faith—and understand—understand that *I know* I am your equal mate, because I can follow you to your heights & depths, as your comrade-mate because I can appreciate *all you do*—tho I cannot do as well myself. If you were a woman, you couldn't do as well as you are doing now either! So there!

I want you to accept me as I am—not to imagine that I am more—perhaps a genius. I know I'm not a genius. The poems of the S-S will be *written* by the Sandburg-S tho the Steichen-S will help with inspiration and love. The big achievements in oratory that the S-S will give the world will be done by the Voice & Brain of the Sandburg-S, tho here again the Steichen-S will help with inspiration and love. The Steichen-S will do a lesser part of the actual world's *work* left by the S-S. The Steichen-S will do some good platform work, I believe—good campaign speeches in *small* halls where it's *talking* rather than *orating*, we want. And the Steichen-S will do some good general organization work—planning—correspondence—circular letters—etc etc. The Steichen-S will do all it can. Paula will reach and reach—knowing that only by *approximating* your *work* can she continue to *understand* it and to understand you and so win more and more love from You. This is a thing that *can be* and *will be*. Paula *is sure* it *shall be*. Paula is sure she will be able to earn your love more and more by becoming more and more your Comrade.

But Paula knows that *if* to be your equal mate she would have to equal your powers of poetic & oratorical expression—then equality would be unattainable. And the S-S would be an illusion.

So Paula wants you to know that *that* isn't her way of understanding Equality between man & woman. Paula sees herself & Cully *equals* tho she knows she never can make poems & orations to equal Cully's. Paula's womanhood and woman's love balances Cully's superior brain-power.

Paula has spoken!

Long and long and stupidly at that. Let this letter be a proof of Paula's deficiencies in powers of expression! 'Tis proof enough—

Paula is sleepy—so sleepy—Good-night, Cully. Many kisses and good-night. Paula is never so sleepy but what she wants and wants to kiss Cully!

You! I kiss you and kiss you—

1. My father had written two articles on women and socialism. The one referred to here was "Socialism and Woman Suffrage." See Appendix B.

78.

[May 3, 1908]
Sunday

I've worked today—on school things—themes & tests—feel relieved at having them out of the way.

Then I took a walk into the country after dinner—saw how green the tree-tops are with putting forth buds and leaves. Saw peach trees with a few blossoms actually full blown! and the pink showing in *all* the blossoms just ready to open!—A lazy day in June[1]—hot—sultry—hardly a breath of air stirring—I threw myself under a tree and rested and dreamed! Of Carl and Carl—of Ess-Ess!—of This Summer!—of the Life Together all the days and days to come!

Now I'm back here with but a few minutes for writing before mail collection.

Got your letters this morning "with love from the heart of Sandy" interfused vibrant all thru them—O You, Sweet, *You to love!* Your good eyes to kiss! Your beautiful voice to listen and listen and listen to. When you come to Princeton for the lecture ("IF!") you must speak those poems to me again that you spoke "Among the Hills"—"When I was a tad-pole and you were a fish"[2] etc—That voice of yours, Cully, with its richness and resonance—O Cully! But I want to hear it!

And you are getting in "baseball form"—are you? Good! And once more, "Good!" I say. And don't forget—it's for the Ess-Ess!

I'm sending you a picture of me with some hesitation. I didn't bring it along with me to "the farm" because the picture shows me as I used to look, maybe (I'm sure I can't know for certain!) some years ago—four years. I look too saccharine-sweet in it for me-as-I-am-today. But I know it won't do you any harm to see me as I used to look before I *lived thru* the real experience of the last four years. That picture shows me still a Child—not grown to womanhood.

Still—maybe you'll find something in the picture that has survived from childhood into womanhood—Maybe you'll see something of me in the picture—Look at it and see for yourself![3]

I get so much joy from having Paul Fournier's picture of you—

the one with the shirt collar turned under—it's really you—the clean-cut chin and jaw—the strong neck—the mouth and ears and brow—and the texture & clearness of skin of Cully (in base-ball trim!)—That's where the big picture (is it by Elizabeth B.?[4]—it surely isn't by Paul F.—Paul couldn't mount it so well—nor so *miss you*—perhaps?—Perhaps!—I don't like Paul's mounting—too fussy and mechanical)—(What a fearful parenthesis!) I was going to say that the big picture isn't *You* at all. It misses the *fineness* of You. The Expression isn't You. The features aren't yours. The complexion is bad—looks pasty—How dared she! (I'm assuming that this is Eliz.'s work—You said she'd done you and that you didn't like her picture—so I'm putting two & two together and—). When you have the *cleanest* skin that ever was—clean not only on the surface—but clean all thru and thru—you, Cully, of base-ball fame! and training! and clean living! Clean living! (My but I'm proud of you—heart!)

But Fournier's "Cully" I have up where I see it the first thing when I enter my room—and where I can see it while I'm writing at my desk. And it's You and You. Almost like seeing you—really—Fournier did a good job—God bless him! again and again for it! I thank Fournier everytime I enter my room. Good for him.—I was bothered about the eyes the first day—but now that I'm used to them I don't mind that.

It's a good picture—shows the *Boy Cully*—clean and strong and *so good!* (Of course the picture doesn't touch some other phases of You—the Poet?—still no—I think the Poet is "imminent" in that picture—I guess you are all there—the potentiality of the whole C.S. tho all these phases are not in active expression maybe at the moment the picture catches you!)

Cully I look at you (*thru* the picture and *past* it—at "YOU") and I say: "I love you and love you—You—clean and strong and good—so good!"

Lilian

1. She means that it is like "a lazy day in June." It cannot be June, as she is still expecting him to come to Princeton for the lecture.

2. My mother did not quote this correctly. The first line of Langdon Smith's "Evolution" is "When you were a tad-pole and I was a fish." My father knew this poem very well, and I have heard him give it from beginning to end, all fourteen

verses, while we sat spellbound, and at the end he would always exclaim, "But why did he take the girl to ritzy Delmonico's?"

3. This must be one of two photographs that my uncle took of her sitting on the steps of the veranda, at the farm.

4. This is probably Elizabeth Buehrmann, a Chicago photographer described by him in a letter to Ivan Swift in January as "recessionist."

79.

Monday, May 4th

Oh, these bourgeois! these conventional sticks with their sense of proprieties etc etc! These Magills!

Mr Magill is beginning to get scared about your lecture—not about *what you'll say*—but about the levity there may be in connection with the idea of my future half's giving a speech here! He's wondering what the pupils will say—how many giggles they'll giggle at the prospect of hearing """"my betrothed"""" give a speech! Miss Steichen's """"betrothed""""! Horrors!

I'm sick of listening to Mr Magill. Have just had a talk with him in which he expressed his doubts—which I wasn't at all prepared for. He had made an appointment with me to arrange for the advertising—and lo when I came prepared to discuss the respective value of handbills and posters and such practical things, he pours out the doubts of his pusillanimous bourgeois heart! Proprieties! Delicacy! Dignity!—And Giggles! Levity!—

Pshaw!

Poor Magill torn between an agony of curiosity to see the man who suits Miss S——, and an agony of fear lest the equilibrium of his little school may be disturbed by levity over Miss Steichen's bringing "her betrothed" down here to make a speech!

Disgusting! They're a disgusting bunch. They train their children so they can't do anything but giggle at mention of marriage—such is their supreme prudery and so do they pass it on to the next generation. And then they somehow sense that it isn't quite as it ought to be when youngsters can do nothing but giggle at the mention of marriage. Ergo—say they—let us remedy this matter—by not mentioning marriage at all before youngsters, or at least by giving the fact of marriage the least possible attention—let's keep it well in the background—

Now I know it would do the boys who like me good to hear you—and get some glimmer of what *you are*. It would do them lots and lots of good—

And as for the gigglers—some have done it so long—the habit is rooted for always and there's no help for such—Some can be helped more or less—and can learn that love isn't a laughable thing, but something beautiful and solemn too.

I was patient and patient with Mr. M. I didn't fly off the handle. I just told him it was up to him. I wasn't going to urge it any more—didn't want him to feel that I was pressing anything upon him. If he wanted the lecture, all right. If not, all right too.

But if the lecture isn't to be given, you shall not come down here for a visit, Cully. Magill shall suffer to this extent at least that his curiosity will not be gratified.—If we plan for a visit at all, I'll come up to Chicago. We could have a better time there than here anyway—we'd have some freedom there. Here absolutely none. I told you what sort of a town it is. Conventional on the surface—underneath debauched, a social sink (insanity, feeble-mindedness, etc etc.—) rotten. The only decency they know is Conventionality. The Chaperon!—They know that they themselves cannot be trusted to be decent unless they are watched! That's their morality.—

Oh the pity of it! (No, no! I just wanted to say "darn them"—but that's not the idea—) Poor poor decayed Princeton! Oh the pity of it!—

And the apple-blossoms are sweet here and the thrush sings and the lawns are well-kept—houses comfortable and pretty even—and the women wear beautiful clothes—but—*of love they know nothing—of ideals they know nothing*—

The whistle is blowing—must run again to make the mail! Princeton giggling the while! (It's out, you know, about our marriage-to-be, thru members of the board—so Princeton knows!)

Goodbye!

Lilian Steichen, 1903, by Edward Steichen.

Princeton High School, 1907 (Bureau County Historical Society).

Faculty of Princeton High School, from the 1907 yearbook. Lilian Steichen is on the bottom row, left (Bureau County Historical Society).

THE FACULTY.

"If we imagine no worse of them, than they of themselves; they may pass for an excellent group."

MR. MAGILL
PRINCIPAL.
"We'll praise him for all that is past;
and trust him for all that is to come."

MISS STETSON
SCIENCE.
"She hath many nameless virtues."

MISS SCHNABELE
MATHEMATICS, GERMAN.
"She is a woman, therefore may be wooed:
She is a woman, therefore may be won."

MR. JOHNSON
COMMERCIAL.
"O, what may a man within him hide
Though angel on the outer side."

MISS RATTRAY
LATIN.
"And still they gazed and still the wonder grew,
That one small head could carry all she knew."

MISS LISTER
DOMESTIC SCIENCE.
"For nothing lovelier can be found in woman
Than to study household good."

MR. YOUNG
PHYSICS, CHEMISTRY AND ARITHMETIC.
"Nature hath framed strange fellows in her time."

MISS COLE
MUSIC, ENGLISH.
"A musical head—foolish heart."

MISS STEICHEN
EXPRESSION, LITERATURE.
"The prophetic soul of the wide world dreams of things to come."

MISS STERN
ENGLISH.
"Quips and cranks and wanton wiles,
Nods and becks and wreathed smiles.

MISS GREENE
COMMERCIAL.
"The joy of youth and health her eyes displayed,
And ease of heart her every look conveyed."

[10]

Faculty of Princeton High School, as described in the 1907 yearbook (Bureau County Historical Society).

Lilian Steichen, in "that Graeco-Gothic white thing you have on in that picture" (Letter 16), by Edward Steichen.

"Mother *is such a mother* . . . joyous always, glad for the work" (Letter 14). Lilian Steichen with her mother.

Lilian Steichen Sandburg, holding her daughter Margaret, with her father.

80.

[May 4, 1908]
Monday evening

I wish and wish I could have been with you Saturday night—Paula was tired—tired—and O I wish I could have been smoothing back your hair—holding you close where you belong!

The lecture was good—them's my sentiments, only more so—and yours are more so—Says Traubel,[1] "When you find a right word, all history looks on and hurrahs." We must have a protocol and an entente cordiale so to arrive at what "genius" means. For I will insist till the cows come home that you are a GENIUS. Spelled with capitals. So.—

All your letters, all your talk, your face, your breath, your assents and dissents, the whole of you tells me all the time that I'll never plummet any depths nor touch any heights but you on your pinions will be right alongside, every once in a while pulling me to leeward or wind where I ought to be.

You're a genius!—Paula—

A genius is a variation from the type, an individual, prophetic of a new type. A genius may never be heard from, yet it's a genius just the same. Achievements are "incidentals"—aside from all the deeds of one's life is the life, the soul and body of the individual.

What the world has not had enough of is Great Companions. Ol' Walt dreamed in a dream he saw a city, a city of great men and superb women—and the quality that led them was the quality of "robust love."[2] But O me, I'm getting into a big theme here—it winds off on the borderland between science and poetry.

All history looked on and hurrahed to-day when I hit on how we make the start! What do you say, Paula?—there the last week in June, we're just about due at Marinette at that time and we take boat from Milwaukee up north to the lumber country. So?

Miss Thomas gives me her congratulation—puts you as the acme.—The best of all of them on the S-S forthgoing is Ed—he "hopes, hopes O so hard, Paus'l, and loves"[3]—the prayers of him and an understanding go with us.

You say I have but little idea of your limitations. Yes—isn't what I have for you to fill in your limitations, so far as I can, just as you fill in my limitations, in a thousand thousand ways? You! you wonder-woman! isn't it because you know where the orator and poet fall short—where the boy fails and gropes for your hand—isn't it because my limitations criss-cross all over yours that all of me cries out for the all of you? O Paula Paula we are living a Lie—a Lie—away from each other—we were made to be near each other—to grope together in the dark—to stand on the peaks together in the sun—sun-crowned—we-two—I cry out and cry out for YOU—you the blundering wonderful girl that knows me—to you my heart goes, blind to what's been and what will be, saying YOU ARE—

Cully *

* such as he is

1. Horace Traubel (1858–1917), an American author and editor, was a socialist and follower of Eugene Debs. His *Chants Communal* (1904) and other poems show the influence of Walt Whitman. He was a friend of Whitman during the poet's later years in Camden. My father had two volumes of his *With Walt Whitman in Camden* (1906). I have been unable to identify this quote.

2. "A city of great men"—is from Walt Whitman's "I Dreamed in a Dream" (1860). The third line goes "Nothing was greater there than the quality of robust love."

3. From Ed's letter to Paula, which closes, "I am glad for you Paus'l and *hope* it will turn out right—hope oh so hard—and love you.—Ed." Evidently she had received this from Ed and sent it on to him.

81.

[May 5, 1908]
Tuesday

Do you know, Cully, there will be just seven more weeks of school after this one! Then the farm! June 12th! And in two more weeks the S-S—Kitty to see the lines of fun in Micky's face—and Paula to hear Carl's beautiful voice and to look into his good eyes—for always and always!

The days are beginning to drag here in Princeton. I know I couldn't stand a whole year of this hunger and yearning—and living among shades. Shades, that's what these people here are to me. And my work—mere busy-work—make-believe!

And with you—you say the separation means that much of your energy is diverted into poetry etc that might be utilized practically in the movement were the Ess-Ess all there in person!

In both cases, what a waste! L.S. occupied with busy-work—when she might be doing some Real Work herself in the Movement besides helping you concentrate *your* energies on it. All this dreaming that we both are doing—might be transformed into *vital doing*—if the Ess-Ess were together—

But these slow seven weeks will pass! The last two on the farm with mother will be *living* anyway. And you'll be at "the farm" yourself part of this time—won't you?—And then you're doing the Big Work, the S-S work for the movement right now! Good and good! The time must pass swiftly with you!—It's poor L.S. that's the severed member—the real Life of the S-S is in the District where C.S. is—Good and good. The time can't drag so with you! At least you don't live among unrealities! No, you are among the big real things with which the S-S is to live. You are in the atmosphere of our Home!—

Paula feels herself the Exile—far from the S-S home. And how Paula loves and loves the breath of home Cully sends in the good letters. The love—the peace—of Home!

Yes, we've got a Home already. Wherever two souls are One in love and loyalty, there is Home!

Paula ought to be ashamed of herself for letting the corners of her mouth turn down so to-day!

Let's call Kitty in!

[Enter Kitty]

Says Kitty:

For all your blarney, Mickey, see what I'll do to ye. There!—How d'ye like it?—Here's another bite! and another!—Now *will* ye be good and not pester Kitty with your everlastin' blarney! You, Mick!—What? Ye say ye won't be good!—Ye must be talkin' blarney!—Oh, but Kitty knows a cure—she's kissing you and kissing you—so smothering all the dear blarney, Mick!

Oh, ye can't get ahead of Kitty, Mick! Might as well give it up!
—says Kitty—

82.

Tuesday

I study and study the calendar these days hoping that I can find some way of figuring it so the time of waiting won't seem so long—But no matter how I count the time, it's sure to come out *too long*.

Right now my place is with you! So! Yes—you to stroke back my hair—you to listen to—you to put my arms around and to kiss—You—Cully—Heart!—Oh, to come home to you and relax utterly, just be "myself," so perfectly free with you—as you with me, you too "just yourself"! That's what home is! Where two hearts or more are gathered together, and nothing of strangeness keeps them apart separating them into "thee" and "me." The two hearts are One Heart! That is home. Where we don't know "which is which," *there* is Home! Where the one heart is perfectly open and free with the other, there is Home!

Our Home *is*—It is waiting for us. All that is needed is that we-two touch hands. Wherever we-two are together, there is Home! All the parts of a Home assembled! I'm Home-sick! Heart!

I hope you'll find time to run out to the farm for a day. Telephone mother from Mil. or from Menomonee Falls or from Hartford—or write her.

R.R. 17, Menomonee Falls.

Mail-time again. I missed the mail yesterday. Must run now.—Was at school late today entering grades! For the last time but one!

Good-bye—Love—Love—

P.S.—Return Ed's letter—if you have it by you—please. Hurrah for the lumber country & the lake trip—June-end!

83.

Wednesday—May 6

You understand and accept the lecture! Of course!—Paula accepts your definition of "a genius"—and acknowledges that she's guilty, in your sense of the word.—Perfect agreement again!

I don't know whether it's grades or the weather or what—but I've felt more than usually oppressed by a sense of loneliness here. Paula so alone among these Philistines who can *understand Nothing! feel nothing!!* All they know is parties and luncheons and receptions and clothes. Ugh!

And Paula must live among them—brimful of joy (the cup overflowing and overflowing—and still it's not full!!)—and no-one to talk to!—except on paper and over wireless!

When we meet face to face, Cully, what talk there will be!—of gestures and looks first, before articulate words which are too halting and slow and never *can* say all anyway. Just to look into your eyes, Cully, that is all the talk I want! Just the touch of your hand, Carl, that is all sympathy and understanding I want!

I hope you got my letter at Hartford. I missed the early evening mail because mail-time has changed. The evening train leaves a half-hour earlier—as I found out when I brought your letter to the post-office at 6:15 yesterday eve.—I'm going to bring this to the post-office now so as to make sure that you'll get it at Schlesingerville all right to-morrow. I'll write you again after supper to Schlesingerville—the letter ought to reach you tomorrow afternoon, leaving here on the night mail.

Paula throws you a kiss—with love and love from a home-sick heart—and another and another kiss! Carl!

P.S. I inclose letter received today from Miss Thomas. You see she "gives us both her blessin'"—poor lonely girl that she is!—

I don't think B will try to hamper us—especially when he sees it's no use—when the registration is an achieved fact!—If B should, I guess for once he'll have Miss T. fighting him!

Of course I know her fighting wouldn't count much—but it would be a prodigy in itself—"worth the money"—for she is so loyal to him always.

84.

Wednesday night May 6, 1908

On the go, on the go all the time.—But Paula—Paula—I wish I could have been with you—helping you to rest. You were tired—tired.—The letters had been plopping in to me, two every 24 hours. Suddenly, I draw blanks, zeros, for 48 hours! At 5 o'clock this afternoon, I hadn't heard from you since last Saturday night—Sunday, Monday & Tuesday, unaccounted for!—I had just so much time to see so many people tt had to be seen today—or you would have gotten a regular cyclopedia of inquiry & murmurings.

—If the Princeton lecture is not a go, you must come to Chicago the 16th. I hope it will be a go, for while you would enjoy the convention, Princeton would be such a meeting-place—we might drive over toward Sheffield, an old battle-ground! Then I want you to hear the Whitman lecture. It has all the tumult & gayety of the S-S in it—*I looked for* YOU *with it!*—It has YOU in it. We don't know where we're going, where we'll be & do & what become.—But OUR impulses & intuitions are sacred.

A *Mr.* Stewart here, who is "a literary man" & has stuff regularly in the Atlantic and Century—(Lord help him!)—says I present a fine life-philosophy in splendid English (I was so pleased he should approve of my English—him a-writin' for the Atlantic) and sublime force, but tt I don't interpret W.,[1] who was such an egotist; tt what I say of W. might all cling about an old cookstove!—So.

Mister Stewart is unique.

Both Schlesingerville & Hartford will be ready for meetings in latter June—latter June!—it will be fun!

So, if it's not a go at Princeton, then make it Chicago—whatever Paula's heart tells her—Paula's Heart!

I send the collection for to-night's lecture on.

We will get a system going tt can't be beat, dear. A lot of things in the air I feel.—The shelter-fund will grow, while we're laughing, loving & growing—you in the ways you decide on—I in mine.

The "Merrie England"[2] of America hasn't been written. Benson,[3] nor Spargo,[4] touch it.—Whether our "Conversations in Socialism" will touch it—we'll see!

Love to you—love and love—"it hammers at my heart the whole night thru."[5]—I kiss your lips—Breath of my Breath—Heart of my Heart!—Lilian!

Carl

1. Walt Whitman.

2. Robert Blatchford, an English socialist, wrote *Merrie England* (1894) in the form of letters to "John Smith of Oldham," in which he tried to bring him to a realization of the wretched condition of the poor in England and to convince him of the value of socialist principles and ideas. The title is, of course, ironic. My father liked this idea and followed it up to a point when he wrote his "Letters to Bill," which were published later in *Lafollette's Magazine* (1909). See Appendix B for one example.

3. Allen Louis Benson (1871–1940), author of *Confessions of Capitalism* and *Socialism Made Plain,* which appeared serially in the Milwaukee *Social-Democratic Herald.* He wrote many leaflets for distribution by party members at meetings.

4. John Spargo was a socialist, born in Stithiana, Cornwall, in 1876. He came to the United States in 1901 and was active as a writer, lecturer, and worker in the socialist cause. *The Bitter Cry of Children* and *Capitalist and Labor* came out in 1906. The most recent at this time was Spargo's *Socialism: A Summary and Interpretation of Socialist Principles.* He was a friend of Morris Hillquit and worked with the New York Socialists. At the National Socialist Convention in Chicago in May 1908, they went against Eugene Debs and nominated James Carey for president, but without success. Debs received the party's nomination.

5. This quote from Ivan Wright's poem "The Want of You" is not correct; it contains the same mistake (in the third line of the second verse) that she had made in her letter, which may mean that he is actually quoting from her letter. See Letter 69.

85.

Thursday—May 7

VI! Another finger down! And mother's letter today says the early date is all right with her, provided we stay on a week! Our staying on after the knot-tying pleases mother so much—it will make it so much easier for her—so much more natural. If we were to run off right after the ceremony it would seem as if the ceremony itself meant "So long" to mother—which it doesn't.

And the week will be great! The Second *Great Week* at the Farm! the memories of our First "Great Week" will be entwined with the experiences of the Second "Great Week"! We will visit the site of the House in the Woods! And we'll try the Parcels Post again "Among the Hills"! You, Carl, your dear arms—and sweet eyes—and all!

Your sweet eyes!—Today the proofs came of the pictures Ed took of you—and he's got the eyes! Bless Ed—he's got the eyes! I love the pictures and love them—talk to them—"h'm" to them—kiss them! You dear sweet Boy, *You!* You, clean and true and good—so good!

Six!

This is the half-way house!

It's VI weeks since March 27 when we started out to the farm together!

In VI weeks from now (June 20) the marriage and we start on our life-together with a week—Our Second Great Week at the farm!

Then about June 27, Ho for the lumber-country, by boat on our Lake Michigan! Maybe there'll be a glorious storm—tossing spray—big waves—lightning—thunder! Maybe! Or perhaps serene sunny skies—and at night a firmament of stars and the crescent baby-moon sailing placid quiet in the West! Maybe!—Whatever weather the gods send—'twill be our choice!—So, ye gods, don't worry about what weather to give us! Toss up a penny—heads "Rain"—tails "Fair!" The S-S loves all sorts of weather—the S-S understands all the different moods of lake and sky!

As for where the ceremony is to be performed, at the farm or in Mil.—mother has a preference for the farm but she says she wants us to have it where we want it—only if we have it in Milwaukee mother will be with us. It's a feeling mother has—she wants to be there—but whether it's the farm or Thompson's house doesn't matter much to her. So it's up to us to decide. I don't care which—tho as far as *sentiment* goes I prefer the old farm too. But really sentiment doesn't amount to much with me in this matter—and besides a different sort of sentiment would be gratified by doing up the business in the most perfunctory way "at the minister's house"—it would be a royal lark!—On the basis of sentiment I suppose it's really "six of one and half a dozen of the other"—I say we decide it on the basis of this practical consideration: Which place would Thompson (or Gaylord) prefer? Would they really enjoy coming out to the farm? It would mean a day's outing—perhaps that's more time than they'd care to give up to festivity! Thompson is such a hustler!—Perhaps on the other hand they'd enjoy it!—You know Thompson and Gaylord better than I do—so it's up to you, Carl, to find out which way would suit our officiating-ministers-of-the-gospel!—If we were on a street-car line it would be easy enough! You know the poor railroad connections—but we could call for them at Granville and take them back to Granville, then the R.R. trips would not be so tiresome for there wouldn't be all the long waits at Granville. Or they could come all the way from Mil. with horse & vehicle of some sort—tho they wouldn't know the road so I suppose that wouldn't be practical.—If I could think of some way of making it really enjoyable for Thompson and Gaylord, I'd like to have them come out to the farm. But I don't seem to hit the right plan—I almost think Milwaukee is the better place, as far as I can see.

But you can see *farther*—it's up to you—you know them better—can tell what would suit them.—

As far as we-two are concerned I fear we won't be much interested in Gaylord or Thompson (or in the Lord Jesus Christ) that day—when we start again on our life-together after the weeks of separation, of living the lie!—We won't even *notice* whether we're at the farm or in Milwaukee!—We'll see each other—not much else!—(I almost think Mil. would be best! I don't believe we'll prove very entertaining hosts to G. & T. that day! After the weeks apart, we'll want just each other, I do believe!)

I shall address this letter to the Globe—another by the same mail to 344 Sixth—so you'll be sure to get a letter wherever you inquire first.

You didn't give me any address for Friday—so I couldn't get a letter to you that day—

Good-night—Carl, My Love, I kiss you Good-night!

Lilian

P.S. I inclose a letter from Elsie—Good. Isn't it? Hoch das Wunderkind—Here's to the Wunderkind—Hip! Hip! Hurray! Only the German is not slangy.

ENCLOSURE

April 24, 1908

You *dear* girl—

Your letter has just come and I am so happy. I hoped it would be so, for I could see even from your first letter how fine he is, and what a splendid all-round chap! I am so happy for both of you.—He is wonderful, I am sure—any one could see it from the poems—and I take it that that is only one part; and *you* are wonderful—and there you are!

Awfully glad that you have decided to be married—it is the only way—and well worth the trouble. Only let it be *this* summer and not the one after. If you will be poor anyway, what does it matter? Waiting is Hell—not so much in its immediate as in its after-effects. It is a bad physical strain I think—and one of those villainous subterranean ones that make serious inroads on vitality. And if there is any sine qua non for marriage it is health. Nothing else matters in comparison. Take me as a horrible example.

We are planning to sail for America early in September, and owing to scatter-brained not ordering passage before this, seem to be up against paying $90.00 instead of $75.00 which was our maximum! But anyway, we probably couldn't have done better. It is infuriating to have everything cost so much more than it did a few years ago—and no improvement in the article offered. Ought to mean a socialistic boost—yes? Yours for the Revolution.

How I long to see the good brother. I shall write to him some six weeks before I leave here to give him due warning. Wasn't it splendid that you saw him—and that the three of you were together for such exhilarating days. I rejoice in them and in the fine feelings you must be having in the spring of Princeton. Now that you have all this to think of, it won't be so lonely. And with a fine definite culmination ahead of you, the months will slip by joyously. If you do wait a year, Princeton will be good because you won't have to put much energy into it. The Lord bless the Note-Books. But, for my part, I should think you'd be ashamed to take so much time before the fatal plunge, after all your promulgated doctrine of "Haste makes Happiness!" Is it all to curry favor with the Princetonians? I'll bet you it is a sneaking desire to leave your pedestal there after you move out—but I can assure you that they'll forget to wreathe it with flowers, even if you do leave without blot or blemish on your morals. But of course you always were rather a whited sepulchre, and I suppose you want to keep the character.

As a really public-minded citizen the plain duty before you is to leave about May 20, eloping in plain sight, leaving a trail of uncorrected papers in your wake and no grades in your book. *That* would create a furore in which Miss Douglas and I will be as dear little lambs.

As an anarchist—practical, as well as philosophical—I strongly counsel this course of action, and I can conscientiously say that I think you would find it thrillingly satisfactory.

Tell Miss Rattray, please, that some friend of hers (a dam fool—N.B. not necessary to include this!) was here for a few weeks. Misener was her name. I called on her and had her to tea, but no credit is demanded.—And tell Bradford Burleigh that I enjoyed his letter very much—and explain why I can't answer his unless I answer all the others. The same to Santha Roggy [?], please—and any others you think of. I really can't undertake it, as they would just keep it up—and would get no real good from it. And you can see by the scarcity of my letters to you how little energy I have to put into writing.

I keep pretty busy all the time, but the days seem too short. I rest several hours each afternoon. Lacey puts me to bed regularly, in spite of an occasional attempt at resistance. He is adorable, and I am more and more astonished at him every day. It is a good business to be both strong and gentle!

The spring is positively intoxicating. I wish you could have some of these lovely flowers—and could hear the dear birds—nightingales at that! The garden is great—not a "real" garden at all, most of it just a big enclosure and a tangle of flowers, dear, tiny, wild ones, out under the olive trees.

Some nice people have been here in Athens lately for several weeks and I have seen quite a bit of them—Mr. and Mrs. Smyth and Mr. and Mrs. Newbold.—Both women are wonderfully brilliant and a very good sort. I have had good times with them.

I am thankful to say that I am better and much stronger, but it is a slow business. You must be sure to be *well* when you are married. Have a fine reserve fund of health and let the money go to Hell.

Do write lots, and let me know all about everything. You know that I am awfully glad. I am strong for Sandburg. And "Carl" is an adorable name. Hoch das Wunderkind! Blessings on him—and lots of love to you.

As ever,
Elsie Langdon Caskey

86.

Hartford, Wis.
Thursday—again

Bulletin No. III

A gray day, a day of rain, slanting persistent drisly rain—and at times the wind blows in heavy drenching gusts—and here so near "the farm," the House in the Woods, it calls to me The Baptismal Rain, the rain of the first night together!

On us—on We-Two—is all the responsibility, all the risk & folly & glory.—Only those who have lived triumphant lives can advise us—And then we will promise only to listen, not implicitly obey—We listen, yes—and then we do as the Heart of the S-S tells—in accord with the laws passed by the Paula-Carl legislature. Even so—or—Ain't it?

Have to run to catch a mail!

Here goes!

I throw you kisses.—You! Paula!

Sandy

87.

[May 8, 1908]
Friday

I'm sending inclosed two proofs[1]—one of you and one of Berger—Ed sent two proofs of you—the other one I sent on to the farm to be returned "by return mail" so I'll send it on to you next week. Return the one of yourself that I inclose—tho if you want you may keep it over Sunday to show Joseffy! Ed got *Carl* all right—the Wunderkind and the Sweet Boy—Next time he'll get "Cully" too! I love these pictures of you—the eyes are yours sure! So dear—so good—so true! I've been feeling better ever since the pictures came! Maybe that was the Spring tonic I needed!

As for Berger's picture—I think Ed's *got* him—*all of him*. What says his Nibs, the Dook?

Of course the proofs are mere sketches to be changed—filled in—etc. They are pictures in embryo.

Show the proof of Berger to Berger if you care—or not—just as you please. Also leave it with him or not as you please.

The lecture here is off. I guess I'll reconsider what I said about your *not* coming here unless the lecture is arranged for. Maybe Princeton would be a better place after all for a visit. I have an idea! We'll make a lark of it! I'll tell *no-one* about your coming. (Mr. M. was so afraid your lecture would stir the school up. I'll go him one better and say very serious-facedly after you're gone that I told no-one about your visit for fear it would get to the pupils and they would get stirred up!—It'll just about *kill* him to know that you were in town and he didn't get to see you! So we'll punish Princeton!)—But the main thing about my keeping "mum" about it will be that it will leave us absolutely free. If Princeton knows, we'll be invited out to dinners etc.—which we might refuse of course—but it's always more or less hard to turn down people.—We'll live just as we please—have good times in my room, lunches there etc.—and maybe a meal or two at the restaurant—very shocking to Princeton! Then we'll have a day in the woods taking lunch—and you'll see Bryant's Woods with its ravines etc. Also moon-light walks into the country!—Great!—great!—We have no obligations to Princeton! If you'd have given the lecture we might have taken some considerations! We might even have given an evening to a faculty party which Magill would surely have gotten up!—Now we do just as we please!

Could you come Friday afternoon?—(I'll be free from 3:30 on.) And stay over till Monday morning—? That would give us Friday evening—all Saturday and all Sunday!

The expense would be the same whether you came here or I go to Chicago.

Tell me which you would prefer—Chicago has its points of course—but Princeton is lovely in Spring—Here we could get more quickly into the country etc.—have beautiful walks!

And if you're broke—you know I hold the S-S funds in trust. We have $28.00 (I don't believe I told you that I got the Five you sent from Appleton all right).

Don't be foolish and starve yourself to save a few dollars—but send in a requisition on the bursar!

Also don't work too hard to make our funds $50.00 to start on—We can start on less—and why shouldn't I have the fun of adding a little to the Starter-Fund—Why?

Keep your good health—and don't be over-strenuous—

Must stop now—to make a mail!

In a week we see each other! Hip Hip—Hooray—! Hip!—etc etc—

P.S. Will try to write another note this evening—so as to reach you Saturday—Will send it to Globe Hotel.

1. During that week at the farm, my uncle took several photographs of my father. Three of these turned out very well and were entirely different studies.

88.

[ca. May 8, 1908]

P.S.[1]—I add a mystic line: "The letter will never be written!"—That proof is a wonder—I don't know why. What will the artist say when he knows I look on it as great stuff for publicity use! Am going to get Joseffy's judgement & then return it right away.

A beautiful day here at "the farm." We were going to sing "The Vacant Chair" but nobody remembered the air. Out on the parade-ground (between the studio & the garden, you remember) a bright half-moon shines down, a big silver star burns and flares as for joy—all is balm & quiet.

I haven't heard anything wrong about Klingers[2] or Kipers [Keipers] so I guess everything is allright.

Your explanation for Magill of why the lecture will not be a go at Princeton is the unexpected but good. We will try some later time for r-r-revenge-rolling the r's.

Paula, I can't write seriously here. I'm careless—careless!—It's the woods—and the You-You!—that's lingering around here.

Always
Carl

1. The letter starts "P.S."

2. George Klinger's farm was on one side of the Steichen's Little Farm and Phillip Keiper's large farm on the other. This was a gentle joke, for my grandmother was a great talker and seemed to know all that was going on in the neighborhood without trying to find out.

89.

[May 8, 1908]
Friday evening

Just back from a faculty luncheon and have time for a few words. All thru the luncheon Mr. Magill and I *argued*. Interest *vs.* Discipline in education. He had a dozen little backers—I stood gloriously Alone (the *Presence* of course with me as always—that's why I stood "gloriously" alone instead of "lonesomely" alone).—After luncheon, Mr & Mrs Lovejoy[1]—the only outsiders present—told me they thought I was probably in the right! But I seemed so happy sustaining my end of the argument alone and unabetted that they didn't butt in with their support!—They didn't know why I was so happy alone!—When I told them later on, aside, that I was going to take a partner in the work of renovating the Old World—they said "Good!" They had taken each other as partners and the life-together had been great.—They gave us a Cheer!—The two of them are about the nicest people in Princeton—tho they have Magill-itis slightly too! They gave me their approval when I went for Magill hard—but they did so not without misgivings!—By the way Mr L. said "Be sure and bring THE MAN to see us if he comes to Princeton!"—You see! But we won't have time to waste on even the best of Princetonians!

In a week, Cully! Yes—and Yes!—in a week!

To-morrow morning maybe I'll get a letter from you from Milwaukee—and will know whether you can come to Princeton or whether I'm to come to Chicago.—I hope you'll come here for the country is lovely with Spring! Today we had sun-shine after a week of rain and clouds—everything was radiant! A glow over all—and all things fresh, lush, full of sap and life! The trees are leafing out so fast it will be summer before you get here (if you don't hurry). And the violets have started out blooming afresh after the rains. The peach and cherry blossoms are gone—the apple blossoms are going—but the lilacs and fragrant flowering currant have arrived! Princeton smells sweet and looks like a great garden! You must see Princeton—and We-Two must see it together! I haven't half seen it with you away! There'll be such fun and gay laughter and "sweet-fooling" here on the brown roadways—and in the wooded ravines where the little brook winds and gurgles in Bryant's Woods—and under the beautiful old trees in the moonlight and starlight—I hope you'll come.—In Chicago of course there'll be the Convention.—I'd enjoy it only I'm so starved for a sight of you (maybe a bite of you, Micky!) that I'll not be in the right mood for the Convention, I fear. Perhaps I'm only imagining this. Perhaps at the Convention I'd be carried away by the She-Devil of a Socialist in me—instead of giving myself up to wonder at Carl's good true sweet eyes and wanting to kiss and kiss them! Perhaps! Just now I feel that it would be better in Princeton, where We-Two would be alone together—living and loving in the eon-old world of elemental things: odor of lilacs, music of bird and brook, and moonlight over all.—

Love and love from
Lilian

1. This was Elijah Parish Lovejoy, the son of Owen Lovejoy, who was named after his uncle, the martyred abolitionist murdered by a mob. Mrs. Lovejoy was one of the judges of the elocution contest in April.

90.

[May 9, 1908]
Saturday

Today I received Carlyle's Cheer and Challenge to the S-S! (And if it isn't *Carlyle's*—it might have been! And Carlyle meant to say all that to Us anyway!—Poor Carlyle—he can't come to the Shack! tho we'd love to have him, wouldn't we, Carl? Past and Present!—Past and Present!) [1]

The envelope was stamped Oshkosh—So you've been in Oshkosh again. If I had known you'd have gotten a letter there. Didn't you go to Schlesingerville? I wonder whether you got what letters I did write this week—they weren't as many as usual and I fear you missed some of them even so.

The Sat. night lecture I mailed Sunday. That you got I know. Then Monday night I mailed 2 letters addressed to Oshkosh—I missed the 8 o'clock mail so they didn't leave Princeton till Tuesday morning. Tuesday I mailed one letter to Hartford. Wednesday one to Schlesingerville. Thursday I didn't mail any letter for I had no address for Friday. Friday I mailed you 3 letters to Milwaukee (*1* to 344 Sixth and *2* to Globe Hotel). And now Sat. evening I'm sending off this note—tho "Wot's de use?"—you won't get it till Monday for there's no delivery to-morrow of course in Chicago.

I hope you'll be able to come to Princeton—Spring is so lovely here. But if you can't come on account of the convention (I noticed only to-day that the convention lasts over into the following week—so Saturday & Sunday the 16th & 17th may be important Convention days that you ought not to miss)—if you can't come here, I'll come on to Chicago. I'm off downtown and will mail this—tho—"Wot's de yuse"? You won't get it tomorrow.

Paula

P.S. Paula is prosy to-night! What do *you* say, Cully??

1. Thomas Carlyle's *Past and Present,* published in 1843, showed his distrust of social legislators and hatred of laissez-faire policies.

91.

[May 9, 1908]
Saturday

Your last 2 letters to Oshkosh, ten Schlngrville[1] letters & the one here, just read!—and read again! What with yesterday afternoon & last night (it was 11:30 for the mother and me)[2] & walking in to M. Falls[3] this morning, & now all these letters and letterettes at the office, I'm all Kaflustrated—the air is all flying ribbons and clashing melodies, warbling birds, brass bands—Ess-Esses!—wild circles!

If you could at this late day, swing the lecture, it would count.—You see, the gigglers would sit up. The lecture was built in large part to handle a giggling civilization. *Magill's judgement* (!) would be vindicated. An after-interest would be intensified. It might mean return-dates—for one or for a course of 3 or so next year.—The gigglers are everywhere! The world is Princetonian!—They started when I opened at Hartford. I played them along, softened them into real laughter, & then took them off in a lonely place & hung shot corpses of their dead selves for them. Then I glorified life without giggling—and they gave me an encore—they applauded till Tyner led me up for a final bow.—I made friends for us when we go there for socialism.

It's past recall, I guess, getting Magill around again. But if there's a fighting chance, try to swing it.

I will be needed in the convention[4]—was elected 4th alternate—& don't know for sure about Friday or Saturday.—If I go down, I suppose I'll go on to Galesburg for a day or so, perhaps only a few hours.—All busy now, sweet, writing in a rush—will try to get you a note from the boat to-night—You! great great love-heart of a wonder—Lilian.

Carl

1. Schlesingerville.
2. These two were good companions from the beginning.
3. Menomonee Falls.
4. This letter was written on the stationery of the Social-Democratic party of Wisconsin.

92.

[May 9, 1908]
Saturday Evening
6:30 P.M.

All ready for the trip to Chi. again by boat. This is the 5th time I have made this trip—each time marking varied epochs. And never was life bigger, both with clash & conflict, but with the fine lure of beauty & far stars.

I congratulate myself I weigh 120 pounds more than ever! And the magic of fate!—I look with four eyes—I have twice as many wonderful dreams—& a strange new pair of hands that someway is not so strange & new fumbles around my head & cuffs me & thrills me with little touches—

Paula—such Scriptures as you send to me—throbbing letters—I can't take time to answer all as I want to—But You—You know—Whenever I write YOU, meaning Lilian Steichen, as cognomens go, I want to emphasize it, put something into it tt will make it stand out like an electric sign in the night—YOU!!—so.

It was "worth the money" to hear your mother call me "Carl"—You have been doing some sort of educating—sure![1]

Gave Berger the print of himself. Nothing direct btw [between] us in talk.

Edward Steichen is an artist. We all know our best selves, the selves we love. And he caught a self I pray to be all the time! By what wizardry of sight and penetration, he came to get that phase of me in so little a time, I don't know. It took more than eyes—it took heart & soul back of the eyes.

Such an "infuriating," "thrilling," "awfully" Elsie Caskey![2] There's education to know such a one. You were each other's pacemakers in cussing, I see—a divil-wild two o' yez![3]

At present looking, some of ten Wis. delegates will not be at the convention all the time, wh [which] will mean, I sit & vote & see & absorb & refrain from expostulation, muttering Paul Jones' "I have not yet begun to fight."

(Lights of red & white along the river flash into the dusk. The water repeats each of them instantly, as tho, "Hello! hello Night!" The materialities may not have a language but they seem almost to talk to each other.)

So I may have to be in Chi. Friday & Sat. tho this is not likely. I will let you know as to the outlook. I think Princeton would be the better meeting-place, too. About Wed. or Thurs. we will know.

Miss Thomas is *so* good with me—as tho you had helped her see things—trifles of solicitude she never evinced before.—Is thinking about us. Murmurs a fear tt the district finances will not be large enough (she didn't say for what!) & intimates tt I deserve more speaking dates outside the district.

We will do the best we can with what we have to work with. We will surprise them in increase of income.—But always the literature sales go to the Emergency Fund—& if the rest is not enough, from elsewhere more will have to come.—Mrs. Gaylord phones things look dark with them now, "Win," being unwell, but they've seen worse, & she laughs in cheer & faith.

Such days!—Oshkosh, Hartford, Menomonee Falls, Milwaukee, the lake, Chicago & Princeton & YOU!!

The state convention is June 13—you know?

The prints will get to you on Mon. or Tues. The real Prince a few days later!—will see the Princess!—You're promoted from Duchess if you want to be—because you can *cuss* so.

It's almost dark.—After the boat starts, at 8:30, I shall walk & breathe for an hour & then turn in—I've got plans & details of plans for several things. We will talk about 'em.

Love to you—Paula—heart—love & love—kisses on your lips & eyes—Lilian.

Carl

1. My father had visited the farm a few days before.

2. My mother had sent him Elsie Caskey's congratulatory letter, from which he is quoting. See enclosure to Letter 85.

3. This is, of course, a joke about her "cussing," for my mother was as mild

as a Quaker in that respect, though she did occasionally quote from his letters to let him know that she understood how he felt—at the time of the election, for instance. The reference to Elsie's "cussing" must be to either "Waiting is Hell" or "Tell Miss Rattray, please, that some friend of hers (a dam fool—N.B. not necessary to include this) was here for a few weeks."

93.

Monday—May 11th
After School

Raining again!—The rain is coming down in sheets!—Hope you are comfortable someplace—somewhere—in Chicago! *You,* Carl!—And for week-end, we *would* like sunshine—but we'll be so ineffably happy, any sort of weather will be right! Oh for week-end! WEEK-END!!—And right now it's great to think you are no farther off than Chicago! Only a hundred miles away!

If you can come Friday the best train for you will be the one leaving Chicago 11 A.M. arriving Princeton 2:45 P.M.—(Paula is free at 3:30!)

So glad you were out to the farm and out on the old parade-ground. Before many weeks we-two will be doing sentinel-duty there again.

Tuesday—Wednesday—Thursday—THREE days—III—then Friday—and Carl and Paula together!

You see I always harken back to that—to WEEK-END—happy happy week-end—and so near! so near! Week-end! How the thought of it awakens throbbing Joy—Joy! Friday Lilian will look into Cully's eyes! Friday Lilian will kiss Cully's hair! FRIDAY!

Whether it's to be in Princeton or in Chicago—matters not! It will be Friday—and but III days in between! III!

Oh there's poetry in numbers at times—isn't there, Carl, my Poet?

Hello! Here's the old sun breaking thru the clouds! Good! A Glory of golden light over all this fresh Spring verdure! Everything bathed in a warm radiant light!—The World is fresh after the shower—and all a-glow!

Throbbing joy of fresh young life in the great Out-of-doors! And in the S-S Heart! Paula is radiant—thinking of Carl so near! Paula is all throbbing with joy—to think she can kiss Cully's lips soon SOON!

Oh Micky, Micky—Kitty will tumble your hair so! She'll muss you all up—so she will!—You! Micky Malone!

Kitty

P.S. And the princess sends word to the Prince that when the Real *Prints* arrive (not these mere proofs) then the Prince will wonder!—The Princess can hardly wait to see the real Prints! ((harder still to wait for the Real Prince!)) Tho the Lord alone knows *how long*—how long we'll have to wait—I hope Ed doesn't mean to surprise us with them at our Golden Wedding!!—There's no telling tho?!?—It's the unexpected we expect from Ed!!-? And he was startlingly "unprecedentedly" quick about sending proofs!

Perhaps next Friday here in Princeton! Or in Chicago! Whichever you say! I almost think Princeton would be the better meeting-place!

Must stop now to make a mail—

I send you kisses and kisses by wireless! Soon I'll put my arms around you *really* and give you real kisses—You!—My Love! Breath of my Breath!—Sweet!

Oh—and oh!—and OH!
and H'm! H'm!

All the love that I can love and more and more to Carl from Lilian

---

94.

Monday evening May 11, 1908

I sent my April Vanguard to Ed—or rather I sent your article clipped from it. So I can't send it to Joseffy. Too bad. What's the matter with the office, that they don't print extra copies! I want to know!

Don't I want to get away from this blamed old Princeton tho! Ugh! I feel like smashing a few Princetonian heads! But it wouldn't do any good—no—no—*no*—!

I shall persevere to the end giving them comprehensible interpretations of myself! I am so gentle! *So rational.* If I'd let my ire run away with me—I could give it to them hard, as Elsie used to! My, how she did give it to them! But "Lord, it wasn't economical!" Nothing came of batting them over the head—except that Elsie had the satisfaction of self-expression during the batting process. The Princetonians were stunned for an instant—then recovered, and thought Elsie ill-mannered, lacking in self-control, an unaccountable creature who batted you over the head for no reason at all (they didn't understand the reason—so from their viewpoint it was "for no reason at all").

—I'll keep it up to the bitter end. Preserve serenity, talk down to them, be oh so kind and gentle with them, the poor little creatures!—So I shall help them an inch or two on the way—for even Princeton is "on the way" going somewhere—going to the same place we are going too! And they'll get there—in the course of the ages—even with their snail's pace, they'll arrive! So, Princeton, I'm going to keep on patiently helping you to gain your inch or two!—

But I realize this isn't the Job for me! I shall be glad to shake the dust of Princeton off my shoes—and leave to my successor the task of helping Princeton on.—My job is waiting for me in the District! There I can help people on who will march faster than "an inch a year"—there I'll get some results worth while.

Good-bye Princeton! I say it quick and once for all! (It's not a case of "Good-bye and good-bye with emotional lips repeating"!)

I want to say "Hello!" to Comrade Fox and Hope Fox and to James Larsen and to all! I'm homesick for the District!—

Five more weeks of school—One of exams & Commencement exercises—then Mother & the Farm one week—then Cully! and Cully and Cully!—then the North, Cully and Paula and the District!

The days do go by slow tho—awful slow—tho they're jammed full enough of school work—Grade week again now! The last one until Commencement and final exams!—I haven't been able to work on that "Woman and Socialism" paper yet! It always seems just ahead—the time for it!—Of course if I thought it important enough I could cut out walks and letters, and there would be time all right! But it's not so desperately important as all that. It can wait a little—can't it?—I hope to do it in good time without having to give up walks and talks with you!

Now for grades tho—we'll have them out of the way in a couple of days. Then we can breathe again!

Good-bye—tho it's not an unmixed "good"(bye) either—when we have to say "good-bye"—We-two who ought to be together, by Gum!—Paula wants to be with Cully, to hear his voice resonant beautiful, to see the lines in Cully's face—the tragic ones and the comic ones both! Paula wants Carl & Cully both—and wants them hard!

Paula sends love and love—

95.

[May 12, 1908]
Tuesday morning

Just back in my room from a fine morning constitutional. Fresh morning air. Sunlight bathing the wet lush-green grass and the wet black road—pools standing everywhere and shimmering in the sunlight. Birds singing. Odor of lilacs wafted to me from everywhere—and other sweet Spring odors—of sap rising in the trees—of the rich brown earth—of the new-mown grass—of yesterday's rain—

And Paula's heart singing responsive to all—Paula's face all smiles and gladness! But II days between, now! Wednesday—Thursday—then Friday and Cully!

And Paula will look into Cully's eyes and say: "So you've come—have you?" and Paula & Cully will be together!—lips on lips—heart to heart—

That will be Friday!

Such a lyric week-end as it will be!

Week-End!

II!

And we'll plan—we'll plan!

June 13! The Fates outwitting mother![1] It's not *our* doin's! And mother did so insist the first week I was home she wanted me all to herself! The gods are on our side! June 13!

And the Convention? I get the Daily so I read the *facts* about it. I'll expect you to tell me what it really *means*. You must be getting lots and lots of big impressions—from merely "looking over" the delegates from East and West and North and South. You'll absorb a lot of real knowledge of the American movement as a whole.—And you'll know what you're getting, and how important it is for you to be on the spot Friday[,] Saturday and Sunday. I don't want you to come to Princeton, Carl, if it means you're missing something important at the Convention. You'll know. Maybe a few days more or less will make no difference. Maybe they're the very days that will count most. You'll know.—Also you know I'm a sensible girl; and tho Princeton would be a better meeting-place, Chicago has its points.

Or would this plan be practicable? You stay thru the entire convention—then go thru Princeton straight to Galesburg (or maybe a few hours' stop here) Wednesday or Thursday May 20 or 21 (whenever the Convention is over). Stay in Galesburg till Friday. Spend Friday, Sat. & Sun., May 22, 23 and 24 in Princeton!—I mention this plan as you may not have thought of it.—Tho very likely it would keep you too long from your district—eh?

Paula is strong for planning!

Must start for school now.

Love and love and love to Carl from

The Happiest Girl
Lilian

1. These lines must refer to the date of the Wisconsin Social-Democratic Convention. She thought that this would really mean little time alone with her mother.

96.

[May 13, 1908]
Wednesday

Good. I'm expecting to come to Chicago—leaving here Friday evening about 6:30 arriving Chicago about 9:30.

In case you find you can get away Friday morning or evening—you'll wire me in time. The evening train leaves Chicago 6:10 P.M. arrives here a little before 9—a fine train. If you come on the evening train be sure to wire *in time*—sometimes telegrams are not delivered very promptly here. But I'll inquire at the telegraph office at the depot before I take the train myself. So I guess there's no danger of our missing each other—by your leaving Chicago at 6 and I leaving Princeton at 6:30! That *would* be tragedy!

If you come on the morning train there'll be no danger at all of our missing each other—even if the telegram doesn't arrive. For the 11 A.M. train arrives here about 3 in the afternoon several hours before I would leave for Chicago.

My street and no. are: 323 East Peru St.—You'd better take the bus at the depot to the American House (There are 2 hotels in Princeton—one at the North End near the depot—and the other, the American House at the South End only three blocks from where I room—So you'll want to stay at the American House).

From the American House anyone will direct you to 323 E. Peru St.—corner S. Fourth—Mr Sol Robinson's house—a block south of the High School.

If you come in the afternoon, I'll be at school and so can't meet you at the depot. If you come in the evening I will meet you.

I'm going to put in as much sleep as possible these days. I am not at my best anyway—and shall not be this week-end—Too bad of course, and it makes the Chicago trip a little inconvenient for me. Another reason why I hope it may turn out that you can come here—(provided it will be all right both for the Convention and for you.)—I'll be all right—don't you worry—only I'll have to take more time for sleep and rest than ordinarily—but I'll be all right! Sure, Mike! I pride myself on being a strong sturdy fellow *all* the time—So don't get started on "vain imaginings" because I mentioned this. I referred to it simply to show you that there is this further reason that made me urge Princeton as against Chicago for the meeting-place. It's simply a slight inconvenience. And we won't be able to be quite so strenuous—walk quite so many miles etc—

The time will be so short for talking—planning—etc that we won't want to spare any time for theatre *surely,* Carl. There'll be so *much* to talk—and what with the Convention etc we won't have much time to ourselves anyway.

I'm looking forward to meeting Joseffy—I wish he could be with us at the farm in strawberry season! (tho maybe we won't be at the farm ourselves for strawberry time! But if we are—and if Joseffy is in Chi. he could come up—and we'd have a time!) (Strawberry time is about middle of July, I think).

Yes Cully—plans—and plans—and we'll "go hiking and talk it over"—Chicago has the lake! so much to the good!—And I will enjoy the Convention!—Things don't seem to be moving very expeditiously there from Daily Soc. reports.—Maybe this is a false impression.—Anyway, the Convention must be inspiring. Paula will enjoy it so very much.—So!

Just Thursday to live thru—then Friday and I'm off to Chi.! Will you be at the Union depot at 9:30? Or are there night sessions too at Brand's Hall?[1] And if I'm to pilot myself to Brand's Hall—tell me about where it is—street & cross street.

Hope this reaches you Thursday morning or noon. Would like to get a reply so as to know whether to expect to be met by you at the depot in Chi.—

Friday 9:30!
Carl!

Love from
Lilian

1. Frederick Heath, editor of the *Social-Democratic Herald,* wrote in his column about the location of the convention: "Brand's Hall, on North Clark Street, is not well suited for convention purposes. The acoustics are bad and the big side windows glaring." Curtains were lowered to try to remedy this, but that was of little aid. However, this was where they had met for the Socialist Convention in 1904 and for an important meeting in 1905, so probably there were other factors that made the choice imperative.

97.

[Wednesday evening, May 13, 1908]

If I came to Chicago instead of your coming to Princeton—expect me on the train leaving Princeton about *6:30 P.M. Friday*, arriving Chicago about 9:30 P.M.

Will you be able to meet me at the depot? Union depot.

Lilian

98.

[May 14, 1908]
Thursday morning

Yesterday evening I wrote you definitely about my train. I gave the letter to someone to mail it for me. They *may* have forgotten to do it. So here are duplicate "instructions"! I arrive on Burlington train at Union depot, Chi., 9:30 Friday. If you're not there, I'll wait for you—unless I get different "instructions" from the Dook meantime.

I'll come—*sure*—unless you wire me you're coming here.

Good-bye—

Lilian

99.

Thursday evening

My train arrives 9:15 P.M. instead of 9:30—
Tomorrow, Friday!
Love to Cully

from Paula

100.

On train to Chi.—Friday

Five hours aboard—two hours more—yet—The news butcher is a comrade, locates me by the button—

This afternoon would have been a great afternoon to *write.* I can write 20 words a minute, you know, that would be 1800 [*sic*] an hour. I have pencils & paper & time to write a great speech, & a great poem this afternoon—all I lack is ideas and feeling!

101.

[May 18, 1908]
Monday Night

I am so sleepy I can't write—can't keep my eyes open—Understand your condition Saturday morning when you were so *so* sleepy—You—My Boy!

Good-night! It's no use trying to write—this is just to tell you that I'm sleepy, sleepy—sleepy.

My Boy—My Boy—I love you and kiss you—Good-night!

102.

[May 19, 1908]
Tuesday—Chicago

All aboard—supper with Barker[1] & Joseffy & then for Milwaukee to-night, hitting Sheboygan to-morrow noon.

Ghosts!—Paula—ghosts around the room last night—the ghost of You—your presence—so near you are & so dear you are—so fragrant is the breath of you—so sweet what you leave with me when you go & so fine the tang of what you keep sending when you are away.—When we say "Love and Love" to each other now, it is like the warblers among the spring blossoms—the free glad gushing of new realizations.

And so shall we go on—two eaglets—from country to country.

Not always will it be "spring blossoms"—not always do we want the mad spontaneity of May & flowers. Sometimes it will be from crag to crag across dark spaces we go—but together, ready for any luck—we two.—

Love and Love,
Carl

1. Edwin Barker, for whom he had worked on *The Lyceumite* and *The Billboard*.

103.

You mustn't lose sleep, Liz—Your delectable eyes—your round arms—your bonnie proud head and shoulders—give them the sleep they need—You are the Woman Who Understands—and I want you long and long—in all "the lashing of black waves and in loneliness"—and in all the blare and blazoning of our ultimate doings.

Cully

104.

[Tuesday, May 19, 1908]

Dear Heart:

So it's Sheboygan you go to next. I thought you said Sheboygan Falls. This morning I sent off a few lines to you to S. Falls—no matter—it was *only a few* lines and will come back to me as I wrote my name on envelope.

Maybe when this gets to Sheboygan you will have moved on! You're getting me by wireless these days anyway—aren't you?

I inclose a clipping just received from home about Ed—from one of the Mil. papers the day after Ed left. A friend sent mother the clipping. You return it right off—for I want to send it to Ed *soon.*

Yesterday I was *merely sleepy.* Today I'm happy and happy and happy. The memory is so fresh and alive. I can feel your warm breath on my cheek. I can see your clean true eyes. I can lay my head on your breast and rest—and rest—The memory is so near—so sweet and near!

Such honey-days! The honey-weekend!

And now—3 weeks from Saturday—III! III!—we touch hands again!

And another week—IV from Saturday—and Joseffy and the Life together!

Goodbye now—

Paula

(throwing you a kiss!)

105.

[May 20, 1908]
Wednesday

These are good days—serene—sweet—in the S-S heart "the peace that the World cannot give"!

It's the Presence, Carl—it's the Presence. You with me! As you were with me those two honey-sweet days in Chicago. You with me!

I feel it—there aren't going to be any more lonely days for the S-S. The vivid memory of Chicago days will tide us over these brief three weeks of external separation (for really I don't feel them as weeks of separation—you are so near, Carl. I can touch you—and look at you—and feel your breath!)

Good—good—days!

And, dear, you left some visible tokens—mementos—of wolf-tooth love! You!

And Kitty is glad for it! Glad for the unsightly blemishes! The black and blue marks!

You—you're goin' to be arraigned in court for cruelty to animals! You! Micky Malone!

Says Kitty

P.S. What's your next address?

106.

[May 20, 1908]
Milwaukee—Wednesday

A wonderful spring day with the Spring Song everywhere—a tantalizing laziness over all.—

While I was in Chi. the trees changed some & this morning on the avenues they greeted me with a little unusual haughtiness. We expect to make it up, though.

I am delayed some, in various ways; may not hit Sheboygan till to-morrow—for your messages there!

Several practical things to the advantage of the S-S are on the move—also to the advantage of the S.D.P.!

Such hours as we will have with grass & trees & sky! Heart!

'Twas a bit like home, coming into the Northwestern station & seeing the ghost of you near the ticket window where you passed me the rebuke beautiful.

"Hasn't it been beautiful?"

"No! *Isn't* it beautiful?"

Correct me on my tenses and my moods, Paula.—

You!

Love and love

To Lilian

Carl[1]

1. This letter was written on a copy of the program prepared for the Wisconsin Social-Democrat Convention in June. At the banquet in the evening "Charles Sandburg of Oshkosh" gave a speech on "Our District Organizers."

107.

Wednesday May 20, 1908

Together—we-two! Yes—and ready for any luck! Everything else counts for so very little in comparison. Together! That's the only thing worth considering!—With you, my love, everything is Good. Without you everything would be *Hell.*

The world looks good to us! Such a glad mad sweet world!—And whatever crag-born agony may come to us, the world will still look good—we will see the meaning and understand and love the more for it.—

You—Heart—so near—You—my boy—my boy—we-two, boy and girl—one heart—one life. These two mad feverish days together—such days to look back to and live over again!—But what will the real life together be—when the days lengthen into weeks, and weeks into months, and months into years—always together! together! No feverish haste then—but time for the whole garment of love to be snug! Time and time enough in the eons together!

My Love—my Boy—I kiss you—and love you—and always it is more love, more kisses—never enough!

My Boy—Sweet!

Goodbye from Paula

108.

Thursday—May 21, 1908

I'm sending herewith Elsie's letter to which I referred in Chicago.—One point in it demands elucidation! the allusion to "that comedy of the cheerful yellow back." It was a French erotic comedy. Elsie was studying up French as that's the language at social affairs in Greece. So she sent to a book-store for some modern French comedies as they would be largely *conversations*—and conversational French was all Elsie wanted. Among these comedies was one *turrible* yellow-back comedy, all about the Nuptial Night! And the climax was referred to euphemistically as "La Mystere delicieux et redoubtable"—the delicious and redoubtable mystery!—We laughed much over this comedy. Elsie read it and said it was no good. So I didn't actually read it, but she reported the general drift of it.—And it was ludicrously funny to think of her reading a novel about the nuptial night in order to acquire French vocabulary for polite social intercourse in the salons of Athens! As if that would be a likely subject for conversation!—Yes—we had lots of fun over "that comedy of the cheerful yellow back!"

I'm also inclosing a letter you sent me some weeks ago. I found it cleaning up my desk. I had written some comments on the letter—rather unsympathetic and so didn't send it back to you.—But I'll send it now anyway. The comment has some sense to it—and it's all right since I recognize that it is only *one side* of the question. A mood, merely a passing mood. Significant, as such to you who must come to know all my moods—the savage ones too!—Here in these comments I'm savage.—Today in a different mood I'm big enough to forget to be critical and see the *positive side* of H.L.C.[1] She's a happy heart—good for her! And God bless her! Amen!—

This letter is written "at Home"—The Chicago "Home" is with me still. Home! and Home! Cully is here. I laugh to him and play with him and speak to him and throw my arms around him and listen to his low sweet resonant Voice calling me "My Girl"—and I answer "My Boy."—

And I'm happy—happy in our Home! Mickey teases—and Cully says "Now for the Parcel's Post" and Carl's eyes look at me and call "Paula—Paula!" Oh—it's a Home! Such as never was before! Our Love-Home—our cave for two wild hearts, boy and girl together!

Dear, I send admonitions to take best care of yourself. Soon I'll be present in person to see to it! You, dear! Soon and soon—

Paula loves you and kisses You—You!—Good-night!

1. H. L. Caskey, Elsie's husband.

109.

[May 22, 1908]
Friday

I have your note with love and love—My Boy knows how to throw me kisses so they arrive! arrive across the miles! and bring throbbing joy! Such a Heart My Boy is! My Cully!

Of course T[1] couldn't be expected to see how the S-S would make it. But we *will* make it someway somehow! The way to learn how is to jump in and swim! We'll not learn by standing on the shore and speculating about what swimming would be like! No-one has ever tried it before—what we are going to try to do! We-Two are unique—so who can advise us?—And as you say we shall dissipate doubts and misgivings not by explanations but by actions—we shall *do* the impossible. And T will sit up some! And glad too—he'll enjoy being shown and so will G[2]—they are the best possible sort—eager to see us win out—eager and anxious! Their doubts are all right—what must be expected from everyone outside the S-S unit!—We know. It's a question of life and death. If we-two can't make it go someway, somehow, then we've no business living at all! So! And Paula isn't meditating suicide!!! Paula knows we two *can* make it together. If we try one way and fail—we'll try another. In the end we'll make it, all right—If no other way then along the Starvation Road! Other great souls have won out that way! Browning recommends it when he blames the couples who wouldn't venture on that Road:

> Each life unfulfilled you see;
> It hangs still, patchy & scrappy;
> We have not sighed deep, laughed free,
> *Starved, feasted, despaired,—been happy.*

We'll try it *sans* starvation first, making some demands on the world. But once baffled that way, we'll not give up. Still it will be the S-S together—tho we find no other road open than Starvation Road. There's plenty of precedent! It was the road Marx took!—(Surely no good socialist will question the wisdom of the Marxian way of doing things! You doubting socialist comrades—maybe you think Marx was a celibate! maybe you think Marx had a comfortable bank account!!! Study the life of your Prophet!—and cease doubting!!)

I inclose you a letter from Ed—You will be glad to know there is a color photograph of "Your Girl" at the farm waiting for you. I think we'd better not try to send it on to you—for the plate might so easily break! But it's something to look forward to.—I haven't any idea of how these transparencies will look—so I'm eager and eager to see them. Something extra for June days! as if there weren't enough! (The Cup full to overflowing and there's more to come it seems!)

I'm getting a few more clothes made in view of the fact that we must live in a couple of dress-suit-cases for the summer. That means that I'll have to have a *few* things to serve *many* purposes. It puts out of commission for *this* summer many things that I have but that would take up to much space in the suit-cases. You won't forget to bring your cases with you when you come. I see a trunk is *out of the question* ("being as" our headquarters will be in "suit-cases," no fixed domicile with clothes-closet and trunks!). I'll manage to get all I shall wear the whole summer till September and the farm—in suit-cases—1½ suit-cases and a bag!—

Everything I'm buying is of very good quality—which means much money spent—but I'll have clothes to last some time for all and any occasions—

(If we should try Starvation Road, Carl dear, we could pawn the clothes! See? So in any event they're a good investment!) Anyway I'm not *planning* for Starvation Road. Only I say it would be pretty good business—if nothing else offered! The point is *anything* would be *good, so good*—provided we-two were together. We will try to live 'comfortably,' because so we can reach the masses best—do work for the S.D.P. best. Good agitators are sufficiently fed and decently housed and well clothed. So these things we demand. But if the demand is not met with a supply—why our work of agitation will have to suffer for the time being. But at least we will *live*. We can live gloriously on *any* road that we take *together*—Starvation Road or any other. And if we *do* have to take Starvation Road, not only will we-two be happy then & thereafter—but in the end we'll get away from it and serve the movement too. But apart our happiness would go to the dogs—and so would our serviceableness to the Cause.—

Without being together—life is simply *unthinkable* for the S-S—

And we're going to do great things for the Party this summer! We'll show 'em! Gee—it'll be fun—When the "She-devil of a socialist" is along! We'll do things up fine! That'll be the Answer!

Love and love
to Carl

from Paula

P.S. This will be my last letter addressed Sheboygan. The next goes to Oshkosh.

1. Carl D. Thompson
2. Winfield Gaylord.

110.

Saturday Night

Have looked thru "The Metropolis"—reading a chapter here and there. I really thought The Jungle was great—so I wanted to give "The Metropolis" a fair showing—else I should have thrown the book aside after the first chapter.[1] Sinclair is a perfect Baby to write *so* of New York. He doesn't know what he's talking about. How naive it all sounds! Sinclair's a Baby! a Baby!—And a man has no business being so simple of soul as all that!—What's the use writing such a stupid vulgar book? And why does the socialist press boost it more or less?—Rot! and Rot!

No, Sinclair isn't an artist. Not one character in the book is a live individual. All are types! "The Greedy man" or "The Glutton"! Unrelieved abstract metaphysical types! No blood in their veins! No individuals!—And the villains (Such lots of villains too!) aren't they of the blackest dye tho! not a human trait in them! They're just pure and simple VILLAINS!

Goodbye, Sinclair of the Metropolis! I liked you all right when you wrote about the poor—you seemed to know and love them. But the millionaires you *don't* know! You don't appreciate! That's where you show that you're a small man, Sinclair. Only petty men believe in a Devil. And you believe in a whole class of Devils! Poor Sinclair!

Besides the book is so "unpleasant"—to no purpose.—*To No Purpose.* Unpleasantness is fine, when it takes you to some destination, when it has purpose. Like Shaw's *Plays Unpleasant.*[2]

Goodbye—Sinclair—I'm beginning to wonder whether the Jungle would seem so good on second reading!—

In III weeks the III. Convention! There was the Men. Falls Konvention! Then the Chicago Konvention! Now III weeks ahead, No. 3.—the Milwaukee Konvention! And not III weeks either—no—II and a half. Such Conventions we have! But then we are so Konventional—you know!

(This I'm saying to get those three slaps on my forearm! for I couldn't earn them by calling you a mystic for what you said about Christ and Galilee—which was *realistic* not mystic. So.)

I'm off downtown now—to the dressmakers! These things take time too you know!!—

Sunday on the lake shore Paula should have been along—loafing with Cully!—and at Neenah working with Carl—Paula wants so hard to be along.—

II and one crooked finger meaning "one half"—

Good! Ain't it? Love and Love to My Boy

Lilian

I send under separate cover article from Everybody's an account of the photos by Ed.[3]

1. Elsie Caskey in Athens felt much the same about *The Metropolis.* She had not read it, merely some reviews that included excerpts, but that was enough. She wrote to my mother: "I read some extracts in a review in some magazine from the book on New York written by the 'Jungle' man, and suffered a severe shock, for I took the 'Jungle' in a rather heart to heart way, you know, and even now thinking of the awful scenes in it gives me a heart-ache. *Well*—if he observed the packing-houses in the way he did New York, I fear that his evidence is vitiated and yellow. Not that it makes any difference in the fundamental principles, only that it disgusts one with human nature. That man, what's his name? Sinclair? seemed to be so *sincere,* straight from the shoulder and real."

2. George Bernard Shaw's *Plays Unpleasant* were *Widowers' Houses, Mrs. Warren's Profession,* and *The Philanderer.*

3. The June 1908 issue of *Everybody's Magazine* had an article titled "Roose-

velt—Taft—La Follette on What the Matter Is In America and What to Do About It" by Lincoln Steffens, with "Photographs specially taken by Eduard J. Steichen" of President Theodore Roosevelt, William Howard Taft, and the White House.

III.

[May 24, 1908]
Sunday

Sandburg number of Vanguard "Honeymoon" number of S.D.H.—we're doing things! Sure! Give a Rouse!

If the Herald Special is to come out the 27th—that'll mean some hustling for you meantime, won't it?

And when would the Vanguard Special come out? Or is that indefinite?—

Yes—I'd have enjoyed Gaylord's "Good! You won't be sorry"—Gaylord is a trump. The S-S says that Gaylord is *all right*. He knows!

And so Thompson is to do the "splicing."—We'll not decide quite yet whether it's to be at the farm or in Milwaukee. The main objection to the farm is that a few people would be hurt if they were left out. Query: Why leave them "out"? There would be no objection to a farm wedding if we had besides Joseffy & Thompson, Miss Thomas, Mr. & Mrs. Mayer[1] (the artist and his wife—good friends of mine who are *all right* except that they're not socialists out & out, tho Louis voted nearly the whole S.D. ticket this spring and they are "sympathizers"—and *good* folk for the rest.—Louis is really an *artist*, you must see his wonderful pictures, mountains and lake things in particular—they're great! We'll see the Mayers someday this June—the paintings and the baby included!—They would enjoy violin and humor and all—Louis might do some "general" stunts himself—he's a bohemian and is capable of wild things when the mood is on him. Joseffy would probably enjoy Louis too!) After this long parenthesis I take a deep breath and resume my catalogue of friends who ought to be invited to the wedding if it's to be at the farm: Miss

Thomas, Mr. & Mrs. Mayer—Mr. Delère[2] (an old family friend—who wouldn't mix well, but it's not likely that he could come on a Saturday as it's a workday for him—still he'd have to be asked—You must meet him too—he used to be awful good to Ed and me when we were kids—very like a real father in many ways—and again like a big brother. I wouldn't hurt him by leaving him out—but I'd hope he wouldn't be able to come because he'll not feel at ease with the Mayers etc. He has voted the Soc. ticket the last nine years! but he's agin' the soc. just the same. There's no convincing him because he isn't the kind of man who "gets ideas" or lets "ideas get him"—He lives on facts, separate unrelated facts. He is incapable of accepting a "faith"—soc. or other)—Miss Thomas—the Mayers—Delère—Mr Whitnall[3] (I expect Mrs Whitnall will be on her way to Europe, so she won't have to be invited—tho if she were in Mil. mother would say she'd have to be invited along with Mr. Whitnall.—Mr Whitnall would mix, all right, in fact first rate. Joseffy & the Mayers would like him and so would you—he'd contribute some sallies of wit too!) (However, come to think of it, Whitnall probably couldn't get off on Saturday either—So that would be another *necessary* invitation, probably *declined*). I guess that's all—tho I believe Victor L. B. would expect to be invited! In fact I think he ought to be invited if Miss T. is—and she would have to be. And it would be all right. Yes. He'd mix too—but wouldn't his presence interfere with Thompson's pleasure? Would it? No—no—I've seen the two together socially having a fine time!—You see then the probable guests would be:

Joseffy
Thompson
Thomas
The Mayers
Berger

And even this short list would probably be cut down by some not being able to come. Berger probably wouldn't come—tho he'd want to be asked. The Mayers might not be able to come on account of their baby—in fact come to think of it—it's almost certain that Mrs Mayer at least couldn't come, for the baby needs her for food! (But Louis might come alone—tho he rarely goes anywhere when May is kept home).

I'm afraid Miss Thomas wouldn't mix well—with Joseffy and Thompson! Tho—who knows?

(Does Cully?)

I don't want to hurt Miss Thomas—(she introduced us too!)—and Miss Thomas and I have been very chummy. I visited with her about five days last Xmas vacation—and she was out at the farm two days last summer and we planned *(then)* for her to spend a week at the farm this summer! So you see—it simply *won't* do to have a farm wedding unless we do invite Miss Thomas.

You see how matters stand. A Milwaukee wedding is *very* simple to manage. We could take Miss Thomas along with Joseffy to Thompson's house and let the two of them be witnesses. The job would be over so soon that the question of compatibility of the witnesses wouldn't cut any ice (Gee! What slang for Lilian!) And it would give Miss Th lots of pleasure.—and she has loving kind eyes—have you ever noticed?—she must have looked very kindly that time when she seemed solicitous about us!—Of course mother would be along too.—

Now the farm wedding I like better in many many ways. What do *you* say? How does the idea of a farm wedding strike you—now that you see what people will have to be invited extra? There's one thing about inviting people that struck me just this minute. That is presents! Most of the people I mentioned have sense enough to know that asking them to the wedding doesn't mean that presents are desired. Still a few might. Berger is conventional enough to take that view!—And maybe a few others would feel that they *ought* to.—That would be *unbearable!*—You know weddings are commonly regarded as a sort of hold-up game!

What do you say to *this* awful possibility! I guess Milwaukee is best! And yet—maybe we could write the invitations in such a way they'd all know we weren't "holding them up" for wedding gifts! Berger is so obtuse about little things—it might be necessary to write plainly in the lower left-hand corner: "No presents accepted"![4]

And so for each person—whatever we thought necessary—a hint for one person—no warning at all to those who would understand anyway. See?

Not that I have any bigotted narrow notions about wedding gifts. Delère will surely give me something—and I won't frown at him and say "No presents accepted!"—It's different with Delère—it's his way—and he has known me so long—has always given me Xmas presents etc—just like one of the family—only *more so*—that is he's more for giving presents being old-fashioned—It will come natural from him—not as a hold-up at all—He gave me things when I was a *little* kid and he's kept it up—and so he has the right.

As for the Mayers, they know me so well—and Mr Whitnall too—they will understand that we're inviting them FOR A WEDDING FESTIVAL & not to bring gifts. They will understand without a doubt.—The Socialists are the ones I'm worrying about—Berger & Miss Th—But we'll give Miss Th a broad hint and Berger an out and out warning in plain English—

So—Cully—this spectre of Wedding gifts need not deter us from the farm wedding!—

What do you say?

I haven't written to mother saying I don't want rings—but I will. If she cares much about it—you get the kind you mentioned—that will wear thru the ceremony!

And say, Cully—do you want printed announcements! Have you a long list of acquaintances whom you wish to inform formally that you have entered the bonds of matrimony??

I haven't any such list of *personal* friends—but maybe mother will want announcements to send to family friends—it's the usual way, you know! And maybe mother will think it isn't a real marriage without! She hasn't broached the subject yet—but she will—or at least I expect so.—How is it? I remember Elsie had a list of several hundred *personal* friends—and her family had a much longer list!—Maybe you are like Elsie in this respect!—Are you?—Or are you like Paula who hasn't any such formidable list. The few people I want to know it, I'll *write* to. Unless you & mother both want announcements—in which case I may send off a few on my own account.—I laughed at Elsie—and she laughed back at me—and we agreed that it was all right to be *different* on such a non-essential.—

Eight Sundays ago we were in the woods alone together! for the first time! And the Parcel's Post was inaugurated! Cully!—Last Sunday we were together—so near—boy and girl in each other's arms.—Three Sundays hence, the Convention. Four Sundays hence, we'll be one day married!

Time! How it passes—and will pass—whereunto?—Whereunto?

Love and love to Carl

from
Lilian

1. My mother had always admired Louis Mayer's paintings, and a few years before had written enthusiastically to a friend, Miss Laura Bliss Lane:

> I've seen Louis Mayer's *Spes*—also a portrait of a girl—, and the "Man is even as a blade of grass—and the glory of man even as the flower of grass" (you know the two heads).
>
> *Spes* means most to me—it is *infinitely good.* The wide reaches of the landscape infinite like nature. The pink clouds absolutely the most luminous I have ever seen except in heaven—these alone would give a sentiment of Hope to the painting. Then the figure of the girl in the shower of apple-blossoms—how she seems to melt in a rapture of Love! and Hope!

My father was later impressed by Mayer's paintings, particularly some of the lakeshore paintings in winter, and he wrote a poem about these, "Louis Mayer's Ice Pictures" (*Breathing Tokens*). Louis Mayer also did a portrait of my father when they lived in Milwaukee.

2. Mr. Delère was another Luxembourger, perhaps one reason why he was an old friend of my grandmother and grandfather, and he was a long-time friend to my mother and father.

3. Charles Whitnall.

4. Since they had the Milwaukee wedding, and in such haste that none of these guests were able to attend, there were no wedding presents.

112.

Monday

At last I have found it—a book that comes near to expressing my socialism. "Hurrah for Jaures!" I knew he was much to the good but I had no idea so great oratory, with so fair logic, serious facts, & sublime sentiment, was in the world-movement anywhere. His oratory I know of scarce anything else to compare with—& his written papers, they please me. He has *sentiment,* Paula. Sentiment!

In so many, so sadly many, socialist souls, the facts of science buzz on the window-pane and the roses of sentiment never flower.

Good-will, something of faith, tt is fine, this Wis. movement has, but the sentiment, ardor, flowing, glowing enthusiasm of Jaures—not yet.

Who in the American movement has dared to write on the topic, "Moonlight?"—J. is the only sclst writer, aside from C. S., who matches you, Lilian, in exclamation points!

Jaures! the S-S greets you!

113.

[May 25, 1908]
Monday

Your letters from the district have in them the whirl of real life—hurricanes—tornadoes—breezes—gales—Good! Here in Princeton there is a dead calm. Nothing doing in the way of *real* things. Plenty of busy-work. And that's all. Two and [a] half weeks more of Princeton for me. I'm beginning to shake its dust off my feet—so eager am I for Good-byes! I'd like to start packing my trunk right now.

I wasn't meant for this life of inaction. I wasn't meant to waste my life on a becalmed sail-boat! idly looking to the East & the West and the North and the South—just *looking* but not *moving* in any direction.—I was made to be a sailor-girl sailing on rough seas with a proud sailor-boy, glad of the high wind and the work of sailing our vessel true! Ho! Heigh-ho!

Such hearts for all sorts of weather we have! We-Two—sailor-boy and sailor-girl—We love the sky—fair or stormy—We love the waters storm-tossed or rippling gently under safe breezes—Only we can't stand being becalmed—inactive. No tropic ease for us! North seas for us—children of the North! North seas with winds and gales and hard weather too—the ever-changing North Seas—skies now blue and fair, now black and lowering! Ho! Heighho!

To the Sailor-boy—the true, proud, glad, mad sailor-boy—love and love from the heart of the Sailor-Girl. We stand on deck amid the spray and the wind (*salt* spray and an *eager* sea-wind), dressed in rough work-a-day sailor clothes, my arms are tight around your neck and you are folding me close and sailor-boy and sailor-girl are kissing each other—free and glad under the wild great sky!

114.

[May 26, 1908]
Tuesday

Just a wee note, dear sailor girl. I'm plugging away at several things now, that I want to get out of the way before the bigger togetherness begins. You know what the Bigger Togetherness is.—These things will all help toward the building of our machine up here.—Yes, buy *good* clothes—they can be hocked in emergencies. People enjoy a certain carelessness in dress about a man, the which is unforgiveable in a woman.—I could do a lot more of effective work if here and there at times, I could shift parts of the job onto somebody. 'Twill be fun seeing how Paula likes the job, what parts she will take to best—O we will make good! But it will be fun getting ourselves assigned to the various parts of the ship—

Good-bye—dear sailor girl—the Son of the Vikings loves and loves her—Two hearts for wayfaring and for sailing—proud, reckless and bold—Difficulty we will know—But defeat—never—never! Free and large and lavish, we shall insolently and triumphantly sail and sail—

115.

Tuesday Night

So that's the sort of Boy *You* are! You! You rip out a section of Ensor[1] to take with you to study! Haven't you any respect for books? Don't you know that books must be handled with reverent care? Are you going to shatter the last idol—you Iconoclast, You!—H'm—So books are to be ripped up! You seem to think that books are for *actual use,* instead of for ceremonial worship!

Cully!—Gee, but I'm glad you're not afraid to rip a book up. You're no mystic book-worshipper! You've met that sort of people tho surely. B is of that type. Books are kept in painfully perfect condition. His library looks like a book-store—the books are so carefully handled, they look unused. That's fetishism, says Kitty Malone—who loves the thought in the books with all her heart—but feels no reverence for the paper and type and binding!

Still, Cully, save the pieces! Paula will want to read Ensor! I got a few peeps into the book thru Thompson at the time the book was out of print so I couldn't get it.[2]—And now I'll wait to read your ripped-up copy. So save the pieces! It ought to be the sort of book that one refers to again and again! So don't rip it to death! Save the pieces!—You proud bad mad dear Boy!

About the Weddin'—I've thought a little further on the subject—and I still feel that if we have a farm wedding we ought to invite Miss Thomas *as witness!* It wouldn't be called a "wedding," tho, and so all the rest could be left out without hurting anyone's feelings. Just the family, minister and witnesses! It would go all right. The Mayers won't care about the ceremony (tho they wouldn't like to be left out if they thought we'd invited other friends generally) and I'll ask them to come out some day the week we're at the farm. B and Wh—won't mind—under the peculiar circumstances they'll not expect it. Delère I'll ask informally but he can't get away on a Saturday I know. So it'll be just Joseffy, Thompson and Miss Thomas.

Yes I really think Miss Thomas ought to be included whether it's to be at the farm or at C.D.T.'s—

Now I like the farm best—so do we all seem to. What do you say to leaving it to Thompson to decide (without his knowing it!). You ask him to do it at the farm. If he seems pleased—doesn't plead that he's too busy—why that settles it. But if he shows that he'd rather not give the time for it, then we'll have it in Milwaukee. Thompson could come on train leaving Mil. at 9:00 arriving Men. Falls 10:30. Or he could leave Milwaukee at 11:10 arrive Brookfield at 11:30—reach the farm about 1 after a 6-mile drive.—In either case there would be time for dinner and ceremony and talk till 5 o'clock when he'd have to leave the farm to drive to Granville or Brookfield to make a train arriving Milwaukee about 7 P.M. There's very little choice about the return train—as there are *no* late afternoon trains—but trains from both Brookfield & Granville arriving Mil. about 7.—

You & Thompson get it settled at the Convention. That will be time enough. It's up to Thompson.

And tell me what you think about having Miss Thomas too. As for the rest I mentioned in an earlier letter, that was a semi-demi conventional-social, overly big-human mood: the rest are out of the question. (Unless you particularly *want* them). (Nothing is out of the question that you happen to want!)

What do you say?

Do you know, Cully, this week is half over—then next week—and the Week after we meet again! So really there's only one week—one full week—apart! Ingenious mathematics! Paula's a shark! Sure!

Anyway it doesn't seem long—

Goodnight—You—Heart—I kiss your lips, your hair—and—Good-night!

Paula

1. Robert Charles Kirkwood Ensor (1877–1958), an English journalist, historian, and poet, was an ardent socialist and Fabian. He edited a book of socialist speeches, which was published in 1904 under the title *Modern Socialism*.

2. *Modern Socialism* was reprinted in 1907.

116.

May 28—1908

I've written mother urging "no rings" on the plea that I gave up wearing rings about 10 years ago because they seemed to me relics of barbarism on a level with ear-rings and nose-rings!—I'm waiting to hear mother's reply.

I'm going to try to get that Woman & Socialism leaflet written over Saturday. I ought to have found time before. But always there's something else that seems more pressing. I've had lots of letters to write—to the farm & to Ed—long ones. And then school-work—and getting clothes made—Clothes do take a lot of time. You can't have any idea of it because you're a mere man and get your few simple things *ready-made!*—Then I have a few social obligations even to Princeton!—especially in view of the fact that I want to enlist the goodwill of a few prominent club-women who may help us get a lecture-date here next year. Maybe this is wasted effort tho—Princeton is so immersed in the past—lectures on Shakespeare or Virgil would be more to their liking—and given by an accredited Ph.D. (damphool)—Still I'm taking the trouble to be social with them—and it may count. The chance is worth considering.

But I *am* going to get down to the writing—Sure! Now I'm off downtown to the dress-makers and a few other necessary errands. Then this evening maybe I'll be able to make a start on "Women Must Enter Politics"—Prosit!

We are working the wireless system hard these days—I find the service excellent! So easy to get you! And such swift and sure replies! Letters are but a small part of our actual communication!

From girl-vagabond to boy-vagabond—love and love—and a long kiss lips on lips.

Lilian

Saturday it will be II[.]

117.

[May 29, 1908]
Friday

Sure—Cully—we are the sort that are in a hurry. We'll make good in the long run in a big all 'round way. And it's fun!—only "You & me" are on the inside of the game and *know* what's coming! We know—so we can wait till we're ripe—we know we'll ripen all right in good time. Others may doubt—who cares! And some day we'll show 'em!

Fate intercepted my work last night. Callers came—stayed till ten—then I watched the storm—a "beaute" it was—for a half hour and turned in tired sleepy.

To-night the Seniors give a banquet to faculty and juniors 7-11! (There's to be dancing etc after the feed). Last Friday it was the Juniors giving a spread to faculty and seniors! Pabulum and pabulum & feed!—All of which means waste of perfectly good time—Sorry!—but can't be helped—Soclsm & Woman will have to wait!

Two weeks from to-morrow the Convention!!

Carl, Carl! I send you kisses—and yearnings. I want so to be along—side by each we-two! Just to feel conscious each of the other's presence! Carl!

Love and love
Your Girl

118.

May 30—
Saturday—Night

Carl—

Sit up and listen—Paula or Lilian or Liz (I don't know which) has something to say:

All this blessed day I've tried to write "An Appeal to Woman." Have scribbled and scratched my head and sat and thought and read and scribbled some more. And just now—after this day of it—I've made up my mind that it's no use. As far as the Cause is concerned I might a great deal better wash dishes in a restaurant and out of my wage contribute a wage-earner's mite toward the party funds! Any leaflet that I could grind out would be but a poor piece of work—the thing has been done better already than I could possibly do.—As far as my own happiness is concerned, I might again a great deal better be a dish-washer in a restaurant. There would be some fun dish-washing for *that* I could do and it's always a pleasure doing a thing you *can* do.

It's no use.

I've been thinking it all over—all my literary efforts from the time when I was ten years old till now. I always had to grind every sentence out. As far as literary expression goes I'm about as defective as I could possibly be, considering that I have good powers of appreciation. I am naturally a Silent Person, says Flavia. I haven't the gift of gab, says Kitty Malone.

This is a solemn declaration—a Pronunciamento!

You must understand, even if the rest don't. About the rest I care very little—whether they understand or not. But *You,* Carl, You must understand me *as I am.* You mustn't have any illusions about me. See? Else you would be loving some Paula-phantasm—not the real Paula—not *me.*

I shall never write for print. I feel as sure of this *now* as of anything that refers to the future. Absolutely positive.

As far as I am concerned it is settled. I'm glad that it's settled. Tho it's a disappointment—for from childhood I had "literary aspirations."—I'm glad it's settled nevertheless. I'm glad I know, so I can give up trying. For it makes me unhappy to be trying and trying to do what one can't do.—The problem of life is to find your sphere—find what you *are* qualified to do and then do it. When you're working at what you *are* qualified to do, work is a joy, though it be only sewing on buttons. But trying to do what is beyond you is sheer agony.

Now I have before made up my mind not to try any more to write. You know it. I wrote you that before this.—Several times I made up my mind "finally" and then someone would unsettle me. Last summer Miss Thompson unsettled me—she didn't convince me, but just unsettled my *sure* conviction that I couldn't write.—And now again *you* unsettled me.—

But it's over now—the doubt. I'm *sure* of myself. Sure I'm no writer. I'll never again try to write. If I ever write again it will be because I have something to say and feel that *I've got to express it*—as I feel about writing letters. Spontaneous expression. Play Art.—But, remember, I feel positive *that time will never come* when I shall feel this spontaneous need to express myself in writing for print. I'm positive of it.

Oh, a committee report—Something of that sort I might do—where the *idea* and not the *expression* was the main thing.[1] My *ideas are* I believe worth while. I have faith in my *reasoning powers*—but not in my powers of expression, for I have none.

Do you understand, Carl? This means somewhat. It's a serious matter. You must get readjusted to this decision of mine—this new revelation of what I am—this new self-knowledge I'm sharing with you. You *must understand.*

I write no leaflet. I write no review of Hunter's Socialists at Work. I write *nothing* for print—not *now* nor hereafter.

So.—

You see—we're beginning to find out what parts of the work I *can't* help you in.

Now for what I *can* do. Set speeches I'll be able to make—for I *have* made them. And I can lead a discussion![2] And I can help with the correspondence.[3] Also I'll be able to sell literature—tho *what degree* of success I'll have in this we can't tell till I actually try it this summer. But I've sold hats—so I ought to be able to sell literature about which I know so much more! and for which I feel a tremendous enthusiasm! So.—And general organization work I ought to be able to do. So.—

Now do write me that you understand. And be sure first that you *do* understand—that you understand that I shall never do any writing for print—not reviews, nor leaflets, nor newspaper work etc. etc.—*You* must understand because *"You are Me."* If I understood but you didn't—don't you see that would mean separation into "Thee and Me," the molecule breaking up!—You would not seem so near me—for you would be nearer a phantom-girl, an illusion, a not-me (who writes!)

I feel greatly relieved.—To know one's limitations is a good and necessary thing for effective work in life. Now that I know what I can't do, I shall put more determination and whole-souled devotion into the work I *can* do.

14 days hence—the Convention—flipping the penny—etc. etc.—II—Two weeks—and we see each other—and find each other dearer than we hoped!—Carl at Chicago was dearer than Carl at the farm. The more we know the more we love. The acme is always ahead. We'll never reach the mountain peak! (There'll never be the other side—the down-grade!)—Always you shall be dearer and still dearer at each further revelation! You—Carl—You whom I may love with all my powers—unreservedly! So that I am really

The Happiest Girl

(because I'm Your Girl)—

Cully—that $4.00 makes it 34.00. But you let me put 6 to it and call it 40.00. It won't be "me" that's putting the 6 to it—*you saved me that much in Chicago*—so the 6 are really from you.

So it's 40.00

1. Later, after they were married, my mother wrote a few of the Lake Shore and Fox River Valley notes for the Milwaukee *Social-Democratic Herald,* when my father was so busy during the campaign that he would have had some difficulty in managing this also.

2. She had done this in Chicago. Some of the socialist readings discussed at their meetings sound formidable. In a letter to Miss Laura Bliss Lane at that time she wrote: "We read and discuss [Antonio] Labriola's *Essays on the Materialistic Concept of History.* It just now occurred to me that very likely you would find the discussion more vital, more significant if you know more about the theory of critical (scientific) socialism."

3. Helping with the correspondence turned out to be a lifelong work.

119.

Memorial Day

I do not mourn the dead—they are dead.—Under the grass-roots the maggots have wrought the decay of their bodies. The graves of the dead mean little to me. I want life to mean more and death to mean less.—All these paradings and masqueradings to-day are a lesson in organization & agitation—which we can do when sentiment is aroused and educated and trained.

You—Paula—are the finest, cheering, beautiful thought I have to-day—not a memory only but a Life you are and an anticipation.

—You—Heart—

Carl

120.

[May 31, 1908]
Sunday Afternoon

This morning I received your Memorial Day letter—also Peggy and Pygmalion and the Remarkable Rocket—also a copy of Hunter's *Sclsts at Work.* So it was a great morning reading.

Wilde's story is as good as Alice in Wonderland. Sometime when we're off playing in the shack we'll reread Alice in Wonderland together. The poetry especially is great—And the Rocket is just as great, maybe greater because it's twentieth century stuff! So glad *you sent me The Rocket*.—Hunter's book is splendid. The *Turrible Kid* knows how to write. Sure. And what to write. Sartin sure.—You'll have to read the book from cover to cover-- it's the kind of book you want to *read thru*—it isn't enough to get the mere general drift of it.—Sure it's the best book on Socialism that's been *written by an American*.

After reading your letter and the stories, and reading a good deal, chapters here and there, in *Sclsts at Work*—I had breakfast-dinner. Shredded Wheat and soft-boiled Eggs (done on my alcohol lamp). A Fine Fletcher dinner.—After dinner a walk. Then I darned stockings. Then bath and hair-wash.—And here I am, my hair still wet, writing to Cully—

I guess I'd better dry my hair now—and leave off writing till it is dry! So Good-bye, dear.

More anon.

Paula

121.

Sunday Night

To resume—I dried my hair all right—then took a short walk—Back to my room—supper of shredded wheat with a few drops of olive oil and that's all—a one-course banquet! Then more of Hunter's book. Then letters, mostly business letters—orders—bills paid—etc etc—lots of 'em. Also a letter to Elsie. Now it's turning-in time, but first I want a few minutes talk with you.

When I was out walking this evening it came over me again—as it has so often before—what an *extra* measure of happiness is mine because I have you to love as you were when you were but a kiddo, besides having you-as-you-are-now to love. You must tell me more of the boyhood days—for I have memorial day wreaths of love to hang on the monuments of those past days. Every incident you tell gives that much more content—substance—to that love that harkens back to your past. Your past isn't a dead thing—for it lives in you to-day. To know you as you are today, I must know you well as you were ten and twenty years ago. It's my right. It's my right to love every inch of you—none shall escape me! You—You—My Boy—My Boy—Mine to love—Mine every corner of your heart and mind—Mine every inch of your body—Mine all your past—your present—your future—Mine to love!

Mine to love! Carl! My Boy—

I kiss your lips with love and love—and love (always "and love" to be added—always after I say love, I know that now it is already more love—so I add "and love")—

Good-night, dear—
Your Girl

122.

[June 1, 1908]
Monday night—
or rather Tuesday One P.M.

—Getting ready for the meeting to-night kept me from writing.—What the hell do I care whether you go in for literary work or not? Don't we each give the other free loose for anything & everything?—We go we know not whither—All I know is you are a great woman, a splendid girl—In some way you will express yourself—*YOU decide on the way*—For me to decide would be the same utter sacrilege as for anyone outside the S-S to decide *we* are unwise in our embarkation.—More on this, when we meet.—You tell me tt whatever way of expression I take for myself is best. What would I be to insist that I know the road of expression You should move along?

—Great you are—great, beautiful, inclusive, daring, quick, original. You are big enough to do as you dam please—I would rather be a poem like you than write poems—I would rather embody the big things as you do than carve or paint or write them—You inspire art—& tt's living!

Cully loves Kitty & Liz—& Carl loves Lilian & Paula—

You may cut out writing, but, Paula—please don't say you'll never pull my hair nor improve my MSS nor a hundred different things I'm too sleepy to name!

Love—Paula
Carl

123.

[June 1, 1908]

Dearest—Here's love and love to My Boy—

I tumble your hair and cover it with kisses and challenge the Parcel's Post to do its best and worst! Oh—it's a day—a DAY—for the Parcel's Post—a glad mild sweet day! June! What will June do to Two-Hearts that were mad in chilly March!?!

More to-night—Adios.

Lilian

124.

June 2

June! June! of roses and the and the WEDDING! Is here! Is here!

The June mornings—dawn—and earliest awakenings—birds shaking songs out freely from full throats and glad hearts—fresh dews on grass and flowers—morning odors sweet and cool—All—All—for Us-Two at the farm—in a couple of weeks or so! Tenting, I hope! So we can see the last glories of starry nights—and the first loveliness of Morning!—

June is here! is here! of roses and dew and birds and the WEDDING! June is here!

And we have another niece, Carl—a May-baby. The "little brother" who was to be called August after Rodin—turns out to be a little sister! (Will she be called Augusta?)[1]

I think two little girls are nice—don't you? But no one in the family seemed to think it could turn out to be a *girl*.

"Mother and child are doing well" says the cablegram. Wish we could see the little thing.

Goodnight and
Love and Love
Paula

1. There was some hesitancy about the name because Edward and Clara Steichen had not considered the possibility of a girl. Clara thought of naming

her Charlotte, after her sister, and Kate, after a friend. My uncle wrote to his mother and father at the farm: "She has a number of names—Charlotte & Kate and I generally call her Mike. I don't know which will last but—I guess we will call her Kate—after our very good friend Mrs. Simpson." However, they gave her as a second name Rodina, so that she was after all named for the sculptor Rodin.

125.

[June 5, 1908]

It's 4 o'clock, Paula, Friday morning. I have been plugging away since six o'clock last night—on the best thing I've done yet—the letter to Dear Bill—the homeliest, fairest, beautifulest piece of socialist literature, the nearest thing to Merrie England, yet done! Cuff the braggart, Paula!

A kiss to you—and now for sleep—

Cully

126.

[June 5, 1908]

Dear Carl—

Hello—and I'm pinching you *hard*—so you'll know it's me!

That's all—only love & love and Goodbye—A week from Sat. (tomorrow) we'll be together!

Paula

127.

[June 5, 1908]

Dear Heart: No word from you to-day by letter. No matter. We've been together all day just the same. I was hearing my classes for the last time—and Carl was marked "Present" with the rest! No absentees this last day.—We had flowers and flowers! Peonies Red—Pink and White! And Roses. And Roses. A deluge of them. No desk visible—or books or anything. Just a mass of flowers! Very sweet of the youngsters really.

I read them Russel's article about S. Carolina slavery—Contract Labor of Convicts.[1] Some of the girls wept! Some of the boys wanted to stay after 12 o'clock thru the dinner hour to hear the rest! What with the flowers and the interest in Russel's article—it was a day! What with Carl calling and calling to me—a sweet undersong: "One Week!"—it was a Great Day!

After school I mimeographed my exam questions for Monday. Now I'm thru supper—bread and pineapple—and waiting for Mrs. Kendall who will take me out to her home (18 miles in the country) for tonight and to-morrow. It will be a good rest—the drive and all.

Goodbye and Love
(and Love!)
Paula

1. Probably the "Report of Hon. Charles W. Russell, Assistant Attorney General, Relative to Peonage Matters . . . Oct. 10, 1907." This may have been something my father sent her.

128.

[June 7, 1908]
Sunday

Here's the cuff, you Braggart, you! Oh, yes Kitty has a strong *four*-ceps too!—You won't ask me to cuff your ears again, Mick, will you? will you?

We're dying to see the Letter to Dear Bill! Yep! *dying* to see it!—Now aren't you sorry you were such a braggart! that you aroused such fatal expectancy! You! Cully!

Oh—I want to kiss you! You!

I! and II!

I haven't told you what mother wrote in reply when I expounded *my* view of the wedding-ring. Mother's heart is set on it—not the ceremony—we could leave *that* out (I shall explode if we have *that!*)—but she thinks we ought to *wear* rings. And here's the reason mother gave: The ring is "an outward and visible sign" of marriage. Travelling, at hotels together etc, people will take *Us* for granted if we wear rings. If we don't wear rings mother thinks our relation will be misunderstood—especially because we're socialists. See? I hadn't thought of this point. I'm very unobserving about such things—never noticed whether or not anyone wore a wedding-ring. But I know it's different with some other people. And is it worth the candle to refuse to conform to the custom of wearing rings—when it may mean misunderstandings of that sort? Mother is more rational than the average person—if she thinks it so strange and so unnatural for us not to wear rings—won't the people in the district, more particularly the women, feel that something is lacking in the S-S!

Now the freer marriage is a question we don't want to provoke discussion about *now*. The world isn't ripe for it—at least not our little corner of the world: the District. So as long as we conform in all other things as far as essential conventions regarding marriages go—I say there's no use halting at such a little thing (so open to public view besides) as wearing rings. I say we cut out the ring ceremony—or perhaps better "cut it down" (for if we're to buy the rings to satisfy the conventional ideas of the District and Practical World generally—why we might as well give mother the extra pleasure of the ceremony—but simplified[)]. The tiniest excuse for a ceremony—as simple as Thompson can make it—will do the hocus pocus of making the rings "real weddin' rings" in mother's eyes.

Now mother herself wrote me very sensibly, stating her idea & reasons, but she said she didn't want us to have the rings on HER account. We shouldn't have them—unless her *reasons* convinced.

And that was right. For I could convince mother I think—and satisfy her—that rings are foolish. Only I don't think they're foolish myself now—the origin of the custom was barbaric of course. But with evolution of marriage the symbolism of the ring has changed. And you know the present symbolism—that is what the common people *today* consider the wedding-ring to symbolize:—a ring has no end, so marital love is endless; "till death do us part" that's the idea of the ring. To some common people this symbolism is definitely known—we were taught it at Catholic Sunday School! To most it's just a vague feeling:—a real marriage means rings somehow or other!

Now I know you are willing to let me decide a point like this. But I want to explain definitely why I've been won over to the ring-idea,[1] as a practical rational concession to the People.

For my own part I don't need any symbolism. I believe our love will outlive the stars—as you do. But neither of us believes in trying to chain love with promises of eternal fidelity. We don't believe in any promises. And we know that no promises of eternal love can make love last forever. Love *is* free: you *can't* chain it—it comes and goes freely—when it wants to go it shakes off easily all the chains that may have been put upon it and that seemed to hold it prisoner while it stayed in reality of its own free will.

All this we know. And I think the Ring, the wedding-ring that is, symbolizes to the people generally today not merely the *faith* that wedded love will last always—but the *promise that it shall.* So I don't like this symbolism. So personally I don't like to wear the wedding ring on this account (the barbaric origin of the custom isn't as sound an argument against it I think—for some customs that are right good now have been evolved from low origin)[.]

But we are not going to argue this question of the futility of *promises* of life-long love. It would hamper us in our chosen work. One thing at a time. Socialism is *the thing* now. We want to steer clear of other issues like religion, marriage, etc.

I know you agree with me about steering clear of these issues. And I think you will agree that in order to steer clear of the marriage issue—we'd better conform to all the conventions that the dear People consider essential. And the wedding-ring is such an essential.

Yap—we'll have to wear weddin'-rings to satisfy the prejudices of the *Proletariat*.

Now your buying the rings out of our starting-fund is out of the question—The Financial Sec'y says the funds cannot be so diverted—as the starting fund will be needed in full for starting!

So I say let me pay for the rings. We'll have to have gold ones as long as we're going to wear them—also mother will want them gold. Do you know whether $20.00 would buy them? If you think they'll cost more, write me how much. But you'll have to write so I get the letter *here* Tuesday. That is you'll have to mail it Monday. You see I *don't* want mother to know I'm buying the rings! Mother would think it very "unwomanly" of me! (Paula is chortling)[.] So I must pay for the rings—*but mother will take for granted that you do the paying*. I'll turn the money over to you at the convention—or better—I'll mail it to you—probably before I leave Princeton.

This is the sensible practical thing to do. You see that—pal—don't you?

You—dear old pal!—

Love and Love—
Paula

1. Nothing in any of these letters astonished me as much as this evidence of my mother yielding to my grandmother on the wedding ring. Certainly they were married without it. We all knew that she had no wedding ring but considered this part of her strong-minded ideas about the "barbaric symbolism" of jewelry that made her give away all her own as a young girl.

129.

Busy and busy—finishing up grades—backwork of delinquents—etc. etc. Such a turmoil and hurly-burly.—And besides trying to get off 2 freight boxes—books etc.

Busy and busy—

I would feel tired and dead but for the thought of You singing in my heart—You—You to love!—And love! And then it is not enough! You!

Paula kisses you.
ONE WEEK MORE

130.

[June 7, 1908]
Sunday

Sacred music to-day—free concert—wild rain & wind impetuous & proud—so. Classifying, reducing, selecting, getting the honeymoon baggage down to a minimum.—O! and O! such a 120 pounds to pay excess on! You're sure an Excess! Paula—You weigh & count—a lump of radium.—

—Comrade Thorn has been observing my habits & now holds tt the greatest point in favor of the tie-up is, tt I need someone to watch over me & keep me straight—"it will pay in the long run." You are to make me behave! You are to curb genius when it gets reckless—a big job—such fun it will be.—Paula, I have worked by *system* & I can do it again. Have several ideas & plans we will plug away at—so our love-idling may be much & often—yes—

Cully

131.

June 8

Dear Cully:

I have more light on the ring question. I've sounded Princeton—which is orthodox American A 1—This is the result. The man need not wear a ring—the woman must! We might scandalize even Hopie and other dear people in the district if I came ring-less. But *you* needn't! It seems that in Europe, at least on the Continent, bride & groom both always wear rings—but here in America lots & lots of men don't.

Of course it isn't fair that I should have to wear the ring & you not! It's the way of the whole darn system!

However—it's a trifle and the physical burden of the ring will be slight. Get a light-weight plain narrow band—the less gold the better—but real gold! I inclose $19.00 (what Cash etc. I happen to have handy) and you're to buy the ring, pal! Spend as little of the $19.00 as possible, and what's left we'll add to the starting-fund. A thin narrow band ought not to cost more than ten dollars. I say "ought"—for this dictum is on the ethical plane. On the practical business plane, I have no idea how much such a weddin' ring "ought" to cost. But I feel sure the concession will be worthwhile—smooth our way thru the district and this old conventional world generally! Remember narrow and thin—pal—for the ring isn't a "splurge"—it's a concession to bourgeois morals—and "an offering" to the Cause. The only reason I say "gold" instead of plated—is that I'll have to wear it a long time and the plating would wear off. It's like clothes—the best are the most economical. Besides mother is another reason.

So—

Yap—We'll have to go to church once in a while to prove we're not agin' the church. We must keep the economic-political issue clear of religious & moral issues. See?

Am off to the post-office. Will register this probably to insure safe delivery—

Love and love—in a hurry—

Paula

And you did *fine* work in the Herald May 30 issue. We're stuck up over it!

132.

Enclosed is Three. And Kitty, Honorable High Turnkey of the Exchequer, Kitty, be careful how you give me money—I am "a son of fantastical fortune" and a spender. We will buy what we need. The rest goes into your hands. Now, having sent you all my money but fifty cents, I have inclination to hustle.

Soon—I see your lips and eyes again—and the Two of Us call out, "Look who's here!"

Cully

P.S.—I send an MSS—don't know just what it's worth—may send it to the mags tt pay for stuff bfr letting the Soc's have it.

133.

[June 9, 1908]
Tuesday

Yesterday I sent you a registered letter to Fond du Lac. Hope you got it all right.

Have sounded a few more people on the ring question—and am surer than ever we ought to concede the point. Incidentally I learn too that the double-ring ceremony is *un*usual. So glad of that. For the practical reason that two rings would cost more—really! So much Mathematics I know—

The bursar reports that she has $40.00 on hand—our starting-fund. And when we add to it the balance that will be left from the $19.00 after you've bought the weddin' ring—our starting-fund ought to be nearly $50.

As long as we have the ring—we might as well have the one-ring ceremony if mother seems to care much about it. In her letter she didn't mention the ceremony—just my wearing the ring afterward. So I really don't know how she feels about it. Maybe she won't care for the ceremony. Maybe she will. It's a non-essential—a little mummery more or less doesn't matter—if it gives mother real pleasure. IF.

And remember my little contribution to the starting-fund and paying for the ring is a secret between us. Mother must not know of it. She wouldn't quite understand.—Anyway it's no one's business but our own. And we understand! We understand!

The news that I'm going to meet Mary & Esther has come.[1] Good! And Saturday is only 4 days off now! IV, Carl, IV! And we meet!

If it were a Saturday later—Mary & Esther might be at the Wedding![2]

And when I see them I'll want to say: And you were near Cully all the years when he was a boy—you ate with him—played with him—shared the common life with him for days and days and weeks and months and years! "How strange it seems"[3] and near—

I hope they'll talk about the days when you were kiddos together—I must know all about it and live it all over with You. For *your* past is *my* past—*our* past.

Now I must start to pack. I leave here at 6 A.M. tomorrow. Lots to do—between now and then!

I will reach the farm Thursday (for I stay over in Milwaukee shopping with mother from Wed noon till Thurs).

Address me there

RR 17, Menomonee Falls

Love and love to the Wunderkind (Gayeties of Jrnlsm is a good caption).[4]

Paula

1. The letter of my father's with this news is among the missing. His sister Esther had written to him, asking why he had not written and then suggesting that he come to Chicago on June 10 or 11 for a little family party with his sisters. Esther's letter is also missing, but his reply to her, on May 25, follows.

Oshkosh, Wis., 5/25/08

Dear dear Esther:—

Your notes about your recital have come to me. You know I'm glad about such things, your making good with your music and being able in art to give pleasure to your friends and the public. You wouldn't reproach me with not writing you if you knew how lean I am and how I am plugging day and night for socialism & the socialist party up here. You will come to see some day, my dear girl, why almost all the great artists, painters, musicians, & dramatists, are socialists or in sympathy with us. Socialism, if you will look into it, you will find means greater art—more of music for more people.

The 10th, 11th, 12th & 15th of June I am dated at Neenah, Chilton, Fond du Lac, and Schlesingerville, Wis. So I can't make Chicago at the time you mention, & as I have other appointments for the rest of June, I do wish you could arrange to come to Milwaukee for the S.D.P. State convention, the 13th & 14th. If you haven't had the lake ride from Chi. to Milwaukee, by all means take this chance to have it. You could take the boat from Chi. the morning of the 13th, getting to Milwaukee in time for the convention opening in the evening. Leaving Sunday night for "the lake by starlight" you could be in Chi. again Monday. This round trip would be $1.50 or $2.00 and $1.00 extra for berth. We ought to have some pleasant hours together, tho I will have some speaking & committee work to do at the convention. And you will meet some great people—people with fine hearts and big souls.—The most of the summer I will be in the farther northern part of the state, about Marinette & Sturgeon Bay, and as this is campaign year it means extra effort all along the line.

Next winter I am going to put in lecture courses in a number of towns up this way, at least five, maybe fifteen. I want to hear your star pieces. If you can only raise hell on the keyboard, in a way *to wake up and give enjoyment to an audience strange to you,* this is your chance to start into public concert work! Honestly, as brother talking to sister, I doubt whether you are reckless and proud and bold enough for public work. But maybe you have changed from a good, quiet, behaved girl into a genius! If you have I will be able to get you dates next winter up here, tho there would probably be hardly anything more than expenses the first season.

Yes—meet me in Milwaukee the 13th of June.

Charlie

Note that there is no mention of my mother in this letter. He seems to have planned a surprise for Esther and Mary. Esther apparently wrote that they would come, and then he wrote to my mother.

2. Since his sisters could not come at that time but wanted very much to be at their brother's wedding, the date was changed to June 15, a Monday evening. After the ceremony Mary and Esther took the night boat back to Chicago.

3. "How strange it seems" is from Robert Browning's "Memorabilia."

4. "Gayeties of Journalism" was later published in the *Social-Democratic Herald*. I found it interesting to see how my mother here adopted his shorthand system of eliminating vowels.

134.

Oshkosh—6/10/'08

Am staying over here because I had openings with the unionists. Was before the electrical workers last night and will have an hour with the trade council to-night.—I send along Miss T's letter. She's just a bit afraid I'm not up on fundamentals. So she explains tt I am not headed nor' by east but nor' by nor' east!

Oho! Kitty Malone—3 days—3 days—Oho!—you'll be put to it—hard put to it again—no good to run nor dodge—You will find yourself surrounded so you can't get away.

Love—And Love
Mickey

135.

Enroute Mil to Men Falls
Thursday—

And I didn't write you yesterday!—My boy isn't getting what's coming to him these days!—Mother and I have been shopping in Mil since yesterday noon and we're fagged out completely—the mother is exhausted—and Paula is done up too.

Will write you from Men Falls to Milwaukee *General Delivery* so you can get it early Sat. morning.

We probably will reach Mil. 9 A.M. Sat.—Union Depot.

Goodbye—and
Love
Paula

Afterword

On the day of the convention, Saturday, June 13, my mother and grandmother came by the morning train to Milwaukee at 9:00, as she had written him. Mary and Esther followed their brother's suggestion to come by boat on Lake Michigan from Chicago. They must have been surprised to meet a prospective sister-in-law, and both liked her very much. However, they were disappointed to hear that the wedding date was set for June 20, since they wanted to be present, but Mary's nursing job would not permit them to come then. My mother probably expected something like this, as can be seen from her letter to him when she first heard that his sisters were coming. To please Mary and Esther, they decided to have the wedding then, while they were in Milwaukee.

They were not prepared for this, since they did not yet have the license, and there was much to do in a short time. My father used to say, referring to this, "We really had to scurry around for the license." He wrote of "going with a beautiful young woman to the Milwaukee County Courthouse for a marriage license. There we learned that the license had to be procured in the county where the bride resided. So Lilian Paula Steichen, residence Menominee Falls, and I journeyed to Waukesha."

The ceremony was performed by Carl D. Thompson at his home, on Monday evening, June 15, with Kate Thompson (Mrs. Carl) and Olive Gaylord (Mrs. Winfield) as witnesses, with Mary and Esther and my grandmother present. Reminiscing, her eyes lighting up, my mother told me of an amusing incident at the time concerning the little Thompson boy, who was only about four or five years old, and very impressed on learning that a wedding would be held in their parlor. He went upstairs and took some artificial flowers from one of his mother's hats, then came down with them and offered them to my mother, saying that a bride should carry flowers. My mother, who detested artificial flowers, was very amused, and thanked him. She held them all during the ceremony, much to his satisfaction.

The honeymoon in Green Bay and the far north was not to be. On the day of the wedding my father received a telegram from his good friend Chester Wright, in Manitowoc, with some serious news; he and the Manitowoc *Daily Tribune* were being sued for libel by William Rahr, who had been criticized for his handling of the county fair. In this crisis Wright asked my father to take his place on the newspaper while he attended to the court case with his attorneys, Daniel Hoan and I. Craite. Not many men would have agreed to do this at such a time, but my father felt that if he refused, he would be letting down a good friend in time of trouble, so he went off to Manitowoc with battle in his eyes. My mother, though very disappointed at the time, thought that he was right to go, but she could not help wishing that Wright had asked someone else to take his place. However, she had to agree with Wright that my father was the best selection for the job, for many reasons. My mother was on the farm all that summer, and later on when he was on the campaign trail, making speeches for Eugene Debs, my father came there to rest in between meetings. It was not until fall, after the Red Special (the socialist campaign train) had passed through Wisconsin, that they were able to settle down in a couple of rooms in Appleton.

APPENDIX A

Juvenilia

The poems in Appendix A are mentioned by my mother in Letters 5 and 6 as the ones she liked best of those he sent her. The three poems in "An Autumn Handful," "The Pagan and the Sunrise," "The Rebel's Funeral," and "A Fling at the Riddle" were published by *To-morrow Magazine* in March and April 1905. "Fragments" and "Identities" are unpublished. Later my father referred to these poems as "juvenilia," and evidently did not think them worth including in *Chicago Poems,* although the "Other Days" section contains some early poems my mother liked and that are mentioned in these letters ("A Dream Girl," "All Day Long," and "Departures," with the title changed to "Docks"). "The Road and the End" is in a prominent place, heading a section with the same name. I found it interesting to note the tremendous improvement in his poetry from the time of the *To-morrow* poems to 1914, when Harriet Monroe accepted some of his poetry for *Poetry Magazine.*

An Autumn Handful

Perspectives
(Inscribed to Saugatuck)

Always in what I love
Is something yet beyond.
I see the lake expand,
The broad blue vista
Lures the gloaming and the dark.
The somber woodland rises
On the further shore
And cool-deep open places
Ask the wanderer to enter.
Transitions on the slopes occur,
And ever half-caught phantoms
Gesture from a hilltop.

But ever farther yet
Is meaning after meaning,
Shadowed in the onset
Of the dusk—over there
Where day-things vanish
Into silhouettes that also disappear.

Backyard Vagaries

Hollyhocks uprise erect and bold
And look wide-eyed to other lands
As though to pass by merely seeing.

Poppies flaunt their discs
And leer at all the weeds
With Oriental indolence;
Deft are they to offer thin red dollars
To the big white sun!

Mock-mournful brown-eyed Susans
Hush the queries of a bumble-bee;
Sunflowers tanned and hardy,
Gaze across the fence at pansies
Pampered in a tended, level bed.

In Illinois

In Illinois
The grass is at the richest of the year.
The rivers curve along the bottoms
Flashing silver faces to the sky,
Though underneath, the crawfish
Burrows far away from azure.
Yellow, scarlet, russet leaves
Spangle all the woodland—
Premonitions hover in the boughs.

The grapes are all empurpled,
Clusters hang along the trellises
Encalmed as though for some event.
Tomatoes redden in the sun,
As proud as any flower
Of their kinship with the soil.
The stalks of corn stand up like grenadiers
With blade and plume and flaunting tassel,
Enranked for battle, onslaught, hardship.

All the places of the air and earth
Seem shaken with expectancy
As though of something done, arrived.

Only now remains
The conquest of the Gatherers.

The Pagan and the Sunrise

Swarthy, dusky, dappled, alive,
Off in the East, reds and purples plash,
And beams of silver suspire and glow,
And a disc! huge, white, and glistering.

Wild and hot, a longing beats in me,
As some lone atom of the sea,
Cast up as spray might palpitate in mutiny.

I am looked at
By that silent, rising, vibrant Thing—
Pierced and quelled and hushed—
And I soothe and caress my stricken eyes
And dare no longer turn toward that Great Face.

The Rebel's Funeral

(An Arrangement in Red and Ochre)

He knew the lure of the Faraway
And where abysms riven deep in darkness were,
He talked across to gracious, wished-for things;
And some half-uttered, dusky honor called him,
Bell-like through a mist of outstretched arms;
He turned, headstrong, hilarious, gay,
He curled his lip and tossed his challenge,
Babbled oaths and launched a vow,
He who passes, recumbent, conquered, rotting.

He fought a fight with those forbidden things
From which we slink away;
He threw the gauntlet down to Law,
And thought to throttle all the Weariness of Life;
He gambled with the stalking Lords of Night
And was awarded for the chance he took,
A meteor!
No star, no sun, nor moon is his.

He fought, defied and gambled,
Bade care begone and laughed,
Then lost himself and wept,
Yet made his way as bold, abandoned musketeers,
With only lives to sell,
March on to bleed and freeze and starve
At haughty looks from damozels with roses in their raven hair.
    Erect, resourceful, sinewy,
    He yelled defiant jeers,
    Or whimsical, he stood—
    A statue! mute as bronze.

He understood not peace, compliance, nor submission,
His work was war, his gladness, battle,
And he found not what he sought;
So now he lies supine, sardonic, thwarted;
His fling with fate is done,
And the gods and the Lords of the Night laugh last:
But he took from them no common thrill,
He who passes, prostrate, vanquished, mouldering.

A Fling at the Riddle

I think to filch a story from the Sphinx,
Outface that old Egyptian questioner,
And cry, "Behold! I know! I know!
I know I do not know!"

Poignantly sad, and beautiful unspeakably,
That we must pass, that all must pass,
And change and pass away again.
Poignantly sad that noble man
With massive sinews girt with gladness,
And women fair as sunsets, morning stars and roses
Pure as frost-embowered grass of winter days,
Must pass into dust and be blown by the idle winds—
Into nothingness?

Into nothingness?
When mystery but threads back into mystery
And you may tumble wonders into space
And sound and plumb in seas of secrets
So you may learn that rocky bottoms bar you
From the nether seas, the seas on seas,
That underlie the oceans we traverse?
What ho! to think our eyes may span such fathoms!

One day despondent, shall you think
That Time and Things spell "Vanity"?
Next day the sun shall rise
So all the earth held atoms glow and tingle,
Madly thoughtless, moaning little sobs
Of thankfulness that this can be—
That here is Life! life! life!
Hurrying, glad, and endless,
New and ever-new, fresh and ever-freshening,
Throbbing and moving onward to change on change,
And men and women and valor and war and want,
And nowhere a soul despoiled and bankrupt
Of some dear fondling of a hope,
Some stray blithe romance, coming, coming, coming,—
Some shining gleam of a woman's hair,

Some trusty tone of a hero's voice,
Some palace, cottage, ship, or child,
Coming, coming, coming,
Coming from out of the great and beautiful Unknown.

Identities

I am back of the quiet bells of evening
And I am the bars of music unforgotten.
I hold the beckoning hand of the statue
And the poem you love, it unlocks me.
I pass into what you ask for
And come back with my outspread hands.
Out of the hurtling storms I teach you
And I am the ship you signal
Far in the dusk on the heaving sea.

Deep in the hearts of stalwart men,
Fair women, moss and stars,
I fasten the braid of thought and love.
Jailed and betrayed in clay,
I shall break and scatter your shape
And strong as the sun and free as light,
We shall roam and roam forever.

Call me no masquerader!
I was your shadow
When planets were blown to form.
I will follow you faithfully yet
In the wildest wrecks of things.
I will linger through halcyon ages
Embodied and glad with you.

I am your soul.

1907

Fragments

In a far time I was a cave-man,
Knew in my veins the snarl,
The crouch, the leap, the thrust and out,
And I made my way in a welter of blood,
Blood and tears and pain.

With the Aztecs I have bowed unmurmuring,
Glad that the sun-god lived,
Glad for the break and close of day,
Glad for an Aztec girl
And the tawny, shapely fingers
That slipped to my hand and held me.

I am a Pagan
And I with the Greeks and Romans
Toiled over rugged and lonely highways,
To triumph, luxury, ravishings.
I knew Phidias,
I stood by him and welled with longing
That the marbles were so mute,
That the loves, the passions, dreams,
Could be but weakly told in stone,
And he was a boy and smiled and said
He could not tell me whitherward.

I was a Goth and I was a Vandal,
Attila and I were friends;
We lived by slaughter and plunder,
We tumbled the gods of an arrogant folk,
We slashed in a nation's heart;
We believed a Story, followed a Cross,
And a man was a lord or a serf.

I am a Christian
And into my life is threaded
A thread from the soul of the Man—
The Man with the brow for thorn and blood.
I learned from him the worth of lilies
And a heart thrown loose, thrown free,
Thrown wide and whole to the world.

I am Columbus
And out over seas uncharted,
I sail my fragile and battered craft;
I may wear chains and languish,
I may fall sick, to brood and curse,
But though I reach no palm-fringed, coral shore,
I will have sailed!
I will have sped o'er the trackless blue,
I will have known the love of the sky,
Rouse of the sea and talk of the stars—
I will have sailed!

I have comrades, out on the seas,
Brothers valiant, dexterous, true;
Their crafts are moving over the tides—
What of the Indies we shall find?

1906

APPENDIX B

Related Letters and Socialist Prose

These letters and articles were written either just before my father and mother first met, toward the end of December, in 1907, or at some time during the period when the love letters were written. At one time or another they have referred to these articles, and this completes the picture drawn by the love letters.

My father looked on Philip Green Wright as a dear friend and teacher, another comrade and poet, and I have often thought that the letters he wrote to Wright after he left Lombard College are as good as a journal of those early years. This letter discusses *The Plaint of a Rose,* which Wright's Asgard Press published in 1908.

Galesburg
December 21, 1907

My Dear Sandburg:—

To-day for the first time I have been able to sit down and really read your letter and its very interesting enclosures. Neither his letter nor yours give any clue as to Mountain's full name! A subcurrent of pathos in his letter and Gobeille's and Edson's.[1] As Gilbert puts it somewhere—"Oh! to have longings for the infinite and be brought face to face with the multiplication table!"[2] Well, well, perhaps when we get the Asgard Press to a point where it also will be more of a reality and less of a dream we can bring out the soul thoughts of some of these good fellows and to again quote from my old favorite Gilbert "gild the philosophic pill"[3] to an extent that we may make our "fellow creatures wise" enough to pay for them. The Plaint of a Rose[4] will be out next week. I am sending cover design to the engravers to-day. It is Betty's work and I hope you will like it. We have really spent a lot of time thinking about it. It must be interesting to be really in the fight and in the inner circles of Socialism. I have a notion that the panic will help the vote somewhat.

I see the Socialist editors are working it in that direction for all it is worth. It may interest you to know that I have had orders for several Incidentals—10 copies at the College, 7 copies to Miss Kidder, 12 copies to Miss Lamkine, 2 copies to Dr. Currier.

Very Sincerely yours,
Philip G. Wright

1. William Mountain, Joseph Gobeille, and Charles Edson.

2. This is a misquote from the Gilbert and Sullivan opera *Patience,* where Bunthorne says to the milkmaid Patience: "Do you know what it is to yearn for the Indefinable, and yet to be brought face to face, daily, with the Multiplication Table?" Although my father liked Gilbert's Bab Ballads, he had never read *Patience,* and perhaps the original would not have appealed to him as much as Wright's misquote, which he must have used in his letter to Carl D. Thompson, as is apparent from Thompson's reply: "Let the infinite longings be tinctured with the intellectual grip of the mastery of the multiplication table. Let us have them both." When he wrote "The Sordid," my father in the last sentence misquoted Wright's misquote from *Patience.*

3. From Jack Point's song in *The Yeoman of the Guard,* one of the last of the Gilbert and Sullivan operas:

For he who wants to make his fellow creatures wise
Must gild the philosophic pill.

4. *The Plaint of a Rose* was a parable of not more than five paragraphs.

Milwaukee, Wis. Dec. 26, 1907

Dear Comrade.—

Yours of the 24th is at hand. Glad you are coming this way. It will be worth your while to stop off at Sheboygan, the Falls and Plymouth and have a talk with the comrades there if nothing more. I shall be glad to see you either Friday or Saturday. We can talk matters over and make it worth while.

I think you need offer no apologies for the litter sermon[1] as you call it. Intellectual excellency and power are inevitably commendable.

Let the infinite longings be tinctured with the intellectual grip of the mastery of the multiplication tables. Let us have them both.

Until I see you, best wishes.

Fraternally yours,
Carl D. Thompson

1. My father appears to have sent him as well as my mother a copy of "A Little Sermon."

The socialist magazine *The Vanguard* published "The Sordid" in April 1908. My mother had always felt strongly about the poor wages of the uneducated, struggling workingwomen of that time, barely making a living wage, and so she must have felt that the third paragraph from the end spoke for her. "It's great stuff—really great—compressed. A thing *really done!*" she wrote him in the postscript to Letter 31. He also mentions it in Letter 48 along with other articles he had written at the time. *The Vanguard* is referred to in Letters 75 and 93.

Evidently none of the socialist editors on *The Vanguard* was a Gilbert and Sullivan enthusiast since the mistake in the last sentence was not caught and eliminated.

The Sordid

It isn't the sad nor the tragic of life that cuts in and hurts one. It is the sordid, the squalid. In the commonplace is somewhat of beauty; but in the dirty, the stingy, the abortive, is the nerve of ugliness. Napoleon at St. Helena, the defeated and exiled, is superb. But Bonaparte, pale and worn and starved, meditating suicide on the banks of the Seine because even his brilliant genius has not been able to supply him a Chance to prove himself, this is not superb, this is commonplace, almost barren, quite dull. Had he jumped in, the reporters would merely have had to describe one more Body of Unknown Man Found This Morning.

"Despair and starvation and death," said a newspaper man to me, "are picturesque and appealing. Their victims have crossed the last bridge. They are in the beyond, on the bosom of the unknown. We can neither help nor hinder them. But these masses of people who live on half-rations all the time, getting just about enough to keep them fed and slept to a point where they can do their work, these half-dead and half-alive millions who move in a dreary twilight of existence, without a real thought or a real emotion their whole lives through, dirty and stupid, cowed and beaten, satisfied with the scraps and rags of living, they constitute neither tragedy nor comedy. Despair and starvation thrill me. But half-rations and satisfaction—that's where I can't get any enjoyment."

Treachery, deceit, poison, seduction, eavesdropping, these are nothing to one in health, with a good steak and coffee before him. The tragic extremes of life we can stand. Sumptuous revelry and utter anguish have their fascinations. It is the dull, monotonous, dead-level of satisfied, half-fed respectability, the struggling millions caught in the coils of ethical, political and juridicial codes dictated by a false economic system, this is the main bewilderment of modern life.

Youth, love, aspiration, ardor, stifled of opportunity, in dirty kitchens with cracked walls, and children born blear-eyed with no choice put to them as to their coming into this world, this is what overshadows the souls of the thoughtful.

Caesar, struck down by his life-long friend, the soldier on the battlefield with a bayonet plunged into his vitals, this is heroic and cheering in some ways. But a man who has toiled all day at useful work, creating stuffs to sustain and comfort human lives, eating oleomargarine on soggy bread and washing it down with chicory, seated at an oil-cloth table-cover set with broken pieces of porcelain, this is the sordid.

A good, beautiful woman unjustly slandered? Ha! the brave knight leaps for his sword. "The Ladies! God bless them!" No gentleman will stand by and see a lady insulted. This is frippery and folly. 'Tis one of the fantasies of our morality, that men will mouth these platitudes when "the man who has the coin" can debauch and pervert by the score and hundreds what women he can find who are victims of economic necessity, who need his coin.

Our ideas of chivalry are changing. You don't have to go forth on a white steed, with sword and lance and coat of mail, in order to be a "knight." The real knights nowadays are working to save womanhood from the miserable wages paid in sweatshops, factories, mills and department stores, wages that usually drive hundreds of thousands to loveless marriages and careers of prostitution.

Not to face these things is cowardice. To look at them and bear them in mind day and night is to get weak, leak pity and mumble in undertones. But to turn away from them is to smother the finer and higher instincts of life.

Chivalry and poetry and chastity are all very well. But those who face the facts and conditions of life without fear or compromise may smile at the truth of Gilbert's lines, "O to have infinite longings and then to suddenly encounter the multiplication table!"

In Letter 1 my mother mentioned receiving *Labor and Politics* along with "A Little Sermon."

Labor and Politics

The working class is more perfectly organized today than ever before. In fact, until the last century the working class had always been practically without any organization.

Today, it has two wings. It is organized in the industrial field and it is organized in the political field.

The trade-union is the working class organization on the industrial field. The trade-union has been fought in every conceivable fashion, and with every weapon of advantage that the capitalist class could find to use. Against fearful odds, the organization has continued. Lock-outs, bull-pens, Pinkertons, blacklists, lies and distorted facts spread by a capitalist press, have been used to prevent labor organization. But against all this, it has come up triumphant, so that today we see organized labor one of the greatest powers in modern civilization. It has obtained higher wages and reduced working hours and all that it has so far gained it holds and guards jealously.

Every advantage which has been secured has been only against a barbarous and cruel opposition. The capitalist press opposed the eight hour day. The workingmen were told, "The more hours you are at work, the less hours you will be drunk. You don't know how to use leisure time. The more leisure time you have, the drunker you get and the more bad mischief you get into." But against these low, stupid slanders, labor persisted, so that today eight hours or less than eight hours of work per day is coming to be looked at as reasonable and right.

You will notice that certain sane, decent, humane measures demanded by labor were granted only after agitation, determined, fearless agitation. As one man has put it, "Sometimes we can win, only by making a hell of a noise." More than twenty years ago, the railroad men began agitation for safety couplers on all cars. Under the old plan of links and pins connecting cars, the slaughter of railroad men was something fearful. Today, it is bad enough—a railroad man has to pay twice as much for insurance as those in "non-hazardous occupations." But it took more than ten years of organized agitation, making a "hell of a noise," to get the public and congress to recognize that it was brutal to sacrifice human lives in order to save a few dollars for the capitalist class. This humane, sensible measure was fought pitilessly by the capitalist class.

These things are cited merely as instances of what the trade-unions have had to struggle against. Today organization goes on, and more and more the workingmen are dictating the terms under which they shall work. They continually demand more and more safeguards around the machinery they work with. Explosions and loss of life are more common in non-union mines than in those where the workers have been wise enough to organize and insist on at least some degree of safety.

The foregoing are some of the phases of the industrial organization of the working class. But it is now becoming more clear every day that industrial organization is not enough. The working class must also have POLITICAL organization or it will taste only sops of justice and not the real thing.

The employers, the capitalist class, are in possession of the powers of government. They own the city governments, the state legislatures and the governors. They own the national government. And they control practically all of the courts of the cities, the states and the nation.

If a strike is on, the capitalist class has the police at its disposal, and the police power combined with the municipal courts has defeated many a strike. With spies in the unions to stir up trouble, and with policemen instructed to use violence on the least pretext, thus starting riots that the newspapers exaggerate and falsify to influence public opinion, the capitalist class has a big advantage. This is a POLITICAL advantage and one that the workers will continually find themselves up against until they get possession of the powers of government.

The militia, upon orders from a state governor, has repeatedly been sent to places where there was no violence, but their appearance in addition to conniving spies, immediately brot disorder. Just the other day, federal troops were sent to Goldfield at the behest of the employers there, when not a single act of violence could be specified and proven. This is an old story. And please think for just a moment, it is these workingmen whose taxes pay the salaries and provide the rations of the soldiers sent against them. This will continue as long as the workingmen fail to use their ballots to put a working class political party in power.

The courts are almost entirely in the hands of the capitalist class. The much advertised William Taft, who is trying to get the Republican nomination for president, when a judge in Ohio, made several decisions that cannot be taken as more or less than insults to labor. Van Wyck, the Democratic judge in New York, tried to legalize the ice trust which was robbing the people of New York by extortionate prices for a necessity of life. These are but passing instances.

The list is almost endless of public officials elected by the votes of workingmen, who have guided their actions and decisions by the interest of the capitalist class.

It was old Commodore Vanderbilt who said, "The public be damned," and it is these shrewd gentlemen who are in practical control of the government today who say, "We will run our business as we please."

It is true that a big fine has been levied on the Standard Oil company but it has not yet been paid, the probabilities are that it never will be, and if it is, the amount in toto is but a drop in the Standard's bucket of profits.

The capitalist class controls courts, legislatures and congress. The question is, "What are we going to do about it? What can be done about it?"

The answer is brief. A political party is now in the field which is a working class party. It is called THE SOCIALIST PARTY nationally—in this state, the Social-Democratic Party. The Wisconsin State Federation of Labor has endorsed its principles and union memberships amounting to more than 250,000 have given their seals of approval to socialism.

With political powers the unions will be able to win where they are now at times beaten. That political power can never be won and held except thru the policies of the Socialist party. It is the only political party with which a workingman can line up and be certain that if it wins he will get what he is voting for.

The objection is sometimes made, "I don't want to throw away my vote." And the Socialist answer to this is, "It is better to vote for what you want and not get it than to vote for what you don't want and get it."

The returns from the recent New York state elections show a Socialist increase of more than 30 percent. At the next national election its vote will equal or surpass that of the People's party in 1892. Mark Hanna said that the next great political contest in this country would be between the Republican and the Socialist parties.

Only thru the Socialist party will the workingman get what belongs to him, the full product of his toil.

My father wrote more than one article on woman and suffrage for the Milwaukee *Social-Democratic Herald,* but this is the one to which my mother referred in Letter 76.

Socialism and Woman Suffrage

Why do Socialists believe that women ought to have the right to vote?

Well, in the first place, because WOMAN IS THE EQUAL OF MAN AS A HUMAN BEING. She is not his equal in physical prowess. She can't do the heavy day's work that a man can generally. And it is possible that woman, in the grand average has not the mental reach, the brain power of man. But the heart-power of woman, the love and service she will give an object of affection, in this she completely surpasses man. Without the sacrificing mother-nature of women, the world would be empty of people. The man who speaks of the "natural inferiority of woman" slanders the woman who suckled him and discredits the wife who is supposed to be his comrade.

The Socialist acknowledges that if women had the right to vote, it probably would not make a great deal of difference in the result of elections. But because woman is a human being and the equal of man, the mothers and sisters and wives of men should have the right to the ballot.

The property of a woman is taxed as that of a man is. Why shouldn't the woman have something to say as to what sort of men shall spend the money she pays in taxes?

The boy of a mother can be drafted for war purposes and sent to the front and torn to pieces by a flying shell. Why shouldn't she have something to say as to the presidents and congresses who hold the powers of war?

Just think of a woman like Ida Tarbell, whose historical writings and industrial studies have made the whole world her debtor, being barred from voting! A superb and brilliantly intellectual woman like Mrs. Raymond Robbins, Minnie Maddern Fiske or Lilian Steichen is barred from the ballot, while thick-necked, leer-eyed politicians, who openly boast that they can buy ballots with whiskey, have the privilege of voting.

Just as we have done and are doing in other matters, we will change public opinion on this ground. In giving women the right to vote, men will but honor themselves, and build toward a greater civilization.

This may be the "Dear Bill" letter my father mentioned in Letter 125 and my mother in Letter 128. My father wrote a series of "Dear Bill" letters in 1909 that were published in *La Follette's Magazine*. Another "Dear Bill" letter was published as a booklet under the title *You and Your Job* by Charles Kerr and by a Philadelphia Socialist press, which did a reprint of 10,000.

Dear Bill:

I used to know a white-haired old man out in a country village. This man had read more and thought for himself more than any other man in the village—nobody had a chattel mortgage on his brain. He was a good listener. He did more listening than talking, and generally when he talked there were long gaps and pauses between his words. But when he did talk, he said things. I remember one idea of his that he used to repeat in different ways, but it generally went about like this, "All of the great things of life are simple. When a man talks to you about something so tangled and snarled and mixed up that he can't make it clear to you, then the chances are that he doesn't know what he is talking about. The man who thinks clearly, speaks clearly. Whatever you actually understand, you will be able to explain."

We used to talk about politics and business and trusts and labor unions, the changes that are taking place over civilization, strikes, lockouts, boycotts, blacklists, bull-pens, "the rich growing richer and the poor growing poorer," monopolies, and all these dangerous new things that nobody had heard of a hundred years back. And this old man was asked one night what he thought was the matter with America and what would have to be done to stop the muttering and thundering of the radicals and revolutionists. And I'm going to try to give you as near as I can, in the old man's words, what he thought was the root of the trouble.

"In human society," he said, "we don't do the same as the bees do in their hives. Among the bees, if there is one that won't work, if there is one that wants to eat honey but won't get out and hustle in the meadows and orchards and bring home honey for the hive, all the bees that work fall on him and sting him to death. Of course that looks kind of cruel and why the bees do it we don't know, except that the instinct has been planted in the bees that work to kill the bee that won't work. And while it's my own private guess that it'll be a long, long time till we get things going among human beings so that there will be no shirkers and all will be workers—I make another guess of my own that until we get things working that way, we will have radicals, revolutionists, single taxers, socialists, communists, monasticists, and people with voices grown hoarse from being raised in protest.

"I believe in human nature," he went on, "I believe that down at the bottom every man wants to do right, and while some of us have more of the right in us than others, every man from John D. Rockefeller down to the street-corner agitator, has something of truth in him. And in the same way that you can't think of Abraham Lincoln apart from the institution of chattel slavery, and in the same way that John Brown, rash and reckless, was pushed on by deep, hidden forces; so there is something deep and right and true, back of these agitators around us to-day, forcing them on to situations that even they can't see clearly ahead of them.

"I have been reading history and science for forty years and from all that I have studied as to how nations are born and grow and then die, it seems to me that just as soon as a nation gets to the point where a small part of the people are rich and a large part of the people are poor—then that nation is starting to die, the death of it is beginning. It seems to be a sort of process of slow decay and if you can't stop the process, that nation will go to its grave. I have seen a certain species of ivy creep and climb up the sides of a sturdy, healthy tree and after a while fasten itself on to the tree in such a way that it no longer got its food and water and nourishment from the soil and the sun and the moisture of the air: it got into the habit of living on that tree; what it needed to keep life going it sucked out of the tree. And the leaves on the tree became less and less, the tree faded and became gray, and in time the heart of it was rotten and it fell.

"It looks to me as if the same fight is on here in America that went on in all the old civilizations—a fight between the bees that get out and bring in the honey and the bees that don't, a fight between the workers and the shirkers, a struggle between a vine that wants to live on the tree and the tree that wants to shake off the vine. How it is all going to end, I don't know. But I have a warm place in my heart for the agitator, no matter how vehement or loud or mistaken he may be.

"The Chinese have a proverb, 'Where there is an idle man, somewhere else you will find a starving man.' So I take it that the voice of the agitator is the voice of the starving. When distress gets keen enough it will make itself heard. When I make a visit to the city and see able-bodied men selling newspapers on the streets, and women with wrinkled faces (looking as though they might have born several children), wrapped in faded shawls, standing on the corners peddling lead pencils, I know something is wrong somewhere.

"This is a big country with some big, clean actions on its record; and if it is true that the rich are growing richer and the poor are growing poorer, I believe we will find some way to stop it. If we don't, the republic will go to smash, that's sure."

He is a very interesting old man, Bill, and sometime I'll write you more about him.

Yours always,
Sandy

APPENDIX C
Other Poems for Paula

These are poems my father wrote for my mother during the waiting period when the love letters were written. In the first, he used the words "hill-born" and "hill-loved," which seem reminiscent of the "hill-flower grace" in "The Dream Girl." They are imaginative and very different. It must be remembered when reading "By the Sea" that he means Lake Michigan, which he thought of as an inland sea.

Paula

The mists of night go trailing all the hills,
They feel their slow grey-ghosted way
And hunt for outlet down the sloughs—
Then fade away for other worlds and other forms.

In the running dusk of an upland rise,
High and far on the end of a slope,
At the rim of the world stands Paula,
Looks to the pit and the dome of worlds
Where dawn leaps out flame-fingered and tressed of gold.

At her hill-born neck and hill-loved shoulders
The sunrise flashes its banner and dream,
Vibrant and flinging with wonder and daring.

The gods of beauty know her all,
The gods of service give her passwords,
Low love-shadows, deep love-lights
Gather and flit to her hands and face.

You Gave

You gave—with your deep blue careless eyes and your
low soft careless voice you gave.
Your heart went thudding under your ribs like a guess
come sure and a bird on the wing.
Your breath was a hot and cadenced pulsing, free as the
urge of a seaward tide.
You threw down the bars to fresh wild things of unimaginable
gardens—
Flowers impassioned and red looked out on our reckless and
memoried moments.

We sat where a pine to the wind was yielding
And one high star to the downgoing sun
Was blazing, disdainful, serene.

By the Sea

Flash of wave and winding foam
And changing blue of shifting sea,
What is the stuff of your great deep heart?
   You restless, perpetual thing?

Calm and surge and playing spray,
Ripple and toss on mighty tide,
Sweep and swing of crumbling comber,
Where is the pulse of your slow grand power?

Listening girl and laughing boy
Looking out from sand and shore,
To the blended tints of cunning shells
Pay the cry of your answering glee!
Give a cheer to the sea!
Give a shout to the foam!
Give a rouse to the ships!
To the far gulls flying, halloo!

To the utterest reach of your seeing eyes,
Give greeting and laughter and listening,
You boy and girl on the bank and sand
By the plangent sea, by the vivid and reckless sea.

The passing days will mount and mount
And year into year intermingle
And into the nets of time and to-morrow
Your lives will slip like grain over fingers.

And in all the days of your slipping lives
You shall see no thing like the sea,
The sea and its foam and ship and gull—
For the sea is life and change and glory,
   The sea is a mad imperious child
   And the sea will have its way.

Middle of May

I am young and I want you and I know you hear me calling.
White blossom sprays on a bush, pools cool, and shadows on the
  road,
Raindrops on the leaves holding silver of the morning sun:
    I am young and I want you.

1908

Index

Italic type denotes page numbers that contain the text of Sandburg poems or prose articles.

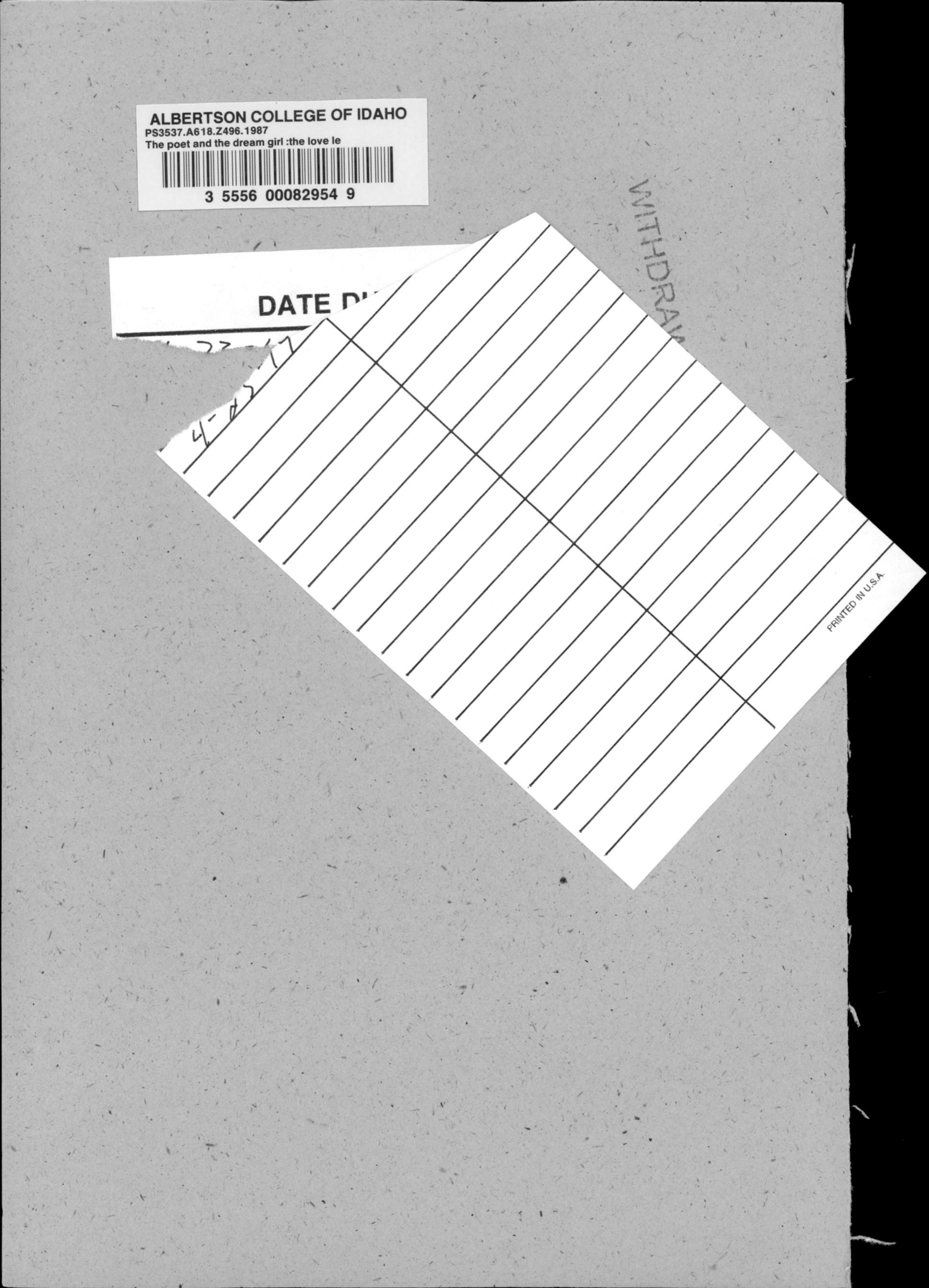
ALBERTSON COLLEGE OF IDAHO
PS3537.A618.Z496.1987
The poet and the dream girl :the love le
3 5556 00082954 9
DATE DU
WITHDRAW
PRINTED IN U.S.A.